W9-BRB-869

Envision It! | Visual Skills Handbook

Author's Purpose

Inform

Entertain

Persuade

Express

An author writes for many purposes including to inform, entertain, persuade, or express. An author may have more than one purpose for writing.

Author's Viewpoint/Bias

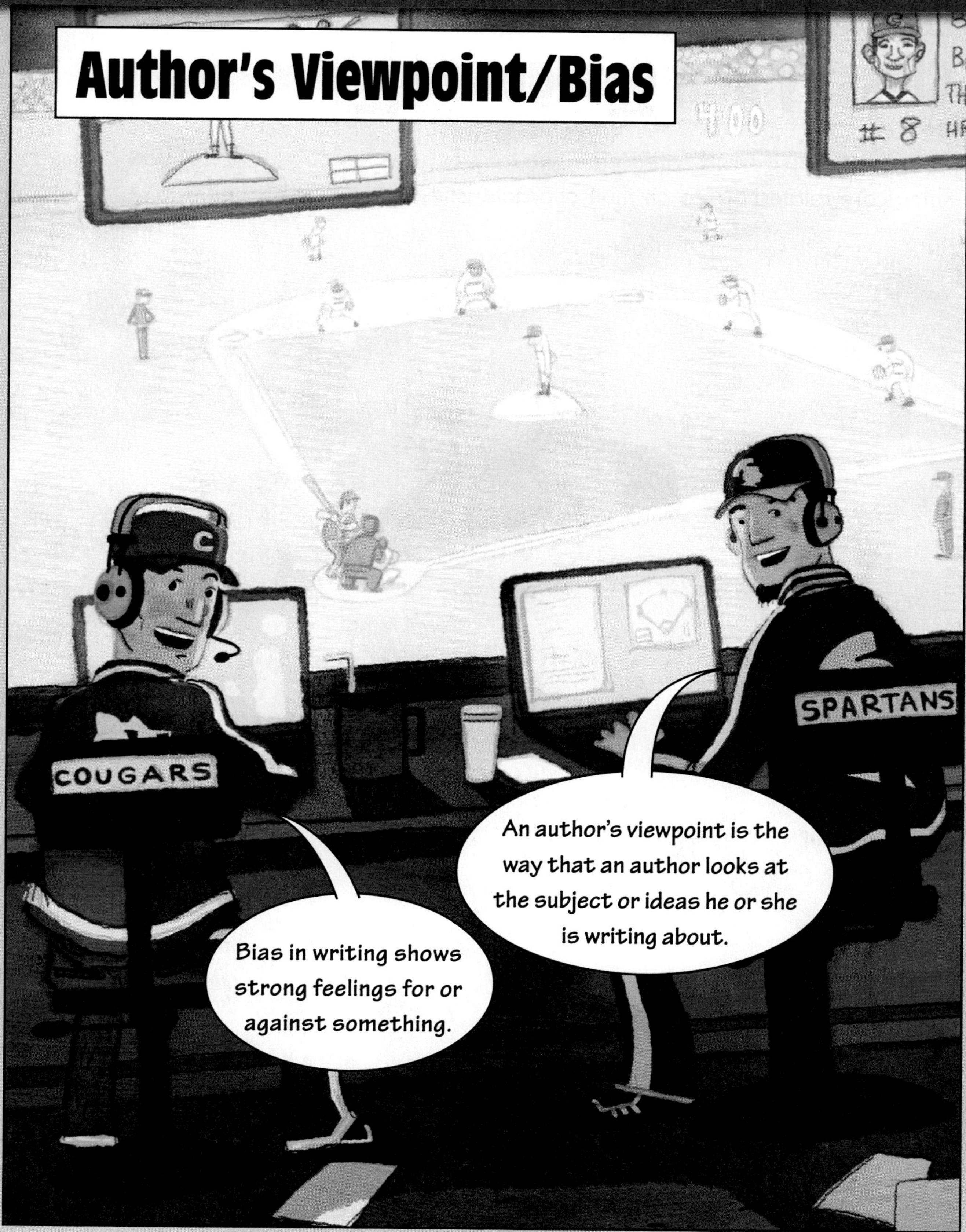

Classify and Categorize

When we classify and categorize, we look at how things are related based on their characteristics.

Compare and Contrast

To compare and contrast is to look for similarities and differences in things.

Draw Conclusions

When we draw conclusions, we make decisions or form an opinion about what we read.

Fact and Opinion

I'm taller than you!

But I'm funnier than you.

A fact is something that can be proved true or false. An opinion can't be proved.

Generalize

To generalize is to make a broad statement or rule that applies to many examples.

You can go faster on a bike than on skates!

Graphic Sources

A graphic source provides information visually, or in a way that the reader can see.

ANIMAL	ANIMAL FOOT PRINT	NUMBER OF SIGHTINGS
		3
		10
		6
		12
		9

Table

A table contains information in rows and columns. Tables allow you to compare facts.

NUMBER OF ANIMALS OBSERVED

Bar Graph

A bar graph arranges information so you can compare or rank it.

Map

A map is a drawing of a place that shows where something is or where something happened.

Diagram

A diagram is a drawing, usually with parts that are labeled.

A Day at the Beach

The End

Literary Elements

Understanding a story requires knowing the four main parts of a story: character, setting, plot, and theme.

Setting - the time and place in which a story happens.

Character - a person or animal in a story.

Plot - the pattern of events in a story.

Rising Action

Climax

Conflict

Solution

Theme - the big idea of a story.

The **Main Idea** is the most important idea about a topic.

Details support the main idea.

Sequence

Sequence refers to the order of events in a text.
We use sequence when we list the steps in a process.

Envision It! | Visual Strategies Handbook

Background Knowledge

Important Ideas

Inferring

Monitor and Clarify

Predict and Set Purpose

Questioning

Story Structure

Summarize

Text Structure

Visualize

Background Knowledge

Background knowledge is what you already know about a topic based on your reading and personal experience. Use background knowledge before, during, and after reading to monitor comprehension.

To use background knowledge

- with fiction, preview the title, author's name, and illustrations
- with nonfiction, preview chapter titles, headings, captions, and other text features
- think about your own experiences while you read

That reminds me of the time we went to the basement during the tornado warning.

Let's Think About Reading!

When I use background knowledge, I ask myself
- Does this character remind me of someone?
- How is this story or text similar to others I have read?
- What else do I know about this topic from what I've read or seen?

Important Ideas

Important ideas are essential ideas in a nonfiction selection. Important ideas include information and facts that provide clues to the author's purpose.

To identify important ideas
- read all titles, headings, and captions
- look for words in italics, boldface print, or bulleted lists
- look for signal words and phrases—*for example, most important,* and others
- use photographs, illustrations, or other graphic sources
- note how the text is organized—cause and effect, problem and solution, question and answer, or other ways

This must be an important idea.

Leonardo da Vinci

Let's **Think** About **Reading!**

When I identify important ideas, I ask myself
- What information is included in bold, italics, or other special lettering?
- What details support important ideas?
- Are there signal words and phrases?
- What do illustrations, photos, diagrams, and charts show?
- How is the text organized?
- Why did the author write this?

Inferring

When we **infer**, we use background knowledge along with clues in the text to come up with our own ideas about what the author is trying to present.

To infer

- identify what you already know
- combine what you know with text clues to come up with your own ideas

I see baking soda foam. Your volcano must have erupted!

SCIENCE FAIR

Let's Think About Reading!

When I infer, I ask myself
- What do I already know?
- Which text clues are important?
- What is the author trying to present?

Monitor and Clarify

We **monitor comprehension** to check our understanding of what we've read. We **clarify** to find out why we haven't understood what we've read and to adjust comprehension.

To monitor and clarify
- use background knowledge
- try different strategies: ask questions, reread, or use text features and illustrations

Let's **Think** About **Reading!**

When I monitor and clarify, I ask myself
- Do I understand what I'm reading?
- What doesn't make sense?
- What strategies can I use?

Predict and Set Purpose

We **predict** to tell what might happen next in a story or article. The prediction is based on what has already happened. We **set a purpose** to guide our reading.

To predict and set a purpose
- preview the title, the author's name, and the illustrations or graphics
- identify why you're reading
- use what you already know to make predictions
- check and change your predictions based on new information

I predict the locations of the state capitals are based on their populations.

Let's **Think** About **Reading!**

When I predict and set a purpose, I ask myself
- What do I already know?
- What do I think will happen?
- What is my purpose for reading?

Questioning

Questioning is asking good questions about important text information. Questioning takes place before, during, and after reading.

To question
- read with a question in mind
- stop, think, and record your questions as you read
- make notes when you find information
- check your understanding and ask questions to clarify

What *does* arachnid mean? Where does it fit in a food chain? Do tarantulas have to adapt to their environment to survive?

Let's Think About Reading!

When I question, I ask myself
- Have I asked a good question with a question word?
- What questions help me make sense of my reading?
- What does the author mean?

Story Structure

Story structure is the arrangement of a story from beginning to end. You can use this information to summarize the story.

To identify story structure

- note the conflict, or problem, at the beginning of a story
- track the rising action as the conflict builds in the middle
- recognize the climax, the time when the characters face the conflict
- identify how the conflict is resolved

Let's **Think** About **Reading!**

When I identify story structure, I ask myself
- What is the story's conflict or problem?
- How does the conflict build throughout the story?
- How is the conflict resolved in the end?
- How might this affect future events?

Summarize

We **summarize** to check our understanding of what we've read. A summary is a brief statement—no more than a few sentences—and maintains a logical order.

To summarize fiction
- tell what happens in the story
- include the goals of the characters, how they try to reach them, and whether or not they succeed

To summarize nonfiction
- tell the main idea
- think about text structure and how the selection is organized

This blizzard is stalling rush hour traffic.

Let's **Think** About **Reading!**

When I summarize, I ask myself
- What is the story or selection about?
- In fiction, what are the characters' goals? Are they successful?
- In nonfiction, how is the information organized?

Text Structure

We use **text structure** to look for how the author has organized the text. Organizations include cause and effect, problem and solution, sequence, or compare and contrast. Analyze text structure before, during, and after reading to locate information.

To identify text structure

- before reading: preview titles, headings, and illustrations
- during reading: notice the organization
- after reading: recall the organization and summarize the text

First, teach your dog how to sit.

Then, teach him how to roll over.

Finally, teach him how to speak.

WOOF!

Let's **Think** About **Reading!**

When I identify text structure, I ask myself

- What clues do titles, headings, and illustrations provide?
- How is information organized?
- How does the organization help my understanding?

Visualize

We **visualize** to form pictures in our minds as we read. This helps us monitor our comprehension.

To visualize

- combine what you already know with details from the text to make pictures in your mind
- use all of your senses to put yourself in the story or text

Let's Think About Reading!

When I visualize, I ask myself

- What do I already know?
- Which details create pictures in my mind?
- How can my senses put me in the story?

Program Authors

Peter Afflerbach

Camille Blachowicz

Candy Dawson Boyd

Elena Izquierdo

Connie Juel

Edward Kame'enui

Donald Leu

Jeanne R. Paratore

P. David Pearson

Sam Sebesta

Deborah Simmons

Alfred Tatum

Sharon Vaughn

Susan Watts-Taffe

Karen Kring Wixson

PEARSON

Glenview, Illinois • Boston, Massachusetts • Chandler, Arizona • Upper Saddle River, New Jersey

We dedicate Reading Street to
Peter Jovanovich.

His wisdom, courage,
and passion for education
are an inspiration to us all.

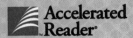
Accelerated Reader®

About the Cover Artist
Award-winning artist Greg Newbold began drawing and painting at age three—and never stopped. His illustrated books for children include *Spring Song* and *Winter Lullaby*. Mr. Newbold also does illustrations for magazines, motion pictures, and food products such as catsup and jelly. He creates his illustrations in a studio next to his house, snuggled in the Rocky Mountains of Utah.

Acknowledgments appear on pages 490–493, which constitute an extension of this copyright page.
Copyright ©2011 by Pearson Education, Inc., or its affiliates. All Rights Reserved. Printed in the United States of America. This publication is protected by copyright, and permission should be obtained from the publisher prior to any prohibited reproduction, storage in a retrieval system, or transmission in any form or by any means, electronic, mechanical, photocopying, recording, or likewise. For information regarding permissions, write to Pearson Curriculum Group Rights & Permissions, One Lake Street, Upper Saddle River, New Jersey 07458.

Pearson, Scott Foresman, and Pearson Scott Foresman are trademarks, in the U.S. and/or other countries, of Pearson Education, Inc., or its affiliates.

PEARSON

ISBN-13: 978-0-328-45566-9
ISBN-10: 0-328-45566-0
5 6 7 8 9 10 V063 14 13 12 11

CC1

Dear Reader,

A new school year is beginning. Are you ready? You are about to take a trip along a famous street— *Scott Foresman Reading Street*. During this trip you will meet exciting people, such as Revolutionary War hero Paul Revere, a cowgirl who lassoes tornadoes, and the brilliant artists behind the special effects you see in movies.

As you read selections about inventions, blues singers, and baseball legends, you will gain exciting new information that will help you in science and social studies.

While you're enjoying these exciting pieces of literature, you will find that something else is going on—you are becoming a better reader, gaining new skills and polishing old ones.

Have a great trip— and send us a postcard!

Sincerely,
The Authors

Meeting Challenges

What kinds of challenges do people face and how do they meet them?

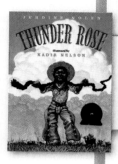

Unit 1 Contents

Week 6

Unit 1

Envision It! A Comprehension Handbook

Envision It! Visual Skills Handbook EI•1–EI•13

Envision It! Visual Strategies Handbook EI•15–EI•26

Words! Vocabulary Handbook W•1–W•13

Doing the Right Thing

THE BIG ? What makes people want to do the right thing?

Week 1

Let's **Think** About Reading!

realistic fiction • science

from *Salsa Stories*
by Lulu Delacre

legend
by Lame Deer

Unit 2 Contents

Week 6

Unit 2

Envision It! **A Comprehension Handbook**

Unit 3 Contents

Inventors and Artists

What do people gain from the work of inventors and artists?

Week 1

Let's **Think** About Reading!

drama • science

persuasive text • science

12

Week 2

Week 3

Unit 3 Contents

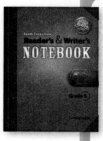

Week 6

Unit 3

Envision It! A Comprehension Handbook

**Envision It! Visual Skills
Handbook EI•1–EI•13**

**Envision It! Visual Strategies
Handbook EI•15–EI•26**

Words! A Vocabulary Handbook W•1–W•13

Don Leu
The Internet Guy

Right before our eyes, the nature of reading and learning is changing. The Internet and other technologies create new opportunities, new solutions, and new literacies. New reading comprehension skills are required online. They are increasingly important to our students and our society.

Those of us on the Reading Street team are here to help you on this new, and very exciting, journey.

See It!

- **Big Question Video**

- **Concept Talk Video**

- **Envision It! Animations**

- **eReaders**

Hear It!

- **eSelections**

- **Grammar Jammer**

- **Vocabulary Activities**

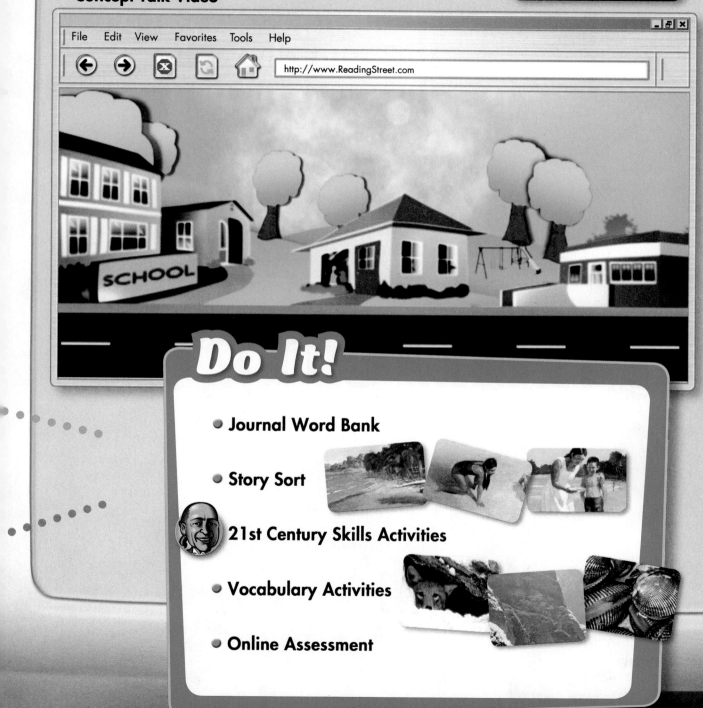

Do It!

- **Journal Word Bank**

- **Story Sort**

- **21st Century Skills Activities**

- **Vocabulary Activities**

- **Online Assessment**

What kinds of challenges do people face and how do they meet them?

Meeting Challenges

Reading Street Online

www.ReadingStreet.com
• Big Question Video
• eSelections
• Envision It! Animations
• Story Sort

Objectives
- Listen to and interpret a speaker's messages and ask questions.
- Identify the main ideas and supporting ideas in the speaker's message.

Oral Vocabulary

Let's Talk About

Courage

- Discuss courage.

- Listen to a classmate's ideas about courage.

- Determine classmates' main and supporting ideas about courage.

**READING STREET ONLINE
CONCEPT TALK VIDEO**
www.ReadingStreet.com

You will learn

3 0 0

Amazing Words ☆
this year!

21

Objectives
● Explain the roles and functions of characters, including their relationships and conflicts. ● Monitor and adjust comprehension using a variety of strategies.

Envision It! Skill Strategy

Skill

Strategy

READING STREET ONLINE
ENVISION IT! ANIMATION
www.ReadingStreet.com

Comprehension Skill

Literary Elements: Character and Plot

- Characters are the people or animals in a story.

- Plot is the pattern of events in a story. Usually, plots happen in sequential order.

- A plot has a *conflict*, or problem; *rising action*, when the conflict builds; a *climax*, when characters meet the conflict; and a *resolution*, when the conflict is resolved.

- Use a graphic organizer like the one below to explain the plot. Then explain Melissa's role and function in the plot.

Problem or Conflict → **Rising Action** → **Climax** → **Resolution**

Comprehension Strategy

Monitor and Clarify

Good readers check their understanding as they read. If you don't understand something you are reading, pause. Ask yourself, *What don't I understand?* Try creating a sensory image to help you understand the story. Then read on to find out what happens.

BRAVE Melissa

Most people around town knew Melissa as a sweet girl who walked her big yellow dog every day. Whether the sun was shining or freezing rain was pouring down, Melissa always walked her dog before and after school.

One winter day, the snow was coming down so fast that the sidewalk became very slippery. Melissa fell and dropped her dog's leash. The dog got confused and kept walking to the beach where he and Melissa would go during the summer. The dog was so confused that he headed toward the lake and accidentally fell through the frozen water.

By this time, Melissa and half the town were at the beach. Without hesitating, Melissa reached her hand toward the dog and pulled him from the freezing water. The dog had always seemed twice her size, but today Melissa looked like a giant. Luckily, both Melissa and the dog escaped serious harm.

Skill What is the story's conflict? How do Melissa's actions influence the story's conflict?

Strategy If you do not understand what is happening, create a sensory image from story details.

Skill What is the story's resolution? How do Melissa's actions resolve the story's conflict?

Your Turn!

⏸ **Need a Review?** See the *Envision It! Handbook* for additional help.

Let's Think About..

▶ **Ready to Try It?** Talk about what you have learned as you read *Red Kayak*.

RED KAYAK

Objectives
● Determine the meanings of unfamiliar words or multiple-meaning words by using the context of the sentence. ● Use a dictionary, a glossary, or a thesaurus to locate information about words.

Envision It! | **Words to Know**

compressions

minute

neutral

grumbled

insistently

intentionally

normally

READING STREET ONLINE
VOCABULARY ACTIVITIES
www.ReadingStreet.com

Vocabulary Strategy for

🎯 Homographs

Context Clues Homographs are words that are spelled the same but have different meanings and sometimes have different pronunciations. For example, *bass* (rhymes with *face*) is a musical instrument, while *bass* (rhymes with *class*) is a type of fish. Use context clues to determine which word (and meaning) is being used. Follow these steps.

1. Read the words and sentences around the homograph.

2. Think about its possible meaning.

3. Reread the sentence and put in one of the meanings.

4. See if the meaning makes sense in the sentence. If not, try another meaning.

Read "Lifesaving Classes" on page 25. Look for homographs. Use context clues to help you figure out the meanings. Use a dictionary or glossary to determine how the words are pronounced.

Words to Write Reread "Lifesaving Classes." Write a paragraph about the job of a lifeguard. Describe how lifeguards prepare and what they need to know. Use words from the *Words to Know* list in your writing.

LIFESAVING
Classes

Normally I spend my summers at my best friend's cottage, but this summer is different. I want to get a job as a lifeguard, so I have to take classes and practice swimming. When I heard that first aid was going to be one of the classes, I grumbled out loud. I don't like the sight of blood. I intentionally avoided looking at the screen during a film about how to wrap wounds. My teacher noticed and insistently asked me about the proper techniques to stop excessive bleeding.

I liked the class about CPR (cardiopulmonary resuscitation), because CPR can really save a person's life. I was surprised by how tiring it is. It is best to work with a partner so that you can take turns doing compressions and rescue breaths. In a drowning case, every minute matters.

Some of the other classes that I'll take this summer are boat safety, rescue diving, and crowd control. I already know how to put the boat in forward, neutral, and reverse from spending summers at my friend's cottage on a lake. I am going to miss hanging out with her, but I'm very excited about becoming a lifeguard.

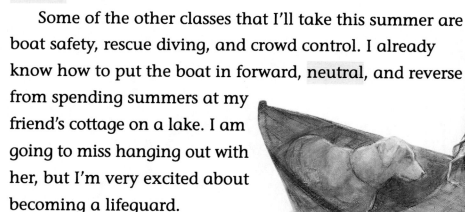

Your Turn!

Ⅱ Need a Review? For additional help with suffixes, see *Words!*

▶ Ready to Try It? Read *Red Kayak* on pp. 26–41.

RED KAYAK

Genre

Realistic fiction deals with characters and events that seem real but are created by the author. As you read, notice how the author makes the characters and events come to life.

RED KAYAK

written by Priscilla Cummings   illustrated by Ron Mazellan

Question of the Week
What inspires people to act courageously?

Let's
Think
About
Reading!

Let's **Think** About...

What do you think will happen to Brady and Tilly as they search for the red kayak?

Predict and Set Purpose

On a cold spring morning, thirteen-year-old Brady Parks sees Mr. DiAngelo's red kayak heading down the creek toward the Corsica River. Brady knows that with the strong winds and the dangerous tides, it is not safe for boating, but he and his friends don't say anything. Now Mrs. DiAngelo and her three-year-old son, Ben, are missing. While Brady's dad and the other rescue workers head downstream, they ask Brady to use his boat to check the smaller creeks. Can Brady and his yellow Lab, Tilly, help find the red kayak before it's too late? And will he remember the rescue training he learned from Carl at the firehouse?

Already my eyes were scanning the shoreline for the red kayak—or a splash of yellow. Mr. DiAngelo had told the police he couldn't remember what clothes his wife or son wore that morning, but he knew they had on yellow life jackets.

I felt excited, but a little panicked, too, as I sped down the creek, squinting into the icy spray and scanning the thick tangle of brown brush and newly budding trees along the narrow shoreline. If that red kayak was out there, I wanted to be the one to find it.

Not too far downstream, a small creek emptied in from the left. As my father's boat disappeared around the bend up ahead, I reluctantly turned my boat up the creek, slowed down some, and kept searching. The bow of the boat settled down, and the wake from behind sloshed up against the transom. Still nothing. Why would there be? Common sense and knowing the currents would tell you that the kayak had drifted downstream, especially with the fast-running spring tides. Unless Mrs. DiAngelo had intentionally paddled up one of the creeks, there was no way they would have *drifted* here.

I was cold. It started to drizzle, and the water froze on my face. I shoved my left hand under my thigh to try to keep it warm. I was thinking that Ben was probably freezing, too—and scared to death by now. I know what being really cold is like. Middle of winter I almost drowned in a cow pond when I was little, maybe eight. J.T., Digger, and I were playing ice hockey, and I fell clear through the ice.

The memory of that accident made me shudder. Abruptly, I leaned over to cut the engine.

Let's Think About...

What clues in the text indicate that Brady might be nervous about searching the creek? **Inferring**

Let's Think About...

Do you understand why Brady's own accident had such an effect on him? **Monitor and Clarify**

"Mrs. DiAngelo!" I hollered at the top of my lungs. "Ben! Can you hear me?"

Nothing.

"Mrs. Di-An-ge-lo!"

Not a sound. I fired up the engine again and kept going.

Up the creek, a couple private docks extended out into the water; then there was a long strip of riprap near a construction site. From that point on, it was just shoreline with trees and a lot of brown cell bush. I kept going, but toward the head of the creek, a marsh taken over by a patch of tall phragmites warned me of shallow water, and I turned the boat around, not wanting to run aground. I sped up and came back down the creek, closer to the opposite bank.

Still no sign of a red kayak or a yellow life jacket. All I wanted to do was open the throttle and head downriver to where the others were searching. My hands ached they were so cold. I stuffed one hand in the pocket and hit the cell

Let's Think About...

Why is it a good idea for Brady to have a cell phone?
Background Knowledge

phone. I pulled it out and saw that I had "1 missed call." Turning off the motor so I could hear, I speed-dialed home to see if Mom knew anything.

"Brady—hi!" she said. "Dad called. He said they found Mrs. DiAngelo."

"They did?"

"Yes. Downriver, near Spaniard's Neck."

"Is she okay?" I asked.

"She's alive," Mom said. "But just barely. They have *not* found Ben."

"They didn't?"

"No. They lost the kayak, Brady. So Ben is out there somewhere in the water in his life jacket."

"Oh, man, it's *cold* Mom—"

"I know . . . I know it's cold. Are you all right? Can you do this, Brady?"

"I'm all right. I'm fine," I assured her. "I need to keep looking!"

I ended the call and put the phone back in my pocket. We had to move really fast now. If Ben was in the water, his time was limited.

Tilly started barking as I picked up speed.

"Quiet!" I hollered.

Let's Think About...

Why does Brady say that time was limited? Reread for clues. **Monitor and Clarify**

Let's Think About...

Why do you think Tilly started barking? **Predict**

31

Let's **Think** About...

What clue suggests that Brady might be close to finding Ben?

Inferring

I wondered if I should waste my time going up any of those little creeks and inlets now that they had found Mrs. DiAngelo downriver. But Tilly was barking up a storm and stood with her nose pointed toward the riverbank, where some of the water curled into a small cove.

It was hard to ignore Tilly's instincts. Once, she barked at the ceiling in our basement so insistently that my father pulled down part of the insulation and found a possum's nest made out of leaves.

"Better not be a squirrel or something stupid like that," I grumbled as I swung the boat toward the cove. I bit my lip uncertainly.

Suddenly Tilly had her front paws up on the edge of my boat. Her tail thumped back and forth, hitting my knees.

"What is it, Til?" I asked, squinting to see through the drizzle.

I slowed down the motor as we approached the narrow channel to the cove. Tall marsh grass obscured my view to the right, but as soon as we had motored around it, I glimpsed the remains of an old dock—a place where J.T., Digger, and I used to fish—and a single, bright spot of yellow.

It was Ben. But as I drew closer I could see that he was motionless, his small body hunched forward, the back of his life jacket caught on a jagged piece of old piling that jutted out of the water like a rotten tooth.

"Ben! Are you okay?" I hollered, pulling the boat up alongside.

His eyes weren't right.

"Move!" I ordered Tilly. Right away she jumped back into the narrow space in the bow.

I flipped the engine into neutral and reached over to pull in Ben. He was a lot heavier than I would have thought, probably because he was so waterlogged. The water was cold too. I grabbed hold of the collar on his life jacket and summoned all my strength to "unhook" him from that piece of wood. For a second, I lost my balance and nearly went in headfirst myself. But I fell backward instead, never letting go, and managed to pull Ben into my boat on top of me. It was a rough landing and I hit my elbow hard on the gunnel. I just hoped I hadn't hurt Ben.

Let's **Think** About...

Why is seeing a spot of yellow so important to Brady? Reread to find out.

Monitor and Clarify

33

The first thing I did was get his wet life jacket off—that and his soaked parka. Then I took off my own coat, wrapped it around him, and put my baseball cap on his head. I rubbed his hands. I patted his cheeks. But he looked terrible lying there on the damp wooden floor of my boat, his face pale as a sheet, his eyes half shut and his lips as blue as a fresh bruise.

I was scared to death because I didn't know what to do! I pulled the cell phone out of my pocket, but my hand was shaking so bad that the phone slipped right out of my grasp, hit the edge of the boat, and disappeared into the water.

"Oh, no!" I exclaimed.

I looked back at Ben. He needed help. I had to quit messing around.

What do I do? What do I do? I was asking myself. *What would Carl do?* And I remembered those guys at the fire station talking about the ABC's. The first thing you did in an emergency was ABC's.

A was airways. I looked at Ben's nose. Clear as far as I could tell. Quickly, but gently—I knew you had to handle cold people carefully because of their

hearts, their hearts can go kind of nuts and not beat right—I rolled him onto his left side. Some water trickled out of his mouth.

"Good," I said out loud. "Good, Ben."

B was what? *B* was breathing. Was Ben breathing?

I pulled the choke out to flood the motor and shut it off so I could hear. But I couldn't hear anything! I put a finger under his nose and didn't feel anything. Was it because my fingers were numb with cold? I stared at his chest, but I couldn't see it moving. Quickly, I felt with two fingers against his throat for that artery, the big one up there under your jaw. But I couldn't feel anything.

No, I decided. Ben wasn't breathing.

Quickly now—I knew I had to—I rolled Ben back onto his back, then I bent over, pinched his nose shut, covered his small mouth with mine, and gave him two breaths. His lips were so cold they didn't feel real.

I checked again. He still wasn't breathing.

C. I remembered that *C* was circulation. Ben needed his blood to be moving around too.

Let's **Think** About...

Do you understand why Brady is trying to find out about Ben's condition? Reread to find out.

⊙ **Monitor and Clarify**

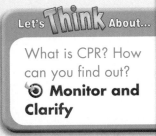
Let's **Think** About...

What is CPR? How can you find out?

🔘 **Monitor and Clarify**

"Oh," I moaned, thinking: *I've got to do it. I've got to do CPR!* I had been taught how—Dad and I took a class at the community center. We practiced on a dummy, and I watched Carl do it more than once. But would I remember?

I tilted Ben's head back a little, pinched his nose again, and started by giving him one breath. Then I sat up, put the heel of my right hand on his chest, covered it with my left, and pressed down. Five times I pressed down. Five compressions. Then I bent over for another breath. Then five compressions. Then another breath. Then five compressions.

I did not think about anything else as I did this. All I was doing was counting and pushing and breathing and praying inside that Ben would start breathing.

"Come on, Ben!" I begged him.

Five compressions. Then another breath. *Breathe, Ben, breathe!*

Ben needed to get to that ambulance fast. I had to get him down to the marina at Rock Hall. It wasn't that far but I wasn't going to get there sitting here in the creek.

Five compressions. Another breath.

I paused long enough to start the motor again and put the boat in gear.

Five compressions. One breath.

Then I headed my skiff in the right direction, grabbed the stern line, and looped it around the outboard's handle.

Back to Ben. Five compressions. One breath.

Quickly, I reached for the stern line and wrapped it around a cleat to keep the motor straight.

Five compressions. Another breath.

As if all that wasn't bad enough, it started to rain hard too.

I ignored it. I ignored the rain, the cold—everything—and just continued. Five compressions, another breath, a quick check to make sure the boat was headed in the right direction.

I glanced up and down, but there was no one in the river. No one! I headed the boat downstream to Rock Hall and kept working on Ben.

Five compressions, one breath. All the way down the river with the rain lashing my face and blurring my eyes until I saw a whirring ambulance light at the landing in the distance.

I kept on with the CPR. I knew I couldn't stop. Maybe I should have. I could have slammed the boat into high gear and opened the throttle. But I also knew that Ben needed me to keep breathing into him.

Let's **Think** About...

What is Brady's focus? How do you know? **Inferring**

37

Five compressions, one breath. We were almost at the landing. I heard someone yell my name, and Tilly started barking. Then more people were hollering, and there was a bank of flashing lights. At least two police cars, an ambulance. It was all a welcome blur. I continued with five compressions, one breath.

Suddenly Jimmy Landers, one of Carl's coworkers, was hollering real loud. "Keep it up, Brady! Keep it up! That's it! Pull the boat in— we've got it! Don't stop, Brady!"

Things happened even faster after that. Jimmy was down beside me taking over, then lifting Ben up onto the dock, where Carl took him and continued the CPR. Then Jimmy jumped back up on the dock, too, and I saw Carl place his fingers on Ben's neck, checking for a pulse. Someone else pulled in the boat while Carl and Jimmy kept working on Ben, even as they carried him to the ambulance.

Before a policeman closed the back doors of the ambulance, Carl shouted, "We've got a pulse!" There wasn't time for him to say anything more. The doors were closed and the ambulance took off, siren wailing, lights flashing.

Completely out of breath, I stood on the landing—I don't have a clue how I got there—and watched the lights disappear. I thought about how we were all going to be on that rescue show. We were all going to be on *Rescue 911,* I thought. All of us, I bet. Tilly, too.

Let's  About...

Why wouldn't Brady know how he got to the landing? Reread for clues.

⊙ **Monitor and Clarify**

A policeman came over and put his arm around my shoulders. "Good job, son," he said. He led me over to his cruiser and gave me a jacket. "Go ahead. Get inside and warm up."

"My dog," I mumbled. I was so out of breath I felt dizzy. "I can't leave my dog in the boat."

The policeman called for someone to get Tilly, and both of us, Tilly and I, got in the backseat of the cruiser to warm up.

"They're taking him over to Lester Krebb's field, where they've got a medevac helicopter coming," the policeman told me. He pulled out a notebook. "When you're ready, I need you to give us a little report."

Let's Think About...

Based on the text and the illustration, what can you tell about Ben's situation?
Inferring

Let's **Think** About...

What is the policeman's opinion of Brady? How do you know?
Inferring

I told him how I had found Ben. When the officer was satisfied, he offered me a ride home in the cruiser. But I wanted to get my boat back too. I assured him I could get home on my own.

"I don't doubt it," he said, grinning.

The rain had let up some, so the policeman let us go. He said he would call both my parents to let them know I was okay and that I was headed home.

Back in the boat, I put Ben's life jacket and his soaked parka to one side and picked up my Orioles hat from the floor, where I'd done the CPR on Ben. It must have fallen off when they picked him up. It felt a little strange, putting that hat back on my head after what it had just been through. But my head was cold. And I needed to get started.

Everyone else had left the landing by then. It was over. I began to feel a little relieved. Tilly and I headed upriver just as it started to rain hard again. But Carl's voice—*We've got a pulse!*—echoed in my ears, and I smiled. I think I could have driven through a blizzard right then. I felt both drained and elated.

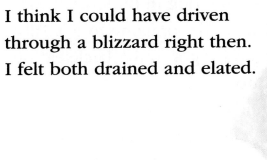

I'll tell you this: I am not the type of person who prays very much. Hardly at all really. But about a minute later, I stopped that boat right in the middle of the Corsica River, in the pouring rain, to fold my hands. I just sat there with the engine in neutral, resting my head against the fingers of my tightly folded hands, because it had just hit me what happened. I'm not saying I cried, mind you, but I did have tears in my eyes.

I thought about how it all happened. About fate. I mean, what if Dad hadn't been working in the shop that Monday? Normally, he'd be out on the water. If he had been, he wouldn't have come to get me out of school. There wouldn't have been the extra person to check the little creeks and coves the way I did.

I knew then I would never be the same person anymore. Because that day on the Corsica River, the day I lifted Ben off the piling, I had straddled the invisible line between life and death that runs down all our lives every second—with every breath we take. And thanks to some good luck and timing—thanks to Tilly, too—I had pulled Benjamin DiAngelo from one side to the other.

Let's Think About...

Do you understand what Brady means by "I had straddled the invisible line between life and death"? Reread to find out.

Monitor and Clarify

41

Envision It! Retell

READING STREET ONLINE
STORY SORT
www.ReadingStreet.com

Think Critically

1. Think about the challenges Brady faced to rescue Ben. What do you think makes people act to save others? What would you have done? **Text to Self**

2. The author includes many details about the creek, shoreline, and channels. Give some examples of these details. Why do you think she included those details in this story?
Author's Purpose

3. What are some of Brady's character traits? Explain how these character traits affect the incidents in the story. Did his character traits foreshadow or give rise to the story's future events?
Literary Elements: Character and Plot

4. What are the "ABCs" that Brady refers to? How does he use them to help Ben? Try creating a sensory image to help you understand the scene.
Monitor and Clarify

5. **Look Back and Write** Reread the question on page 27. Write an explanation of how Brady helped when others were in danger.
TEST PRACTICE Extended Response

Priscilla Cummings

Priscilla Cummings grew up on a dairy farm in western Massachusetts where she developed a love for animals and nature. As a girl, she enjoyed doing many outdoor activities with her family, such as camping and hiking. She also loved to write stories about the farm animals.

After graduating from the University of New Hampshire, she worked as a newspaper reporter. Many of the skills she learned working as a reporter helped her to write novels. She says these skills helped her "transform the spark of an idea into an entire book."

As an adult, Ms. Cummings moved to Maryland, and after several years, she began to write about nature she observed. She wrote picture books about animals in the Chesapeake Bay. Later, she began to write novels. One of her first novels, *Red Kayak,* was selected by the American Library Association as one of the Best Books for Young Adults.

Here is another book by Priscilla Cummings.

Chadwick Forever

Use the *Reader's and Writer's Notebook* to record your independent reading.

43

Objectives

● Write essays with specific facts, details, and examples in an organized way.

Expository

Directions

Directions explain to readers the steps they need to take to complete a task. The student model on the next page is an example of a set of directions.

Writing Prompt In *Red Kayak,* a character uses his knowledge of CPR to help save the life of a younger child. Think about something you know how to do well. Write clear, step-by-step directions for that activity.

Let's Write It!

Key Features of Directions

● explain a process in steps

● describe steps in order

● are often numbered or have clue words that show order

READING STREET ONLINE
GRAMMAR JAMMER
www.ReadingStreet.com

Writer's Checklist

Remember, you should . . .

☑ explain the steps in order.

☑ include facts and details in an organized manner.

☑ use clue words to help show sequence.

How to Make Your Own First-Aid Kit

You've just been asked to put together a first-aid kit for a family camping trip.

First, make a checklist of basic first-aid supplies. Some items are cotton balls, rubbing alcohol, antibiotic cream, assorted bandages, gauze pads, adhesive tape, scissors, insect repellent, anti-itch cream, and a thermometer.

Next, look in the place in your home where first-aid supplies are kept. Do you have enough of everything for the number of people camping? Have an adult look at your list. Should anything be added? If so, add it now.

Then, gather all your supplies in one place. This will give you an idea of the size of box you're going to need. A strong, waterproof box would probably be best.

Now, pack the supplies in the box. Do it carefully; try to organize items so they can be easily found.

Finally, label the box FIRST-AID KIT, so it's easy to identify.

Oh, one last thing! Have a fun and safe time camping!

Genre Directions explain how to do something.

Writing Trait Directions are often **organized** by the sequence, or order, of steps.

The **four kinds of sentences** are used correctly.

Conventions

Four Kinds of Sentences

Remember **Declarative** sentences make a statement and end with a period, **interrogative** sentences end with a question mark, **imperative** sentences give commands, and **exclamatory** sentences end with an exclamation point.

45

Objectives
● Understand the details in a text to complete a task, solve a problem, or perform an action. ● Make connections between and among texts.

Genre
How-To Text

● How-to texts explain how to do or make something. However, they can also tell you how to follow a certain procedure.

● Most how-to texts contain a sequence of activities needed to carry out a task or procedure.

● Some how-to texts use numbered steps that tell the order of what to do.

● Read the article "What Will I Do in an Emergency?" Look for elements that make this article a how-to text. Then imagine that you are facing an emergency. What procedure are you following?

What Will I Do in an Emergency?

Have you ever thought about what you would do in an emergency?

In most places in the United States, dialing 9-1-1 on a phone connects you to people trained to help in an emergency.

When is the right time to dial 9-1-1?

Only call 9-1-1 when there is a REAL need or emergency.

⚠ There is a **FIRE** and you need firefighters.

⚠ There is a crime and you need the **POLICE.**

⚠ Someone is seriously injured or ill and you need an **AMBULANCE** and emergency medical technicians.

Before dialing 9-1-1, try to know the exact location of the emergency. If you are not at home, look for street names, big signs, and names on buildings. This information will help responders get to the location.

OK. You know what kind of help you need and where the emergency is.

1. Dial 9-1-1. Stay on the phone until the dispatcher comes on the line.

2. When the dispatcher answers, calmly and clearly tell what the emergency is and the type of help you need.

3. Give the location of the emergency.

4. The dispatcher will ask you for your name and address, and sometimes your phone number too, so he or she can call you back if you get disconnected.

5. Listen to and answer each of the dispatcher's questions.

6. End the call only when the dispatcher says it is OK to hang up.

You have done your best and help will be on the way.

Think it through and practice what you need to do. Then you'll be ready to meet the challenge.

Let's Think About...

How do the numbered steps explain how you should talk to a 9-1-1 dispatcher? **How-To Text**

Let's Think About...

Reading Across Texts Imagine that you see Ben from the shore before Brady gets to him. Think about the steps you would take in the 9-1-1 call process.

Writing Across Texts Based on your list, write a dialogue between a caller and a 9-1-1 dispatcher about Ben. Try to complete all six steps in the 9-1-1 call process.

Objectives

● Read aloud grade-level texts and understand what is read. ● Determine the meanings of unfamiliar words or multiple-meaning words by using the context of the sentence. ● Listen to and interpret a speaker's messages and ask questions. ● Participate in discussions by raising and considering suggestions from other group members and by identifying points of agreement and disagreement. ● Give organized presentations that communicate your ideas effectively.

Let's Learn It!

READING STREET ONLINE
ONLINE STUDENT EDITION
www.ReadingStreet.com

Vocabulary

Homographs

Context Clues Homographs are words that are spelled the same but have different meanings. You can use context clues to help you know which meaning is used. Think of all the meanings of the word. Then decide which meaning makes the most sense in the sentence.

Practice It! Reread *Red Kayak.* Look for words that are homographs. Copy the sentence with the homograph from the story. Then write a sentence of your own that uses another meaning of the homograph.

Fluency

Expression

Using different tones of voice as you read helps show the adventure in a story. You can express suspense and excitement by varying the rate at which you read and the loudness of your voice.

Practice It! With a partner, practice reading aloud page 34 of *Red Kayak.* Change the speed, volume, and expression of your voice to show the suspense and excitement in the story. Be sure to give each other feedback.

48

Listening and Speaking

When you participate in a discussion, ask and answer questions with detail.

Interview

In an interview, one person asks another person questions. The purpose of an interview is to find out what the person knows about or has done.

Practice It! With a partner, conduct an interview with Brady Parks about his rescue of Ben. Work together to prepare the interview questions and possible responses. One person should act as Brady while the other acts as the interviewer. Then change roles.

Tips

Listening . . .

- Listen to a speaker's messages.
- Ask questions during the interview for clarification.

Speaking . . .

- Make eye contact with your interview partner.
- Speak clearly to communicate during the interview.

Teamwork . . .

- Elicit suggestions from other group members.
- Consider suggestions from other group members.

Objectives
● Listen to and interpret a speaker's messages and ask questions.

Oral Vocabulary

Let's Talk About

Challenges in Nature

● Discuss ideas about challenges in nature.

● Listen to a classmate's ideas about challenges in nature.

● Ask a classmate questions about challenges in nature.

READING STREET ONLINE
CONCEPT TALK VIDEO
www.ReadingStreet.com

51

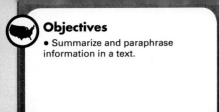
Envision It! | **Skill Strategy**

Skill

Strategy

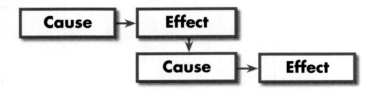

READING STREET ONLINE
ENVISION IT! ANIMATIONS
www.ReadingStreet.com

Comprehension Skill

🎯 Cause and Effect

- An effect is something that happens. A cause is the reason why something happens. A cause may have more than one effect, and an effect may have more than one cause.

- Clue words such as *because* and *since* can help you identify causes and effects. If there are no clue words, ask *Why did this happen? What happened as a result?*

- Analyze how causes and effects are organized to understand relationships.

- Use a graphic organizer like the one below to write three of the causes and effects from "The Real Thunder and Lightning" on page 53.

Cause	→	Effect

Cause	→	Effect

Comprehension Strategy

🎯 Summarize

Active readers summarize to check their understanding. As you read "The Real Thunder and Lightning," summarize the main ideas and leave out unimportant details so that you maintain the text's meaning.

The Real THUNDER and Lightning

Some tall tales and myths provide entertaining reasons for why things happen in nature. These stories are fun to read, but the real reasons can also be interesting.

The real cause of lightning is electrical charges. Inside a storm cloud, a strong positive electrical charge may form near the top, and a strong negative charge may form near the bottom. When these opposite charges flow toward each other, lightning flashes inside the cloud. When opposite charges flow from one cloud to another, lightning flashes between the clouds. When negative charges at the bottom of a cloud move down toward positive charges on Earth, lightning flashes from the cloud to the ground. Watch out!

Thunder happens only when there is lightning because lightning causes it. Thunder results from the rapid heating of the air along a lightning flash. The heated air expands. As a result, it creates a sound wave. Then the claps and rumbles of the thunder are heard.

Skill What clue word at the beginning of this paragraph lets you know that there is a cause-and-effect relationship here?

Skill What causes lightning that flashes from a cloud to the ground?

Strategy What ideas and details would you include in order to maintain meaning in a summary of this passage?

Your Turn!

⏸ **Need a Review?** See the *Envision It! Handbook* for additional help with cause and effect and summarizing.

▶ **Ready to Try It?** Use what you have learned about cause and effect and summarizing as you read *Thunder Rose*.

53

Objectives
● Determine the meanings of unfamiliar words or multiple-meaning words by using the context of the sentence.

Envision It! | Words to Know

branded

constructed

devastation

daintily   resourceful
lullaby   thieving
pitch   veins

READING STREET ONLINE
VOCABULARY ACTIVITIES
www.ReadingStreet.com

Vocabulary Strategy for

🎯 Homonyms

Context Clues When you read, you may come across homonyms. Homonyms are words that are spelled the same but have different meanings. For example, *feet* can mean "units of measurement" or "the end parts of the legs." You can use context clues to determine or clarify which meaning is being used.

Using the *Words to Know*, follow these steps.

1. Reread the sentence in which the homonym appears.

2. Look for clues to the homonym's meaning.

3. If you need more help, read the sentences around the sentence with the homonym.

4. Try the meaning in the sentence. Does it make sense?

Read "The Tale of Carrie the Calf" on page 55. Use context clues to help you determine or clarify the meanings of homonyms you find.

Words to Write Reread "The Tale of Carrie the Calf." Imagine you are Carrie the Calf. Write a story in the first person about a typical day in your unusual life. Use words from the *Words to Know* list in your story.

The Tale of Carrie the Calf

From the moment she was born, we knew Carrie the Calf was different. Her eyes were as black as pitch, and she was as strong as a bull. Instead of blood, she seemed to have a magic potion in her veins. Overnight, she grew fifty feet tall. Morning found her daintily eating the tops of trees.

It was hard getting enough for her to eat! We would give her one hundred bales of hay for breakfast, but by lunch she would be over at the next ranch, eating its trees and anything else in sight. This thieving did not make her too popular. It also caused considerable devastation around the country. Then the time came to brand the calves! How could a 150-foot-tall calf be branded? We quickly constructed a 200-foot-tall fence to hold her in. She just smiled, hopped over it, and then ambled off to find another forest to eat. To catch Carrie, we needed to be more resourceful.

Next, we made a set of speakers as big as a house. We broadcasted a soothing lullaby that could be heard over three states. Soon Carrie was sleeping without a care.

Your Turn!

 Need a Review?
For additional help with homonyms, see *Words!*

 Ready to Try It?
Read *Thunder Rose* on pp. 56–73.

by Jerdine Nolen • illustrated by Kadir Nelson

THUNDER Rose

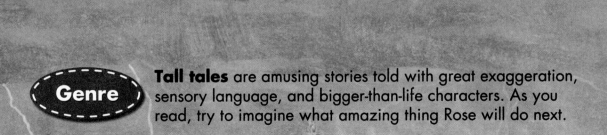

Genre

Tall tales are amusing stories told with great exaggeration, sensory language, and bigger-than-life characters. As you read, try to imagine what amazing thing Rose will do next.

ose was the first child born free and easy to Jackson and Millicent MacGruder. I recall most vividly the night she came into this world. Hailing rain, flashing lightning, and booming thunder pounded the door, inviting themselves in for the blessed event.

Taking in her first breath of life, the infant did not cry out. Rather, she sat up and looked around. She took ahold of that lightning, rolled it into a ball, and set it above her shoulder, while the thunder echoed out over the other. They say this just accentuated the fact that the child had the power of thunder and lightning coursing through her veins.

"She's going to grow up to be good and strong, all right," Doc Hollerday said.

The child turned to the good doctor with a thoughtful glance and replied, "I reckon I will want to do more than that. Thank you very kindly!"

Shifting her gaze to the two loving lights shining on her, which were her ma and pa, she remarked, "Much obliged to you both for this chance to make my way in the world!" Then she announced to no one in particular, "I am right partial to the name Rose."

So much in love with this gift of their lives, her ma and pa hovered over her in watchful splendor. Overcome with that love, they lifted their voices in song, an old song and a melody so sweet and true—a lullaby passed down from the ages, echoing since the beginning of time.

"There is a music ringing so sweetly in my ears," the new-born exclaimed. "It's giving me a fortunate feeling rumbling deep in the pit of me. I'll register it here at the bull's-eye set in the center of my heart, and see what I can do with it one day!"

Rose snored up plenty that first night breathing on her own, rattling the rafters on the roof right along with the booming thunder. There was nothing quiet about her slumber. She seemed determined to be just as forceful as that storm. With the thunder and lightning keeping watch over her the rest of the night, her ma and pa just took to calling her Thunder Rose.

The next morning, when the sun was high yellow in that billowy blue sky, Rose woke up hungry as a bear in spring, but not the least bit ornery. Minding her manners, she politely thanked her ma for the milk, but it was not enough to quench her hungry thirst. Rose preferred, instead, to drink her milk straight from the cow.

Her ma was right grateful to have such a resourceful child. No other newborn had the utter strength to lift a whole cow clear over her head and almost drink it dry. In a moment's time, Rose did, and quite daintily so. She was as pretty as a picture, had the sweetest disposition, but don't let yourself be misled, that child was full of lightning *and* thunder.

Out on that paper-bag brown, dusty dry, wide-open space, Rose often was found humming a sweet little tune as she did her chores. And true to her word, Rose did *more* than grow good and strong.

The two-year-old became quite curious about the pile of scrap iron lying next to the barn. Rose took a good-sized

piece, stretched it here, bent and twisted it there. She constructed a thunderbolt as black as pitch to punctuate her name. She called it Cole. Wherever she went, Cole was always by her side. Noticing how skilled Rose was with the metal, her pa made sure there was an extra supply of it always around.

At the age of five, Rose did a commendable job of staking the fence without a bit of help. During her eighth and ninth years, Rose assembled some iron beams together with the wood blocks she used to play with and constructed a building tall enough to scrape the sky, always humming as she worked.

By the time she turned twelve, Rose had perfected her metal-bending practices. She formed delicately shaped alphabet letters to help the young ones learn to read. For his birthday, Rose presented her pa with a branding iron, a circle with a big *M-A-C* for MacGruder in the middle, just in time, too, because a herd of quick-tempered longhorn steer was stampeding its way up from the Rio Grande. They were plowing a path straight toward her front door.

Rose performed an eye-catching wonder, the likes of which was something to see. Running lightning-fast toward the herd, using Cole for support, Rose vaulted into the air and landed on the back of the

biggest lead steer like he was a merry-go-round pony. Grabbing a horn in each hand, Rose twisted that varmint to a complete halt. It was just enough to restrain that top bull and the rest of the herd.

But I believe what touched that critter's heart was when Rose began humming her little tune. That cantankerous ton of beef was restless no more. He became as playful as a kitten and even tried to purr. Rose named him Tater on account of that was his favorite vegetable. Hearing Rose's lullaby put that considerable creature to sleep was the sweetest thing I had witnessed in a long, long time.

After the dust had settled, Ma and Pa counted twenty-seven hundred head of cattle, after they added in the five hundred they already had. Using the scrap iron, Rose had to add a new section to the bull pen to hold them all.

"What did you do to the wire, Rose?" Ma asked, surprised and pleased at her daughter's latest creation.

"Oh, that," she said. "While I was staking the fence, Pa asked me to keep little Barbara Jay company. That little twisty pattern seemed to make the baby laugh. So I like to think of it as a Barbara's Wire."

"That was right clever of you to be so entertaining to the little one like that!" her ma said. Rose just blushed. Over the years, that twisty wire caught on, and folks just called it barbed wire.

Rose and her pa spent the whole next day sorting the animals that had not been branded. "One day soon, before the cold weather gets in," she told her pa, "I'll have to get this herd up the Chisholm Trail and to market in Abilene. I suspect Tater is the right kind of horse for the long drive northward."

On Rose's first trip to Abilene, while right outside of Caldwell, that irascible, full-of-outrage-and-ire outlaw Jesse Baines and his gang of desperadoes tried to rustle that herd away from Rose.

Using the spare metal rods she always carried with her, Rose lassoed those hot-tempered hooligans up good and tight. She dropped them all off to jail, tied up in a nice neat iron bow. "It wasn't any trouble at all," she told Sheriff Weaver. "Somebody had to put a stop to their thieving ways."

But that wasn't the only thieving going on. The mighty sun was draining the moisture out of every living thing it touched. Even the rocks were crying out. Those clouds stood by and watched it all happen. They weren't even trying to be helpful.

Why, the air had turned so dry and sour, time seemed to all but stand still. And there was not a drop of water in sight. Steer will not move without water. And that was making those bulls mad, real mad. And when a bull gets angry, it's like a disease that's catching, making the rest of the herd mad, too. Tater was looking parched and mighty thirsty.

"I've got to do something about this!" Rose declared.

Stretching out several iron rods lasso-fashion, then launching Cole high in the air, Rose hoped she could get the heavens to yield forth. She caught hold of a mass of clouds and squeezed them hard, real hard, all the while humming her song. Gentle rain began to fall. But anyone looking could see there was not enough moisture to refresh two ants, let alone a herd of wild cows.

Suddenly a rotating column of air came whirling and swirling around, picking up everything in its path. It sneaked up on Rose. "Whoa, there, now just hold on a minute," Rose called out to the storm. Tater was helpless to do anything about that sort of wind. Those meddlesome clouds caused it. They didn't take kindly to someone telling them what to do. And they were set on creating a riotous rampage all on their own.

Oh, this riled Rose so much, she became the only two-legged

tempest to walk the western plains. "You don't know who you're fooling with," Rose called out to the storm. Her eyes flashed lightning. She bit down and gnashed thunder from her teeth. I don't know why anyone would want to mess with a pretty young woman who had the power of thunder and lightning coursing through her veins. But, pity for them, the clouds did!

Rose reached for her iron rod. But there was only one piece left. She did not know which way to turn. She knew Cole alone

was not enough to do the job right. Unarmed against her own growing thirst and the might of the elements, Rose felt weighted down. Then that churning column split, and now there were two. They were coming at her from opposite directions. Rose had some fast thinking to do. Never being one to bow down under pressure, she considered her options, for she was not sure how this would all come out in the end.

"Is this the fork in the road with which I have my final supper? Will this be my first and my last ride of the roundup?" she queried herself in the depths of her heart. Her contemplations brought her little relief as she witnessed the merciless, the cataclysmic efforts of a windstorm bent on her disaster. Then the winds joined hands and cranked and churned a path heading straight toward her! Calmly Rose spoke out loud to the storm as she stood alone to face the wrack and ruin, the multiplying devastation. "I *could* ride at least *one* of you out to the end of time! But I've got this fortunate feeling rumbling deep in the pit of me, and I see what I am to do with it this day!" Rose said, smiling.

The winds belted at a rumbling pitch. Rose squarely faced that storm. "Come and join me, winds!" She opened her arms wide as if to embrace the torrent. She opened her mouth as if she were planning to take a good long drink. But from deep inside her, she heard a melody so real and sweet and true. And when she lifted her heart, she unleashed *her* song of thunder. It was a sight to see: Rose making thunder and lightning rise and fall to the ground at her command, at the sound of *her song*. Oh, how her voice rang out so clear and real and true. It rang from the mountaintops. It filled up the valleys. It flowed like a healing river in the breathing air around her.

Those tornadoes, calmed by her song, stopped their churning masses and raged no more. And, gentle as a baby's bath, a soft, drenching-and-soaking rain fell.

And Rose realized that by reaching into her own heart to bring forth the music that was there, she had even touched the hearts of the clouds.

The stories of Rose's amazing abilities spread like wildfire, far and wide. And as sure as thunder follows lightning, and sun follows rain, whenever you see a spark of light flash across a heavy steel gray sky, listen to the sound of the thunder and think of Thunder Rose and *her* song. That mighty, mighty song pressing on the bull's-eye that was set at the center of her heart.

Objectives
• Provide evidence from text to support understanding. • Read independently for a sustained period of time and paraphrase the reading, including the order in which events occur.

Envision It! | Retell

READING STREET ONLINE
STORY SORT
www.ReadingStreet.com

Think Critically

1. Think about thunderstorms you have been in or watched outside. Compare what you have heard and seen to the storms in *Thunder Rose*. What does this tell you about Thunder Rose's decision to battle the storm?
   Text to World

2. Recall how Rose meets the challenge of the tornadoes. The author has prepared you for this unusual solution. How would the ending be different if you did not know about what happened the day Rose was born? **Think Like an Author**

3. What caused Rose to question her survival? What effect did her song have on the storm?
   Cause and Effect

4. Summarize the events of Thunder Rose's birth. Tell what Thunder Rose says and does after she is born. **Summarize**

5. **Look Back and Write** Reread the question on page 57. Think about one challenge Rose set for herself. Write an explanation of how she faced that challenge.

   TEST PRACTICE Extended Response

Meet the Author and the Illustrator

Jerdine Nolen and Kadir Nelson

Read other books by Jerdine Nolen and Kadir Nelson.

Jerdine Nolen says that as a child she was never bored. There was always something to do with her five sisters and two brothers. Despite all the distractions, Ms. Nolen says she can't remember a time when she wasn't writing and collecting words. "My mother encouraged me to do that. She was always eager to hear my new list of 'favorite words.'"

Once you have a story, Ms. Nolen says, it's important to keep revising and reworking it. "It is like sculpting or wiring the pieces together in a way, so the words on the page have enough life—they could stand up and walk around all on their own."

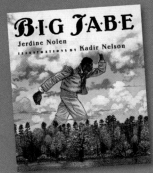

Big Jabe

Kadir Nelson says that as a child, "I always knew I'd be an artist. My mother was so supportive, and she never talked me out of it. I was also fortunate that I had an uncle who was an art teacher. He introduced me to the seriousness of taking care of my gift."

Ellington Was Not a Street

Mr. Nelson has created artwork for *Vibe Magazine*, *Sports Illustrated*, *The New York Times*, and Nike. His paintings can be found in the private collections of famous actors, sports figures, and musicians.

Use the *Reader's and Writer's Notebook* to record your independent reading.

Objectives
● Write creative stories that use sensory details to create a believable setting. ● Use the complete subject and verb in a sentence. ● Write creative stories that include a clear focus, plot, and point of view.

Let's Write It!

Key Features of a Tall Tale

● story events are greatly exaggerated

● has larger-than-life characters

● usually amusing or humorous

READING STREET ONLINE
GRAMMAR JAMMER
www.ReadingStreet.com

Tall Tale

A **tall tale** is an amusing story told with great exaggeration and larger-than-life characters. The student model on the next page is an example of a tall tale.

Writing Prompt Think about a character who is larger than life. Now write a tall tale, using exaggeration to stretch the truth in an entertaining way.

Writer's Checklist

Remember, you should . . .

☑ use an informal voice to tell the tale.

☑ exaggerate deeds done by the main character.

☑ use sensory details to create a believable setting.

Sally Sue to the Rescue!

Sally Sue <u>always tried to be helpful</u>. When she was a toddler, she carried a full-grown horse into the house to play with it. And later, when the farmer's old mule was too tired to work, Sally Sue herself <u>pulled the plow through four acres of crops</u>—in just one hour!

Sally Sue's parents always taught her to be careful of her strength. So she never dug deep holes for fear they would become huge lakes when it rained. And she didn't pull up pine trees to use as pick-up sticks, because she knew the trees were home to many critters.

But one year, there was a terrible drought. No rains fell, and <u>crops, people, and animals were powerfully thirsty</u>.

Sally Sue <u>knew she could help</u>. She stepped over the mountains and grabbed some thick, gray clouds that were hiding. She twisted and shook these overstuffed pillows of water until she got every last drop of rain from them!

From then on, if a drought occurred—it was Sally Sue to the rescue!

Genre
A **tall tale** tells an exaggerated adventure in an entertaining way.

Writing Trait
The writer's **voice** is friendly and informal.

Subjects and **predicates** are used correctly.

Conventions

Subjects and Predicates

Remember The **subject** is who or what the sentence is about. The **predicate** tells what the subject is or does. For example, *Tina and her father* are the subject of the sentence *Tina and her father cook dinner.* The predicate is *cook dinner.*

Objectives

● Use text features and graphics to gain an overview and locate information. ● Make connections between ideas within a text and across two or three texts. ● Make connections between and among texts.

Genre
Expository Text

● An expository text explains a person, place, thing, or event.

● Expository texts include several facts about the subject, often written in categories or classifications. Some texts might also include a few opinions.

● Some expository texts will include graphics, such as charts and photos. These graphics help readers locate information.

● Read the expository text "Measuring Tornadoes." How does the author's classification of tornadoes help you understand the text?

Measuring Tornadoes

BY TRUDI STRAIN TRUEIT

About 800 tornadoes strike the United States each year, resulting in an average of 80 deaths and 1,500 injuries.

It is difficult to accurately measure the high winds inside a tornado, so scientists rely on the Fujita Scale, or F-scale, for help. Created by Theodore Fujita, the F-scale looks at the damage a tornado causes to figure out its wind speed. Nearly 70 percent of the twisters that hit the United States fall into the F-0 and F-1 categories. These weak tornadoes are typically less than 3 miles (5 km) long and no wider than 50 yards (45 m). They usually do little damage—unless they strike without warning.

About 30 percent of tornadoes are strong tornadoes, rating F-2 or F-3 on the scale. Those reaching F-4 or above are called violent tornadoes. Fewer than one in fifty twisters ever become violent, but the most violent tornadoes cause almost two-thirds of tornado-related deaths.

FUJITA SCALE		
RATING	**ESTIMATED WIND SPEED**	**DAMAGE**
F-0 (weak)	**40–72 mph** (64–116 kph)	**Light:** Damage to TV antennae, chimneys, and small trees (about 3 of 10 tornadoes are F-0)
F-1 (weak)	**73–112 mph** (117–180 kph)	**Moderate:** Broken windows, mobile homes overturned, moving cars pushed off roads (about 4 of 10 tornadoes)
F-2 (strong)	**113–157 mph** (181–253 kph)	**Considerable:** Roofs torn off, mobile homes and large trees destroyed (about 2 of 10 tornadoes)
F-3 (strong)	**158–206 mph** (254–331 kph)	**Severe:** Cars lifted off the ground, trains overturned (about 6 of 100 tornadoes)
F-4 (violent)	**207–260 mph** (332–418 kph)	**Devastating:** Solid walls torn apart, cars tossed, large objects become missiles (about 2 of 100 tornadoes)
F-5 (violent)	**261–318 mph** (419–511 kph)	**Incredible:** Homes lifted off their foundations and thrown, straw and grass able to pierce tree trunks (fewer than 1 of 100 tornadoes)
F-6 to F-12 (violent)	**319–700 mph** (512–1,126 kph) or Mach 1, the speed of sound	**Inconceivable:** Though it was once thought tornadoes could reach the speed of sound, scientists now believe F-5 is the top of the scale.

Let's **Think** About...

Identify three facts on this page.
Expository Text

Let's **Think** About...

How does the chart help you to locate information about tornadoes?
Expository Text

Let's **Think** About...

Reading Across Texts Look back at the drawings of the twin tornadoes that Thunder Rose lassoed. Where do you think they would be listed on the Fujita Scale?

Writing Across Texts Describe what you think Thunder Rose's tornadoes did to the farms in her area.

Objectives

● Read aloud grade-level texts and understand what is read.
● Identify and explain the meaning of common idioms. ● Use the complete subject and verb in a sentence.
● Listen to and interpret a speaker's messages and ask questions.
● Give organized presentations that communicate your ideas effectively.
● Participate in discussions by raising and considering suggestions from other group members and by identifying points of agreement and disagreement.

Let's Learn It!

READING STREET ONLINE
ONLINE STUDENT EDITION
www.ReadingStreet.com

Vocabulary

Idioms

Context Clues An idiom is a phrase whose meaning cannot be determined by the ordinary meaning of the words that form it. For example, *easy as pie* means "very easy." You can use context clues—the words and sentences around the idiom—to determine the meaning of the idiom.

Practice It! Look through *Thunder Rose* and find as many idioms as you can. Write down each idiom you find, and think of possible meanings for them. Use context to explain the meanings. Then ask your teacher if the meanings you came up with are correct.

Fluency

Rate

Using different rates as you read helps imitate the flow of everyday speech. Reading more slowly adds emphasis. Reading more quickly adds energy and excitement to a story.

Practice It! With a partner, practice reading aloud pages 63 and 65 of *Thunder Rose*. Focus on varying your reading rate to add emphasis and excitement. Take turns reading and offering each other feedback.

80

Listening and Speaking

Get Ready For Middle School

When you give a presentation, use natural gestures to communicate your ideas.

Storytelling

A tall tale is a humorous and exaggerated version of a heroic story. The purpose of a tall tale is to entertain the reader or listener.

Practice It! With a group, create a tall tale about the adventures of an imaginary character. Include exaggerations and vivid words in your tale. Use body language and facial expressions to make your tale funny and interesting. With your group, tell your tall tale to the rest of your class.

Tips

Listening . . .

- Listen to what the speaker is saying.

- Pay attention to the speaker to interpret his or her story.

- Ask questions to clarify the speaker's point of view.

Speaking . . .

- Make eye contact with your listeners as you tell your story.

- Use complete subjects and predicates in sentences.

Teamwork . . .

- Ask for and consider suggestions from group members.

Objectives
• Listen to and interpret a speaker's messages and ask questions.
• Identify the main ideas and supporting ideas in the speaker's message.

Let's Talk About

Survival

- Share ideas about survival.

- Listen to and interpret a classmate's ideas about survival.

- Determine classmates' main and supporting ideas about survival.

READING STREET ONLINE
CONCEPT TALK VIDEO
www.ReadingStreet.com

83

Objectives
- Make inferences about a text and use evidence from the text to support understanding.

Envision It! | Skill Strategy

Skill

Strategy

READING STREET ONLINE
ENVISION IT! ANIMATIONS
www.ReadingStreet.com

Comprehension Skill

Literary Elements: Theme and Setting

- The theme is the underlying meaning of a story.

- The theme is often not stated. You can find the theme using evidence from the story.

- The setting is where and when the story takes place. Writers use figurative language and details, such as sights and sounds, to describe the setting.

- Use a graphic organizer like the one below to describe the story's setting.

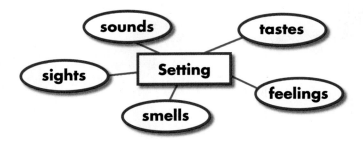

Comprehension Strategy

Inferring

When you infer, you combine your background knowledge with evidence in the text to come up with an idea about what the author is trying to present. Active readers often infer about the ideas, morals, lessons, and themes of a written work.

ALONE

Jesse heard the horses trotting and the wagon wheels creaking even after the wagon disappeared into the thick forest. Soon, those familiar sounds faded. Then he heard nothing but the summer wind rustling the tall prairie grass surrounding his family's log cabin. Jesse was all alone.

Jesse's parents had gone to town to buy supplies for the winter. They would be gone several days. His father insisted that Jesse was old enough to stay alone and manage the farm, but Jesse wasn't so sure.

Jesse milked the cow, weeded the garden, and fixed the latch on the barn door. He cooked his own potato soup and sliced some bread for dinner. That night, alone, Jesse had a hard time sleeping. Wolves howled in the distance. He was trained to use his father's musket and kept it nearby just in case. Each night, he lay in bed, nervous.

On the sixth day, Jesse heard a familiar sound. It was the wagon coming down the trail. His parents were home!

Skill After reading the title and first paragraph, which of these is the story's most likely theme?
(a) the beauty of nature
(b) love of animals
(c) surviving by yourself

Skill What figurative language does the author use in the story? Does it help you visualize the setting?

Strategy Make an inference about how Jesse is feeling at the end of the story. What evidence from the text supports this inference?

Your Turn!

⏸ Need a Review? See the *Envision It! Handbook* for additional help with theme, setting, and inferring.

▷ Ready to Try It? Use what you've learned as you read *Island of the Blue Dolphins*.

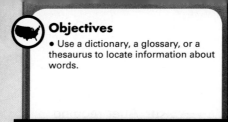

Envision It! | Words to Know

lair

ravine

shellfish

gnawed
headland
kelp
sinew

READING STREET ONLINE
VOCABULARY ACTIVITIES
www.ReadingStreet.com

Vocabulary Strategy for

🎯 Unknown Words

Dictionary/Glossary Sometimes when you read, you come across a word you do not know. You can use a glossary or dictionary to find out the meaning of the word. A glossary is a list of important words in a book and their meanings. A dictionary lists all words, in alphabetical order, and gives their meanings, pronunciations, syllabications, and other helpful information.

Choose one of the *Words to Know* and follow these steps.

1. Find the word in a dictionary or a glossary.

2. Read the pronunciation to yourself.

3. Read all the meanings given for the word.

4. Choose the meaning that makes sense in your sentence.

Read "Island Survival" on page 87. Use the glossary or a dictionary to help you determine the meanings, pronunciations, and syllabications of this week's *Words to Know.*

Words to Write Reread "Island Survival." Write a story about a wild animal that lives on an island. Use words from the *Words to Know* list in your story.

Island Survival

Have you ever imagined being shipwrecked on an island? What would you do to survive? First, you would take a look around to see how you could get food, water, and shelter. A lot would depend on what kind of land your island had.

A rocky, hilly island might have a cave you could use as your home—unless it was already a lair for a wild animal. As you explored, you would keep an eye out for things you could use for building or for hunting. Small trees growing in a ravine might be cut down to build a lean-to.

If you were able to hunt game, you might save parts of animals to use in your home. After you gnawed the flesh, you would have hides to make a blanket. Sinew could serve as a kind of rope. In shallow waters you would find shellfish to eat. The kelp floating there could be used as "wallpaper" or even as food.

If your island had a headland, it would provide a good high point from which to look out for rescue. You might build a fire there to draw the attention of passing ships.

Your Turn!

 **Need a Review?**
For additional help with using a dictionary or glossary to determine the meanings of unknown words, see *Words!*

 Ready to Try It?
Read *Island of the Blue Dolphins* on pp. 88–99.

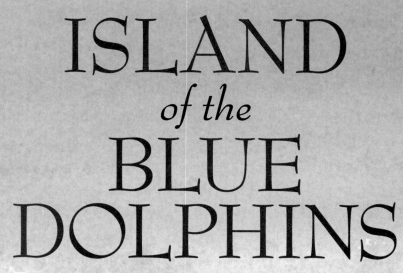

ISLAND
of the
BLUE
DOLPHINS

by Scott O'Dell   *illustrated by* E. B. Lewis

Question of the Week
How do people survive in the wilderness?

Genre

A **novel** is an extended work of fiction that contains story elements, such as setting, plot, and theme. As you read this novel excerpt, keep asking yourself how each incident gives rise to future events.

From 1835 to 1853, a young Native American girl named Karana lived alone on a rugged island seventy-five miles off the coast of California. The author has fashioned this story out of the few facts known about her.

Karana and her people lived on the island until Aleut hunters killed some of the men. A friendly ship later took her people off the island, but she stayed there to be with her brother, who was left behind by the ship's crew. After her brother was killed by wild dogs, Karana faced the challenge of living alone on the island.

The Island of the Blue Dolphins was my home; I had no other. It would be my home until the white men returned in their ship. But even if they came soon, before next summer, I could not live without a roof or a place to store my food. I would have to build a house. But where?

That night I slept on the rock, and the next day I began the search. The morning was clear, but to the north, banks of clouds hung low. Before long they would move in across the island, and behind them many other storms were waiting. I had no time to waste.

I needed a place that was sheltered from the wind, not too far from Coral Cove, and close to a good spring. There were two such places on the island—one on the headland and the other less than a league to the west. The headland seemed to be the more favorable of the two, but since I had not been to the other for a long time, I decided to go there and make certain.

The first thing I found, which I had forgotten, was that this place was near the wild dogs' lair. As soon as I drew near to it the leader came to the opening of the cave and watched me with his yellow eyes. If I built a hut here I would have to kill him and his pack. I planned to do this anyway, but it would take much time.

The spring was better than the one near the headland, being less brackish and having a steadier flow of water. Besides it was much easier to reach, since it came from the side of a hill and not from a ravine as the other one did. It was also close to the cliff and a ridge of rocks which would shelter my house.

The rocks were not so high as those on the headland and therefore would give me less protection from the wind, yet they were high enough, and from them I could see the north coast and Coral Cove.

The thing that made me decide on the place to build my house was the sea elephants.

The cliffs here fell away easily to a wide shelf that was partly covered when the tide came in. It was a good place for sea elephants because they could crawl halfway up the cliff if the day were stormy. On fair days they could fish among the pools or lie on the rocks.

The bull is very large and often weighs as much as thirty men. The cows are much smaller, but they make more noise than the bulls, screaming and barking through the whole day and sometimes at night. The babies are noisy too.

On this morning the tide was low and most of the animals were far out, just hundreds of specks against the waves, yet the noise they made was deafening. I stayed there the rest of the day, looking around, and that night. At dawn when the clamor started again I left and went back to the headland.

There was another place to the south where I could have built my house, near the destroyed village of Ghalas-at, but I did not want to go there because it would remind me of the people who were gone. Also the wind blew strong in this place, blowing against the dunes which cover the middle part of the island so that most of the time sand is moving everywhere.

Rain fell that night and lasted for two days. I made a shelter of brush at the foot of the rock, which kept off some of the water, and ate the food I had stored in the basket. I could not build a fire because of the rain and I was very cold.

On the third day the rain ceased and I went out to look for things which I would need in building the house. I likewise needed poles for a fence. I would soon kill the wild dogs, but there were many small red foxes on the island. They were so numerous that I could never hope to get rid of them either by traps or with arrows. They were clever thieves and nothing I stored would be safe until I had built a fence.

The morning was fresh from the rain. The smell of the tide pools was strong. Sweet odors came from the wild grasses in the ravines and from the sand plants on the dunes. I sang as I went down the trail to the beach and along the beach to the sandspit. I felt that the day was an omen of good fortune.

It was a good day to begin my new home.

Many years before, two whales had washed up on the sandspit. Most of the bones had been taken away to make ornaments, but the ribs were still there, half-buried in the sand.

These I used in making the fence. One by one I dug them up and carried them to the headland. They were long and curved, and when I had scooped out holes and set them in the earth they stood taller than I did.

I put the ribs together with their edges almost touching, and standing so that they curved outward, which made them impossible to climb. Between them I wove many strands of bull kelp, which shrinks as it dries and pulls very tight. I would have used seal sinew to bind the ribs together, for this is stronger than kelp, but wild animals like it and soon would have gnawed the fence down. Much time went into its building. It would have taken me longer except that the rock made one end of the fence and part of a side.

For a place to go in and out, I dug a hole under the fence just wide and deep enough to crawl through. The bottom and sides I lined with stones. On the outside I covered the hole with a mat woven of brush to shed the rain, and on the inside with a flat rock which I was strong enough to move.

I was able to take eight steps between the sides of the fence, which gave me all the room I would need to store the things I gathered and wished to protect.

I built the fence first because it was too cold to sleep on the rock, and I did not like to sleep in the shelter I had made until I was safe from the wild dogs.

The house took longer to build than the fence because it rained many days and because the wood I needed was scarce.

There was a legend among our people that the island had once been covered with tall trees. This was a long time ago, at the beginning of the world when Tumaiyowit and Mukat ruled. The two gods quarreled about many things. Tumaiyowit wished people to die. Mukat did not. Tumaiyowit angrily went down, down to another world under this world, taking his belongings with him, so people die because he did.

In that time there were tall trees, but now there were only a few in the ravines and these were small and crooked. It was very hard to find one that would make a good pole. I searched many days, going out early in the morning and coming back at night, before I found enough for a house.

I used the rock for the back of the house and the front I left open since the wind did not blow from this direction. The poles I made of equal length, using fire to cut them as well as a stone knife which caused me much difficulty because I had never made such a tool before. There were four poles on each side, set in the earth, and twice that many for the roof. These I bound together with sinew and covered with female kelp, which has broad leaves.

The winter was half over before I finished the house, but I slept there every night and felt secure because of the strong fence. The foxes came when I was cooking my food and stood outside gazing through the cracks, and the wild dogs also came, gnawing at the whale ribs, growling because they could not get in.

I shot two of them, but not the leader.

While I was building the fence and the house, I ate shellfish and perch which I cooked on a flat rock. Afterwards I made two utensils. Along the shore there were stones that the sea had worn smooth. Most of them were round, but I found two with hollow places in the center which I deepened and broadened by rubbing them with sand. Using these to cook in, I saved the juices of the fish which are good and were wasted before.

For cooking seeds and roots I wove a tight basket of fine reeds, which was easy because I had learned how to do it from my sister Ulape. After the basket had dried in the sun, I gathered lumps of pitch on the shore, softened them over the fire, and rubbed them on the inside of the basket so that it would hold water. By heating small stones and dropping them into a mixture of water and seeds in the basket I could make gruel.

I made a place for fire in the floor of my house, hollowing it out and lining it with rocks. In the village of Ghalas-at we made new fires every night, but now I made one fire which I covered with ashes when I went to bed. The next night I would remove the ashes and blow on the embers. In this way I saved myself much work.

There were many gray mice on the island and now that I had food to keep from one meal to other, I needed a safe place to put it. On the face of the rock, which was the back wall of my house, were several cracks as high as my shoulder. These I cut out and smoothed to make shelves where I could store my food and the mice could not reach it.

By the time winter was over and grass began to show green on the hills, my house was comfortable. I was sheltered from the wind and rain and prowling animals. I could cook anything I wished to eat. Everything I wanted was there at hand.

Objectives
● Provide evidence from text to support understanding. ●Write responses to literary or expository texts and provide evidence from the text to show that you understand the text.

Envision It! Retell

READING STREET ONLINE
STORY SORT
www.ReadingStreet.com

Think Critically

1. You read about Karana living alone on the island for less than a year. Think of what her chances are of surviving for many years on the island. What do you think your chances of surviving many years on the island would be? Why? Text to Self

2. The author chose to tell the story in first person, as if Karana were speaking to the reader. If you were the author and chose to write Karana's story from the third-person point of view, how would the story be different? Think Like an Author

3. Write a sentence that states the theme of the story. What evidence can you find to support the theme?

   Literary Elements: Theme and Setting

4. Karana mentions that her sister taught her how to weave baskets. What can you infer about the values of Karana's culture from this detail? Inferring

5. **Look Back and Write** Look back at page 97. Cutting poles for a house was physically challenging for Karana. How did she meet this challenge?

   TEST PRACTICE Extended Response

Scott O'Dell

Island of the Blue Dolphins was Scott O'Dell's first book for young people. It won the Newbery Medal and became a best seller. The idea for the book came when he found an article about a young girl, Karana, who lived alone for eighteen years on an island off the California coast. "*Island of the Blue Dolphins* began in anger, anger at the hunters who invade the mountains where I live and who slaughter everything that creeps or walks or flies," Mr. O'Dell wrote.

After *Island of the Blue Dolphins,* Mr. O'Dell wrote another twenty-five books for young people. He believed that writing stories for young readers was more rewarding than writing for adults. His young readers wrote him letters and asked many questions. One of the frequent questions was, "What's the most important thing a writer should do?" His answer was to stick with it. "Writing is hard, harder than digging a ditch, and it requires patience," he said.

Mr. O'Dell died in 1989.

Here are other books by Scott O'Dell.

The Black Pearl

Carlota

Use the *Reader's and Writer's Notebook* to record your independent reading.

Objectives

● Write letters that communicate ideas, include important information, contain a conclusion, and use the correct format and style.

Let's Write It!

Key Features of an Invitation

● may be informal or formal

● gives important information about an event or plan

● sometimes asks for a response

READING STREET ONLINE
GRAMMAR JAMMER
www.ReadingStreet.com

Expository

Invitation

An **invitation** is a note or letter that invites someone to attend an event. It includes important facts, such as the date, time, and place. The student model on the next page is an example of an invitation.

Writing Prompt Think about a place important to you that you would like a friend to visit. Write an invitation asking your friend to join you there. Use specific details.

Writer's Checklist

Remember, you should . . .

☑ include important information to convey ideas.

☑ use appropriate conventions, such as the date, salutation, and closing.

☑ give a sense of closure to the letter.

An Invitation to a Friend

Saturday, July 4, 20___

Dear Cameron,

My family is going to a Huron County park in three weeks. When Mom said I could invite a friend to come with me, I thought of you!

What: Hiking, fishing, and a picnic lunch

When: 7 A.M., Saturday, July 25

Where: Huron County's Sandy Pond Park

Dad said he'll bring fishing stuff for both of us!

Also, if it's all right with your folks, my parents said you can come home with us afterward and spend the night!

My mom will give your parents a call on Friday to talk about the plans, or they can call my mom on her cell phone: 202-555-9692.

Anyway, find out if you can join us. I sure hope you can make it!

Your friend,

Jason

Writing Trait
The invitation **focuses** on important information.

Genre
An **invitation** requests someone's attendance at an event.

Independent and dependent clauses are used correctly.

Conventions

Independent and Dependent Clauses

Remember An **independent clause** can stand alone as a sentence. A **dependent clause** cannot stand alone. For example: *They lived in the country house* (independent clause) *until they finished school* (dependent clause).

Objectives
● Understand the details in a text to complete a task, solve a problem, or perform an action. ● Interpret information in maps, charts, illustrations, graphs, timelines, tables, and diagrams. ● Make connections between and among texts.

Science in Reading

Genre
How-To Text

● A how-to text is a type of procedural text. Some how-to texts explain how to solve a problem. How-to texts may contain a sequence of activities needed to solve a problem.

● Illustrations and maps can present information to help you perform a procedure or gain an overview of the article's contents.

● Some how-to texts explain information with questions and answers.

● Read the article "Seven Survival Questions." Look for elements that make this article a how-to text. What problem does the article solve?

SEVEN SURVIVAL QUESTIONS

by Buck Tilton
from Boys' Life *Magazine*

When you're lost, being a good leader can mean the difference between life and death. John Gookin, an authority on wilderness survival at the National Outdoor Leadership School (NOLS), shares his expert advice:

1 Boys' Life: Why do people get lost?
Gookin: Reasons vary. For one thing, people go out prepared for one activity, but they end up doing another. They may plan to go fishing, for instance, but then decide to leave the lake and try rock climbing. That often leads to trouble.

The other big mistake is over-correcting for minor navigation errors. Instead of calmly retracing their steps, people head off in the wrong direction at a fast pace.

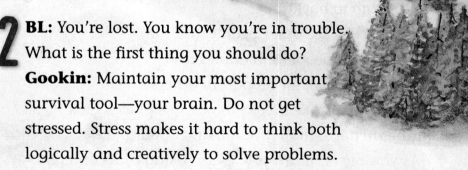

2 **BL:** You're lost. You know you're in trouble. What is the first thing you should do?

Gookin: Maintain your most important survival tool—your brain. Do not get stressed. Stress makes it hard to think both logically and creatively to solve problems.

Sit down. Drink some water. Collect your thoughts. Breathe deeply. Look at a map. Try to decide where you are, and then try to backtrack to known territory. Avoid anything that looks like a shortcut.

Let's **Think** About...

What sequence of activities should you follow in question 2? **How-To Text**

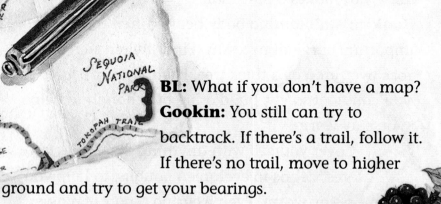

owl feather

Let's **Think** About...

How does the map on this page help you understand the information in the text?

3 **BL:** What if you don't have a map?

Gookin: You still can try to backtrack. If there's a trail, follow it. If there's no trail, move to higher ground and try to get your bearings.

Keep your group together. If you can, eat and drink and rest often. When you're tired and thirsty, it's easier to make bad decisions.

Blackberry

4 **BL:** Are there things you should do while you're trying to backtrack?

Gookin: If you see other people, ask for directions. Lost people sometimes are embarrassed to ask for help from others.

Stay visible. Take breaks in obvious places such as trail junctions, high ground, and open spaces.

As you move, mark your path. Using rocks or logs or tree limbs, build arrows that point in the direction you're traveling. The arrows will help guide searchers and you, too, if you need to retrace your steps.

Let's Think About...

How do the illustrations on these pages help you understand the information in this text?
How-To Text

5 **BL:** What if you can't find familiar terrain?

Gookin: Find a safe place to spend the night while there is still plenty of light. Stay calm.

6 **BL:** What makes a place safe?

Gookin: Maintaining body heat is often the most important survival necessity. Find shelter such as a rock overhang or a thick tree. High ground is best. If you can do it safely, build a fire big enough to help you stay warm.

Cover yourself with anything available, from forest debris to evergreen boughs, to help you stay warm. Even wearing a pair of glasses helps hold in a little bit of heat. Make a bed of green boughs if the ground is cold or snowy.

Huddle as a group, like spoons in a drawer. Don't expect a great night's sleep. You'll be lucky to get catnaps.

Stay near a trail in case others pass by.

Fir

TOP SURVIVAL DOS:

- Stay calm.
- Be methodical.
- Drink water.
- Keep warm.
- Build a fire—it's good for signaling and warmth.

TOP SURVIVAL DON'TS:

- Don't take risks or shortcuts.
- Don't act impulsively.
- Don't hike after dark.
- Don't avoid people. Ask for help.
- Don't lose your spirit. Think positive thoughts.

7

BL: What about the next day?

Gookin: Make yourself easy to find. Stay put, and sit in open spaces or on high points.

Searchers most easily spot geometric shapes (like a triangle or SOS) from the sky. Build one or more using your gear or anything else available, including people. Keep any reflective material out in the open. Signal mirrors are excellent survival tools. Used correctly, they can be seen for 20 miles. If you don't have a mirror, improvise with glass or even eyeglass lenses. A smoky fire can also be seen from far away in calm conditions.

Let's **Think** About...

Reading Across Texts If Karana listed survival tips for life on her island, what might they be? List these tips.

Writing Across Texts Look at your list. Choose the tip that you think is most important and write a paragraph explaining your choice.

Objectives

- Read aloud grade-level texts and understand what is read.
- Use a dictionary, a glossary, or a thesaurus to locate information about words. • Follow, restate, and give oral instructions. • Participate in discussions by raising and considering suggestions from other group members and by identifying points of agreement and disagreement.
- Give organized presentations that communicate your ideas effectively.

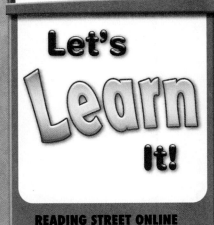

Let's Learn It!

READING STREET ONLINE
ONLINE STUDENT EDITION
www.ReadingStreet.com

Vocabulary

Unknown Words

Dictionary/Glossary If you are unable to determine a word's meaning from the context, look up the word in a dictionary or glossary. You can find the meaning of the unknown word, along with its part of speech, syllabication, and pronunciation.

Practice It! Identify three words that you don't know from *Island of the Blue Dolphins*. Look up each word in a dictionary or glossary, using the syllabication to pronounce each word. Write down the part of speech. Write the definition that best fits the word as it is used in the text.

Fluency

Expression

Using different tones of voice as you read helps to show how the characters feel. Adjust your voice to reflect what is happening in the story and to express the characters' emotions.

Practice It! With a partner, practice reading aloud page 91 of *Island of the Blue Dolphins*. Use different tones of voice to represent the way Karana feels. Take turns reading and offering each other feedback.

Listening and Speaking

Get Ready For Middle School

When giving a presentation, use conventions of language to communicate your ideas.

How-to Demonstration

A how-to demonstration describes how to do an activity. The purpose of a how-to demonstration is to teach others how to make an item or do an activity.

Practice It! Create a how-to demonstration about building a structure. Use *Blue Dolphins* to decide which kinds of tools and materials to include. Write detailed steps and order them. Then present them to your class, and restate the steps when necessary.

Tips

Listening . . .

- Follow oral instructions that involve a series of related actions.

Speaking . . .

- Use conventions to effectively communicate each step.
- Use gestures to communicate the action to be taken in each step.

Teamwork . . .

- Identify points of agreement and disagreement.
- Obtain suggestions from other group members.

Objectives
● Listen to and interpret a speaker's messages and ask questions.
● Identify the main ideas and supporting ideas in the speaker's message.

Oral Vocabulary

Let's Talk About

Personal Challenges

- Discuss personal challenges you have faced.

- Listen to and interpret a classmate's ideas about his or her personal challenges.

- Determine classmates' main and supporting ideas about challenges.

READING STREET ONLINE
CONCEPT TALK VIDEO
www.ReadingStreet.com

129

CANADA

You've learned
0 3 0
Amazing Words
so far this year!

Objectives
● Ask different types of questions about a text. ● Identify the facts in a text and prove that they are facts.

Envision It! | **Skill Strategy**

Skill

Strategy

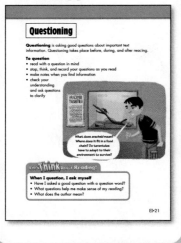

READING STREET ONLINE
ENVISION IT! ANIMATIONS
www.ReadingStreet.com

Comprehension Skill

🎯 Fact and Opinion

- You can prove a statement of fact true or false. You can do this by using your own knowledge, asking an expert, or checking a reference source.

- A statement of opinion gives ideas or feelings, not facts. It cannot be proved true or false.

- A sentence may contain both a statement of fact and a statement of opinion.

- Use a graphic organizer like the one below to help you determine and verify facts in "A Special League."

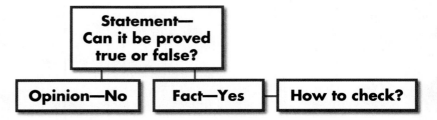

Comprehension Strategy

🎯 Questioning

As you read, ask yourself questions. You can ask a literal question, which can be answered by looking at or recalling information directly in the text. The answers to your questions can help you recall and understand what you read.

A Special League

African Americans have played baseball since the sport began. For many years, however, they were not allowed to play on the same team as white players.

In 1882, the first African American teams were formed. Unlike earlier players, these players were paid to play, because they were more fun to watch.

Skill Does this sentence contain a fact and an opinion?

The National Negro League (NNL) was founded in 1920. Another league, the Eastern Colored League, was founded in 1923. These leagues gave talented athletes the chance to play and gave fans the chance to see the best baseball players of all time.

Strategy Do you have any literal questions to ask here? If so, write them down.

The NNL became very popular in the 1930s. From then until 1950, teams played in the East–West All-Star Game, attended by up to forty thousand fans! Yet things were not so easy for African American players. They had to travel more often and play more games than white players. They made less money. In some places they were refused hotel rooms.

In 1947, professional baseball became integrated. That year, African Americans were allowed to play with whites in the major leagues. Meanwhile, television was starting to show baseball games. These events eventually led to the end of the NNL.

Skill What could you use to verify this article's facts?

Your Turn!

 Need a Review? See the *Envision It! Handbook* for help with fact and opinion and questioning.

Ready to Try It? Use what you've learned about fact and opinion and questioning as you read *Satchel Paige*.

Envision It! | Words to Know

confidence

outfield

windup

fastball

mocking

unique

weakness

READING STREET ONLINE
VOCABULARY ACTIVITIES
www.ReadingStreet.com

Vocabulary Strategy for

🎯 Antonyms

Context Clues Antonyms are words with opposite meanings. You can use analogies, or comparisons that show relationships, to help you understand antonyms. For example, *cold* is to *hot* as *few* is to *many*. Sometimes an author writes an antonym near a word to help readers understand the word.

1. Use what you know about antonyms to complete this analogy: *weakness* is to *strength* as *illness* is to _____.

2. When you read a word you don't know, reread the sentence with the unfamiliar word. Look for an antonym or context clues.

3. If you find an antonym, try using it in place of the unfamiliar word. Does it make sense?

Read "Play Ball!" on page 115. Look for nearby antonyms to help you determine or clarify the meanings of this week's *Words to Know*.

Words to Write Reread "Play Ball!" Write a paragraph about a baseball game you've seen. Use words from the *Words to Know* list in your writing.

Play Ball!

Many young people dream of becoming a great baseball player. Only a few will be able to do this. One reason is that you must first have a lot of talent. Another is that you must be willing to work very hard. With work comes skill. With skill comes the confidence a great player needs.

For a pitcher, every windup and throw of the ball helps him or her learn something. Whether learning to deliver a smoking fastball or a dancing curve, the pitcher must master difficult moves. A hitter learns with every at-bat which pitch should go by and which should be slammed into the outfield. Even the mocking "Heybatterbatterbatter" of the other team can help build a hitter's concentration.

Being dedicated, the great player of tomorrow is willing to work on a weakness until it finally becomes a strength. The really great player is unique. He or she has passed the common level of play expected and has invented a style that stands out. Every player who tries hard and loves the game, though, is a winner, no matter what.

⏸ **Need a Review?** For additional help with antonyms, see *Words!*

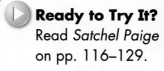

▶ **Ready to Try It?** Read *Satchel Paige* on pp. 116–129.

Satchel Paige

by Lesa Cline-Ransome
paintings by James E. Ransome

Question of the Week
**How do we face
personal challenges?**

Genre

A **biography** tells about a person's life. Look for
how the author presents major events in Satchel
Paige's life.

Leroy "Satchel" Paige earned his nickname as a young man. He carried suitcases—satchels—for passengers at Union Station in Mobile, Alabama. Satchel was a natural athlete. People said that by the age of ten he could outpitch grown men. So in 1923, at the age of 19, he decided to earn his living as a baseball player. In those days baseball was a segregated sport. African Americans were forced to play in their own leagues, separate from whites.

As a semipro pitcher, Satchel developed his own unique style. He'd pick up a tip here and there, put his Satchel spin on it, and polish it off with a brand-new name. Got so Satch began to think of his pitches as his children. The "hesitation" was his magic slow ball. The "trouble ball" caused all sorts of havoc. And then there was the "bee ball," which, according to Satch, would "always be where I want it to be."

There was an odd way about his pitching. He would stand
tall and straight as an oak tree on the mound. His foot looked
to be about a mile long, and when he shot it into the air, it
seemed to block out the sun. Satch's arm seemed to stretch
on forever, winding, bending, twisting. And then there was
that grin he flashed just as he released the ball. It seemed
to say, "Go ahead, just try and get a hit off of that."

"Strike one!"

And you never saw it coming. I mean, one minute it was
there, plain as day in his hand, and then, all of a sudden . . .

"Strike two!"

It was in the catcher's mitt. The batter would strain his
eyes, squint a little.

Here it comes, got it now.

"Strike three!"

Just like that. All over.

"Next batter up!"

"Give it to 'em, Satch. Show your stuff," fans and team-mates would shout. And he did. Every time. Folks would pack the stands to see how many Satchel could strike out in one game. He made the crowds laugh with his fast talking and slow walking ("A man's got to go slow to go long and far," he'd say), but mostly he made them cheer. Never in his nine-teen years had he heard a sweeter sound. The more cheers he heard, the more his confidence grew. A kind of confidence that made him call to the outfield with the bases loaded and the last hitter up to bat, "Why don't you all have a seat. Won't be needing you on this one."

Wherever the crowds went, a good paycheck followed, so he made sure to keep them coming. After just one year he was playing in the Negro major leagues for the Chattanooga Black Lookouts, and the folks were still cheering and shouting, "Give it to 'em, Satch. Show your stuff."

There were two major leagues back in 1924, when Satchel was called up. Because the white major-league ball clubs wouldn't allow blacks to play in their leagues, blacks had created their own in 1920 and named them the Negro Leagues. The white major-league players enjoyed trains, hotels, hot meals, and short seasons.

Negro League players were often refused meals in restaurants and rooms in hotels. They ate on the road and slept where they could—in train depots or on baseball fields. They played two, sometimes three games a day, nearly every day, in a season as long as the weather would hold. And when the season ended in America, Satch went right on playing and traveling in other parts of the world.

Life in the Negro Leagues suited Satchel. He was a traveling man. One city could never hold him for long. He moved from Alabama, where he played with the Birmingham Black Barons, to Tennessee, where he played with the Nashville Elite Giants, and to Pennsylvania, where he played with the Pittsburgh Crawfords.

From the first breath of spring till the cool rush of fall he would ride. Sometimes he joined his teammates on rickety old buses, bumping along on back roads studded with potholes so deep, players would have to hold on to their seats (and stomachs) just to keep from spilling into the aisles. But mostly he drove alone, in cars that would take him wherever he wanted to go. The fans would always be waiting in the next town. Their wait could be a long one—he was never much for keeping anyone's time but his own.

Once he reached his mid-thirties, the joys of traveling began to wear thin for Satchel. He found himself longing for a more settled life and the comforts of a home. In 1941 he finally found it in the warm smile and tender heart of Lahoma Brown. Satch rested his travel-weary legs and happily began his second career as husband and father. But even though he had finally found what he thought he'd been searching for, it was only a year before he took to the road again with his first and only true love—baseball. His family would have to wait.

Satchel's teammates were in love with the game, too. And out of that love grew players better than anyone could ever dream. His teammates included "Cool Papa" Bell, a hitter who ran bases so fast, if you blinked you'd swear he'd never left home plate. Oscar Charleston was an outfielder who could tell just where a ball would land as soon as it hit the bat. And then there was Josh Gibson, who some said could hit a ball so hard and so far, it would land somewhere in the middle of next week. Because of his powerful hitting and home run record, Josh was sometimes called "the black Babe Ruth," but many wondered if the Babe should have been called "the white Josh Gibson."

Back in 1923, when Gibson and Satch were teammates on the Pittsburgh Crawfords, they were considered a mighty powerful duo. Posters for the Crawfords read,

Josh Gibson and Satchel Paige
THE GREATEST BATTERY IN BASEBALL
Gibson guaranteed to hit two home runs and
Paige guaranteed to strike out the first nine men.

"Someday we'll meet up and see who's best," they would often joke with each other. In 1942, soon after Satchel's return to the road, they got their chance.

Josh Gibson of the Homestead Grays

It was September 10, 1942, the second game of the Negro World Series. Satch's team, the Kansas City Monarchs, was in a heated best-of-seven matchup against the Homestead Grays, led by Josh Gibson. Toward the end of the game, Satch decided to raise the stakes. With two outs in the inning and one man on base, he walked two players so the bases would be loaded when Josh Gibson came up to bat. "Someday we'll meet up and

see who's best" rang in Satch's ears as he prepared to face the man who would now determine the fate of his team and Satch's reputation. Satchel called to Josh, "Remember back when we were playing with the Crawfords and you said you was the best hitter in the world and I was the best pitcher?"

"Yeah, I remember," Josh called back.

"Well, now we're going to see what's what," Satch said.

With a ball in hand and a grin on his face, Satch told Josh, "I'm gonna throw a fastball letter high."

"Strike one!"

Josh shook his head, tightened his grip on the bat, and resumed his position as he tried to stare into Satchel's eyes.

But Satch stared straight ahead at Josh's knees. His coach back at the Mount Meigs School had always told him, "Look at the knees, Satch. Every weakness a batter has, you can spot in the knees."

"Now I'm gonna throw this one a little faster and belt high," Satch said during the windup.

"Strike two!"

In typical Satch style, he called in a mocking voice, "Now I got you oh-and-two and I'm supposed to knock you down, but instead I'm gonna throw a pea at your knee."

"Strike three!"

Josh never moved the bat. Satch slowly exhaled the breath he'd been holding since the windup. It was over. He'd done what he'd come to do.

"Nobody hits Satchel's fastball," he said through a smile as bright as the sun. "And nobody ever will."

129

Objectives
• Identify the language and devices used in biographies and autobiographies, including how authors present major events in a person's life. • Read independently for a sustained period of time and paraphrase the reading.

Envision It! | Retell

READING STREET ONLINE
STORY SORT
www.ReadingStreet.com

Think Critically

1. Both Brady from *Red Kayak* and Satchel Paige face challenging situations. Brady must save another person's life, and Satchel must play against his athletic match. Compare how Brady and Satchel respond to these challenges. Do they respond with confidence or with fear? **Text to Text**

2. A good biographer must select which details to include about the subject's life. Lesa Cline-Ransome wrote about Satchel's personal life. Do you think it was important to include this information? **Think Like an Author**

3. *Satchel Paige* is full of facts and opinions. Reread pages 118–122. Then list as many statements of fact and statements of opinion as you can find.
Fact and Opinion

4. What information about Satchel Paige would you like to know that the author did not tell you? How might you find the answers that you're looking for?
Questioning

5. Look Back and Write Look back at page 128. What is the "typical Satch style" that the author is referring to?

TEST PRACTICE Extended Response

130

Meet the Author and the Illustrator

Lesa Cline-Ransome and James E. Ransome

ALL-STARS

Lesa Cline-Ransome & James E. Ransome

James E. Ransome, the illustrator of *Satchel Paige,* has won many awards for his work. He and his wife, Lesa Cline-Ransome, who wrote *Satchel Paige,* live in upstate New York with their four children.

Mr. Ransome says that he did not have the opportunity to meet artists or visit art galleries while growing up. "I do not remember how my interest in art began," he writes, "but I do remember that some of my first drawings were of hot-rod cars and images copied from the pages of comic books and the Bible." Mr. Ransome says, "What makes illustrating books so exciting is that not only am I learning about the characters, the environment they live in, and the history of the period, but I can also allow the story to dictate the palette and design that I use to illustrate it, thus giving each book an original, different look and feel."

Lesa Cline-Ransome was working in the fashion world in New York City when she became interested in education. She started teaching and then turned to writing for children. Ms. Cline-Ransome says she is comfortable working with her husband. She says that she trusts his artistic judgments, and that he sometimes comes to her for ideas about how to illustrate a story.

Here are other books by Lesa Cline-Ransome and James E. Ransome.

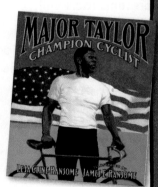

Major Taylor: Champion Cyclist

The Wagon

Reading Log

Use the *Reader's and Writer's Notebook* to record your independent reading.

Objectives

• Write essays with specific facts, details, and examples in an organized way. • Show agreement between subjects and verbs in simple and compound sentences. • Write essays that help the reader understand key ideas and details.

Let's Write It!

Key Features of a Newsletter Article

- typically tells about an event, an idea, or a person

- presents facts with supporting details

- includes direct quotations that enhance the article

READING STREET ONLINE
GRAMMAR JAMMER
www.ReadingStreet.com

Newsletter Article

A **newsletter article** gives facts and details about a subject. The student model on the next page is an example of a newsletter article.

Writing Prompt Think about a person who is interesting to you. Write a newsletter article about him or her, giving details, facts, events, and quotations to describe his or her experiences and personality.

Writer's Checklist

Remember, you should . . .

✓ include specific facts, details, and examples.

✓ guide and inform readers' understanding of key ideas by answering the following: Who? What? When? Where? Why? How?

✓ provide direct quotations, if possible.

Lifeguard Fran

Fran Jones is 17, and to earn money, she works every summer as a lifeguard at one of the state beaches.

Being a lifeguard is a huge responsibility, and Fran has to stay aware. Several times, she's spotted swimmers in trouble. When that's happened, she's raced to the beach with a flotation device, swum out to the swimmers, and helped them get back to shore.

When she's working, Fran sits in a tall chair that has a ladder leading up to it. From up high, she gets a good view of the swimmers. She says, "Because it is difficult to watch every swimmer all the time, I try to identify swimmers who do not seem to be strong swimmers. I focus on them, but I try to scan all the other swimmers too."

To get her job, Fran passed a lifesaving test for lifeguards, CPR training, and a written test. Only then was she certified to work on state beaches.

Without lifeguards such as Fran, we would not be able to swim as safely at our favorite beaches and pools.

Writing Trait Precise **word choice** makes information clear and easy to understand.

Compound and complex sentences are used correctly.

Genre A **newsletter article** tells about a person, a place, an event, or an idea.

Conventions

Compound and Complex Sentences

Remember A **compound sentence** contains two simple sentences joined by a comma and a conjunction, such as *and, but,* or *or.* A **complex sentence** contains an independent clause, which can stand alone, and a dependent clause, which cannot.

133

Objectives

• Identify the language and devices used in biographies and autobiographies, including how authors present major events in a person's life. • Make connections between and among texts.

Social Studies in Reading

Genre
Biography

- A biography is the story of a person's life, written by another person. The author of a biography may use language and literary devices, such as metaphors, in presenting a person's life events.

- Biographies are usually written in the third-person point of view, using words such as *he, she,* and *they.*

- Read "Roberto Clemente: A Baseball Hero." As you read, identify the literary devices and language that make this selection a biography.

Roberto Clemente
A BASEBALL HERO
by Edgardo Rivera

Roberto Clemente was many things. He was as fast as lightning. He was one of the greatest hitters in baseball history. He was also a Hall of Famer. Most importantly, Roberto Clemente dedicated his life to helping others.

Roberto Clemente was born August 18, 1934, in Puerto Rico. In Puerto Rico, the game of baseball is not just a game, but a way of life. Like other Puerto Rican kids, Clemente grew up dreaming about playing in the major leagues.

A T L

Isabela
Aguadilla
San Sebastiá
⊙ M
San Germán
18Y

When he was 17 years old, Clemente tried out for scouts from many different teams. What the scouts saw amazed them. He had a cannon for an arm. He hit the ball out of the park. His dream of playing professional baseball finally came true when the Pittsburgh Pirates drafted him in 1955.

At first, playing in the major leagues was not easy for Clemente. Like Satchel Paige, Clemente endured insults and name-calling from angry crowds and opponents. He was forced to eat and sleep in different restaurants and hotels than his teammates.

Despite this, Clemente went on to become one of the greatest baseball players of all time. He won several awards, including Most Valuable Player, and was voted an All-Star twelve times. The Pittsburgh Pirates also went on to win the World Series in 1960 and 1971.

Let's **Think** About...

What literary devices does the author use in the first paragraph on this page? What major events from Clemente's life does the author include?
Biography

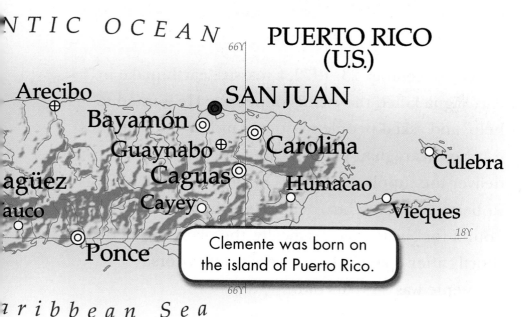

Clemente was born on the island of Puerto Rico.

Clemente wanted to help the people of Nicaragua.

Let's **Think** About...

What language does the author use that indicates this is a biography?
Biography

On December 23, 1972, a massive earthquake in Nicaragua killed thousands of people. He wanted to help, and asked people to donate money and supplies for the Nicaraguan people. Clemente decided to deliver the supplies himself. On December 31, 1972, Roberto Clemente boarded a plane in Puerto Rico bound for Nicaragua. Tragically, the plane crashed shortly after takeoff. There were no survivors. Clemente was 38 years old.

To honor his memory, Clemente was inducted into the National Baseball Hall of Fame just a few months after the tragedy. The U.S. Congress also awarded him the Congressional Medal of Honor in 1973.

The spirit of Roberto Clemente continues to live on today. Outside PNC Park in Pittsburgh stands a statue of Roberto Clemente. Written on the statue are the words "The Great One." This is how Clemente will always be remembered.

Let's Think About...

Identify the language that indicates that you are reading a biography.
Biography

This statue of Roberto Clemente stands in Pittsburgh.

Let's Think About...

Reading Across Texts Compare and contrast the experiences of Paige and Clemente. Did they face similar obstacles? How did they overcome those obstacles?

Writing Across Texts Write a paragraph explaining how Paige and Clemente overcame their obstacles.

Objectives

- Read aloud grade-level texts and understand what is read.
- Write analogies with antonyms you know. • Explain how different messages in various forms of media are presented. • Examine the different techniques used in media.
- Show agreement between subjects and verbs in simple and compound sentences. • Listen to and interpret a speaker's messages and ask questions.

Let's

Learn

It!

READING STREET ONLINE
ONLINE STUDENT EDITION
www.ReadingStreet.com

Vocabulary

Antonyms

Context Clues Sometimes you can find an antonym, or a word with an opposite meaning, to help you determine the meaning of an unknown word. Look in the words and sentences near the unknown word for an antonym that might give a context clue to the meaning of the unknown word.

Practice It! Choose three vocabulary words from *Satchel Paige*. Write an antonym analogy using each word, for example, *cold is to hot as light is to _____*.

Fluency

Appropriate Phrasing

Punctuation Clues Use punctuation as a guide as you read. Pause at commas, dashes, or periods. Use an excited tone with exclamation points.

Practice It! With a partner, practice reading aloud page 128 of *Satchel Paige*. One partner acts as narrator and reads the umpire's dialogue, while the other reads Satchel's dialogue. Use punctuation to help guide your reading.

Media Literacy

Change the volume of your voice and your reading rate to keep listeners' interest.

Sportscast

In a sportscast, a reporter tells about a sports event in an informative and entertaining way.

Practice It! With a partner, prepare a sportscast about the meeting between Satchel Paige and Josh Gibson. Your sportscast should describe what happened during the game. Describe the camera techniques you would use, and discuss how a sportscast is different from online sports news.

Tips

Listening . . .

- Listen to the speaker's message.
- Ask questions to clarify the speaker's perspective.

Speaking . . .

- Make eye contact with your listeners.
- Use compound sentences with correct subject-verb agreement.

Teamwork . . .

- Consider suggestions from group members.
- Identify points of disagreement.

Objectives

• Listen to and interpret a speaker's messages and ask questions.

• Identify the main ideas and supporting ideas in the speaker's message.

Oral Vocabulary

Let's Talk About

Life in a New Country

● Share ideas about moving to a new country.

● Listen to and interpret a classmate's ideas about life in a new country.

● Determine main and supporting ideas in your classmates' messages.

READING STREET ONLINE
CONCEPT TALK VIDEO
www.ReadingStreet.com

Objectives

● Analyze how the organization of a text affects the way ideas are related.

Envision It! | **Skill Strategy**

Skill

Strategy

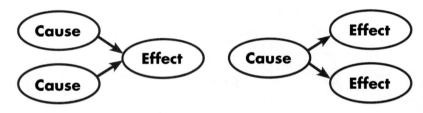

READING STREET ONLINE
ENVISION IT! ANIMATIONS
www.ReadingStreet.com

Comprehension Skill

Cause and Effect

● An effect is something that happens. A cause is why it happens.

● Sometimes an author will use clue words such as *so* and *because* to show cause-and-effect relationships.

● The ideas in a text may be organized by causes and effects.

● Use a graphic organizer like the one below to show the causes of immigration. How do these causes help you understand the ideas presented in the text?

```
( Cause ) ──┐
            ├──> ( Effect )
( Cause ) ──┘

( Cause ) ──┬──> ( Effect )
            └──> ( Effect )
```

Comprehension Strategy

Text Structure

Text structure is the way a writer organizes a selection. A text may describe events in sequence, or in a cause-and-effect pattern. Active readers use text structure to help them understand what a selection is about. As you read, look for text structure.

COMING to the UNITED STATES

Imagine getting on a boat and leaving your homeland. You cross miles and miles of ocean to go live in a country you have never been to before. The people speak a different language, eat different foods, and wear different clothes.

If you did this, you would be an immigrant. Throughout U.S. history, many people have immigrated to this country. People continue to immigrate today. The largest number of immigrants arrived between 1880 and 1930. During this period, about twenty-seven million people came to the United States. Why?

In some cases, people came for freedom of religion. Some people came to escape wars or famine in their homelands. Other immigrants came to make money or pursue job opportunities. They left countries that had fewer jobs and fewer business opportunities than in the United States. These immigrants were willing to work hard to make better lives for themselves and their families.

Skill What clue word does the author use in this paragraph? Where do you think you will read about the causes?

Skill What are some of the many causes of immigration?

Strategy What kind of text structure does the author follow? Why do you think the author chose this structure?

Your Turn!

⏸ **Need a Review?** See the *Envision It! Handbook* for additional help with cause and effect and text structure.

▷ **Ready to Try It?** Use what you have learned about cause and effect and text structure as you read *Ten Mile Day.*

143

Envision It! | **Words to Know**

barren

deafening

prying

lurched
previous
surveying

READING STREET ONLINE
VOCABULARY ACTIVITIES
www.ReadingStreet.com

Vocabulary Strategy for

🎯 Multiple-Meaning Words

Context Clues Some words have more than one meaning. You can find clues in nearby words and sentences to decide which meaning the author is using. These context clues can help you determine or clarify the meaning of a multiple-meaning word.

1. Think about different meanings the word can have.

2. Reread the sentence in which the word appears. Which meaning fits?

3. If you can't tell, then look for more clues in nearby sentences.

4. Put the clues together and decide which meaning works best.

Read "A New Place to Live" on page 145. Use the context to decide which meaning a multiple-meaning word has in the article.

Words to Write Reread "A New Place to Live." Imagine you are a construction worker building a skyscraper. Write a journal entry describing what you see and hear as you work. Use words from the *Words to Know* list in your journal entry.

A New Place to Live

On Tuesday, the foreman started his day by surveying the barren lot between two existing homes. His crew of workers had done a great job the previous day clearing away the old home. He felt confident that this crew could accomplish his goal. He wanted to build a brand-new house within a month.

The workers were ready for the challenge. The foreman explained what he wanted finished by the end of each day. Today he wanted the ground prepared for a foundation. Every crew member knew his or her job. The first sound was the prying open of the bulldozer door. This was followed by the deafening sound of the jackhammers as they broke up an old sidewalk. The bulldozer lurched forward and began to pile dirt in one spot. Teams of workers carried lumber from a truck to the lot. Everywhere the foreman looked, he smiled.

Your Turn!

 Need a Review?
For additional help with multiple-meaning words, see *Words!*

 Ready to Try It?
Read *Ten Mile Day* on pp. 146–159.

Question of the Week

What challenges do immigrants encounter?

TEN MILE DAY

AND THE BUILDING OF THE TRANSCONTINENTAL RAILROAD
Written and Illustrated by Mary Ann Fraser

To Monument Point

Start of
Ten Mile Day

PROMONTORY MOUNTAINS

Promontory
Summit

Camp
Victory

Finish of Ten Mile Day

Genre

Expository texts tell the story of an event or a series of events that really happened. As you read, think about how the author arranges the information about the event.

147

Before the 1860s, no railway ran all the way across the United States. In fact, there weren't any tracks at all west of Omaha, Nebraska. But in 1862, Congress passed the Pacific Railroad Act, and the task of joining the coasts by rail began. The Union Pacific team started out building west from Omaha, and the Central Pacific team began in Sacramento, California, and built east. Promontory Summit, Utah, was chosen as their meeting place.

When Charles Crocker, the construction boss for the Central Pacific, learned that the Union Pacific had set a record of a little more than seven miles of track laid in one day, he claimed that his men could lay ten miles. The president of the Union Pacific said it couldn't be done, and offered ten thousand extra dollars to the team if they could succeed.

Early in the morning of April 28, 1869, Crocker and James Strobridge, his right-hand man, called for volunteers for the difficult task ahead. Each crew was promised four times its normal wages if it could meet the challenge. Nearly all of the team leaders stepped forward. Fourteen hundred of the Central Pacific's best laborers, both Irish and Chinese, were selected out of the almost five thousand volunteers.

At 7 A.M. all eyes rested on Charles Crocker as he steadied his horse beside the grade. The crews knew it would take sixteen railroad flatcars to carry everything they needed to lay two miles of track. Five trains, each made up of an engine and sixteen flatcars, now waited. Some stood at the end of the rails and others were parked on the sidings, the tracks built beside the main road. Wooden ties had already been placed along the entire ten mile route. Everything was set to go.

With a sharp command to the bosses, Crocker's arm rose and fell. The hogger, or engineer, on the first train pulled hard on the whistle cord, and a shrill blast pierced the cold, damp morning air. The race had begun.

Chinese laborers leaped onto the flatcars of the lead train. The noise was deafening as sledgehammers knocked out the side stakes and rails tumbled to the ground. The clanging of falling iron continued for eight minutes, until the first sixteen flatcars were empty.

As the supply train was unloaded, three men rushed to the end of the rails, what they called the end o' track. The three pioneers scrambled ahead to the first loose ties. Then they began lifting, prying, and shoving to center the bare ties on the grade.

The emptied train steamed back to the siding, and men hurried to load iron cars with exactly sixteen rails and thirty-two rail joiners, or fishplates, each. A crew of six Chinese workers and an Irish boss hopped aboard.

To the right of the track two horses were hitched by a long rope to an iron car. With a yell from the boss, the horses lurched against their harnesses and the cars rolled forward on the track. When the iron car reached the end o' track, a wooden keg was smashed over the rails. The iron car rambled ahead as new track was laid, spilling

spikes through the open bottom and onto the ground where they could be used. Dust clouds choked the air.

With the iron car moving steadily along, eight Irishmen lay rails just ahead of its rolling wheels. These "ironmen" were Michael Shay, Thomas Daley, George Elliot, Michael Sulivan, Edward Killeen, Patrick Joice, Michael Kenedy, and Fred McNamare. The four forward men seized the 560-pound, thirty-foot-long rails, while the four rear men slid the rails to the rollers on each side of the iron car. The lead ironmen ran forward. "Down," shouted the foreman. With a loud thud the iron hit the ties within inches of the previous rail. Without a moment to rest, the eight ironmen went back for more. On average, two rails were laid every twenty seconds.

While rails clanked to the ground, the Chinese crew from the iron car loaded fishplates, nuts, and bolts into baskets attached to poles slung over their shoulders. Then they sped up the line, tossing out ironware every ten yards. Where rail ends met, another team fastened the fishplates loosely with nuts and thrusting bolts.

When each handcar was unloaded, the horses were detached from the front and hitched to the back. At a gallop they hauled the empty iron car back to the supply dump. If a returning car got in the way of a full iron car, the empty one was flipped off the track until the full car passed. Nothing slowed the flow of supplies to the end o' track.

After a track-gauge team measured the rails to insure they were exactly four feet, eight and one-half inches apart, the new American and British standard, the rail ends were loosely fastened with fishplates.

Next came the spike setters. Each man picked up one of the spikes lying scattered beside the roadbed, then quickly set it in position with two hits. Another gang of Chinese followed. With three blows from the maul each spike was driven home, securing the rails to the ties.

Some crews had marvelous names. "Fishplate men" tightened the nuts on the thrusting bolts with long-handled wrenches. "Gandy dancers," or "track liners," aligned the rails to the ties using massive

track bars. A foreman would sing out a simple tune with a strong beat. Like the crew on a rowboat, the gandy dancers would all push together on the final beat, aligning the rails.

Following close on their heels, a surveyor directed a rail gang that lifted the ties and shoveled dirt under them to keep the track level.

The last and largest special work team included four hundred tampers and shovelers. They used crowbars, shovels, and tamping bars to pack the ground around the rails. The crew formed three long lines, one on each side of the track and one down the middle. Each tamper gave two crunching tamps to the gravel, or ballast, before moving on, while shovelers filled in where needed.

From the first pioneer to the last tamper ran a line of men nearly two miles long. Like a mammoth machine with hundreds of well-oiled parts, Crocker's men moved rhythmically forward. The ribbon of track rose across the plain at the pace of a walking man. Tired workers were pulled from the line and replaced. But many, including the eight iron men, showed no signs of quitting.

Alongside the grade the telegraph construction party worked frantically to keep pace with the track layers. They set the poles; hammered on the crossbars; and hauled out, hung, and insulated the wire.

The track boss stalked up and down the line, barking out commands and encouragement. The steady hammering of spikes, the rhythmic thud of iron rails, and even the men's labored breathing beat like a drum across the barren plain.

A reporter pulled out his pocket watch and counted the rails as they were laid down. To everyone's amazement, 240 feet of iron were placed in one minute and twenty seconds.

By 9 A.M. almost two miles of track had been spiked and tamped. Even the Union Pacific men, who had laughed at the Central Pacific crews, had to admit it was quality work.

Water, food, and tool wagons creaked up and down the line as the heat rose with the morning sun. Chinese workers wove in and out of the men, delivering water and tea to quench their thirst.

At the front Crocker and Strobridge oversaw every detail. Now and then when something amusing happened, Crocker's merry laugh echoed from his carriage.

With the completion of another two miles of track, the second supply train pulled back to the siding and the third train steamed forward, belching thick clouds of black smoke. Next in line, ready to serve the midday meal, was the so-called Pioneer Train — the boarding house for some of the workers, and the office and living quarters of James and Hannah Strobridge.

155

At 1:30 the whistle sounded, calling a halt for lunch. Whirlwind No. 62, the Pioneer Train locomotive, pushed the kitchen cars up, and the boarding boss served hot boiled beef.

A quick measurement showed that six miles of track had already been laid, spiked, and bolted that morning. Whoops and hollers went up as the news spread among the men. They were now confident they could reach their goal of ten miles in one day, and they named their rest stop Camp Victory.

At 2:30 work began again, but a special crew had to be called in. The tracks were now climbing the west slope of the Promontory Mountains. The climb was steep and full of curves, and the rails had to be bent.

Lacking measuring instruments, this new crew judged the curves by sight. They jammed the rails between blocks and then slowly and carefully hammered them into the right shapes. Every rail now took extra time to mold and fit.

As the afternoon wore on, the foreman continued to ride the line, encouraging the men. Although the horses pulling the iron cars were changed every two hours, they could no longer run up the grade. Now they had to walk slowly up the steep hillside. The rail gang was dripping with sweat, and their muscles must have burned from overuse, but not one man stopped to rest. With each hour another mile of track reached toward Promontory Summit.

By 7P.M. the sun was dipping behind Monument Point. Strobridge signaled for the final blast from the train whistle. The exhausted men cast down their tools, and the day's work came to an abrupt end.

How much rail had the men of the Central Pacific laid? Two Union Pacific engineers took out their surveying chains and began to measure. Everyone waited for the final count. Then it came. The railhead was ten miles, fifty-six feet farther east than it had been the previous evening.

The crews flung their hats into the air, cheering and shaking hands all around. They had done the impossible again. The Union Pacific's record was destroyed, and Thomas Durant lost the bet. A total of 3,520 rails, twice that number of fishplates, 28,160 spikes, and 14,080 nuts and bolts had been placed to complete the job.

The eight track layers were declared heroes and were featured in later histories. Each had lifted over 125 tons of iron. No single crew has ever beaten their record. The Chinese workers had once again proven themselves to their biased rivals. Each team had something to celebrate.

Objectives
● Provide evidence from text to support understanding. ● Read independently for a sustained period of time and paraphrase the reading, including the order in which events occur.

Envision It! | Retell

READING STREET ONLINE
STORY SORT
www.ReadingStreet.com

Think Critically

1. The first transcontinental railroad was a technologically advanced accomplishment in the 1800s. What is a recent accomplishment that we consider technologically advanced? How does it compare to the first transcontinental railroad? **Text to World**

2. The author isn't making up the events of April 28, 1869; they really happened. If you were the author and wanted to add more information about these events, what would you do? **Think Like an Author**

3. Why did the men name the lunch rest stop Camp Victory? **Cause and Effect**

4. How are the events in the text organized? How does it add to the story's suspense? **Text Structure**

5. Look Back and Write Explain in your own words how the railroad crew managed to lay ten miles of track in one day.

TEST PRACTICE Extended Response

MARY ANN FRASER

Mary Ann Fraser is the author of many books. She has also illustrated more than fifty books. Her books are often about animals and nature—two topics she studied and read about from a young age. As a girl, she liked to hike, camp, and care for her pets. Today, she still has several pets, including a dog, turtles, and an amphibian named Newtsie.

Ms. Fraser not only writes about animals and nature, but also about history. Although she didn't like history when she was young, she now believes that "adventure, mystery, and amazing people can be found in the past if we go looking for it."

Ms. Fraser is one of the founding members of the Children's Authors Network! (CAN!) and is also a member of the Society of Children's Book Writers and Illustrators (SCBWI).

Here is another book by Mary Ann Fraser.

One Giant Leap

Use the *Reader's and Writer's Notebook* to record your independent reading.

161

Objectives

- Write essays with strong introductions and conclusions.
- Use and understand the function of collective nouns.
- Write essays that help the reader understand key ideas and details.

Let's Write It!

Key Features of an Expository Composition

- tells about real people and events
- provides a description or explanation of something
- includes a topic sentence, a body, and a closing sentence

READING STREET ONLINE
GRAMMAR JAMMER
www.ReadingStreet.com

Expository Composition

An **expository composition** gives information about a topic. The student model on the next page is an example of an expository composition.

Writing Prompt Many people thought building the transcontinental railroad was impossible. Think of another American achievement that seemed impossible. Now write an expository composition about it.

Writer's Checklist

Remember, you should . . .

✓ research your topic, if possible.

✓ establish your main idea in a topic sentence.

✓ capitalize names of organizations, acronyms, and abbreviations.

✓ use common, proper, and collective nouns correctly.

✓ have an effective closing paragraph.

The Race to the Moon

In 1958, the United States created NASA, the National Aeronautics and Space Administration. President John F. Kennedy wanted the United States to put a person on the moon by the end of the 1960s.

There were many challenges that NASA had to face. First, there wasn't much time. There were also not enough people employed at the space agency, NASA. So President Kennedy increased NASA's budget from $500 million to $5.2 billion, and more people were hired. With this support, NASA was given a real chance to reach its goal.

Secondly, NASA dedicated all its resources to reaching the moon. A **team** of specialists needed to be hired. NASA also had to make sure that the astronauts would be safe, so they performed expensive test missions.

On July 20, 1969, American astronauts landed on the moon aboard the space shuttle mission Apollo 11. The American **public** was excited: No person had ever stepped foot on the moon before. NASA achieved an incredible feat.

Writing Trait Organization
The essay is organized with a problem-and-solution structure.

Common, proper, and collective nouns are used correctly.

Genre
An **expository composition** explains something about real events.

Conventions

Common, Proper, & Collective Nouns

Remember A **common noun** names a person, place, or thing in general, and is not capitalized (city). A **proper noun** is capitalized and names a specific person, place, or thing (Seattle). A **collective noun** names a group (class, public).

Objectives
● Analyze whether Web sites and other digital media are formal or informal.

21st Century Skills

Texting is fun, but **e-mail** can be even better. Share documents and work on a common project in school. E-mail skills get you ready for the world of work. Yes, e-mail can be pretty useful!

● E-mail is short for "electronic mail."

● Writers sometimes organize e-mails like friendly letters, often using informal language. Some e-mails may use formal language, especially if they are about business or research.

● Read "Working on the Railroad." Think about the language used in the e-mail and on the railroad museum Web site. Is the language used formal or informal?

Working on the Railroad

Rachel is gathering information for a school report on how Chinese immigrants helped build the transcontinental railroad. She logs on to the Internet and visits the Web site of a railroad museum. At the site, she finds an e-mail address to contact for more information.

The site gives an e-mail address to contact for more information. Rachel decides to e-mail the Web site.

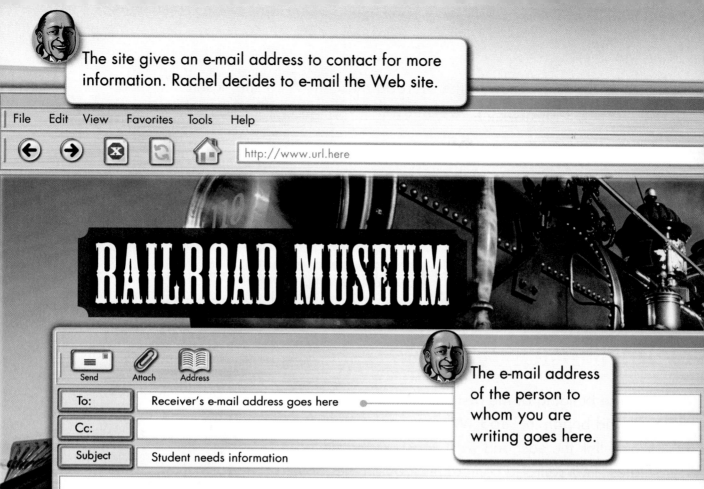

File   Edit   View   Favorites   Tools   Help

http://www.url.here

RAILROAD MUSEUM

Send   Attach   Address

The e-mail address of the person to whom you are writing goes here.

To: Receiver's e-mail address goes here

Cc:

Subject   Student needs information

Dear Ms. Lee,

I am doing research for a school report on Chinese immigrants. I just visited your Web site. I read about the transcontinental railroad. Does your museum have any information about Chinese immigrants who worked on the transcontinental railroad?

Thank you, Rachel

Rachel's e-mail uses formal language because it is about her research. How would the language she uses be different if her e-mail were written to a friend?

In this section of the railroad museum Web site, Rachel finds an article that gives her some useful information.

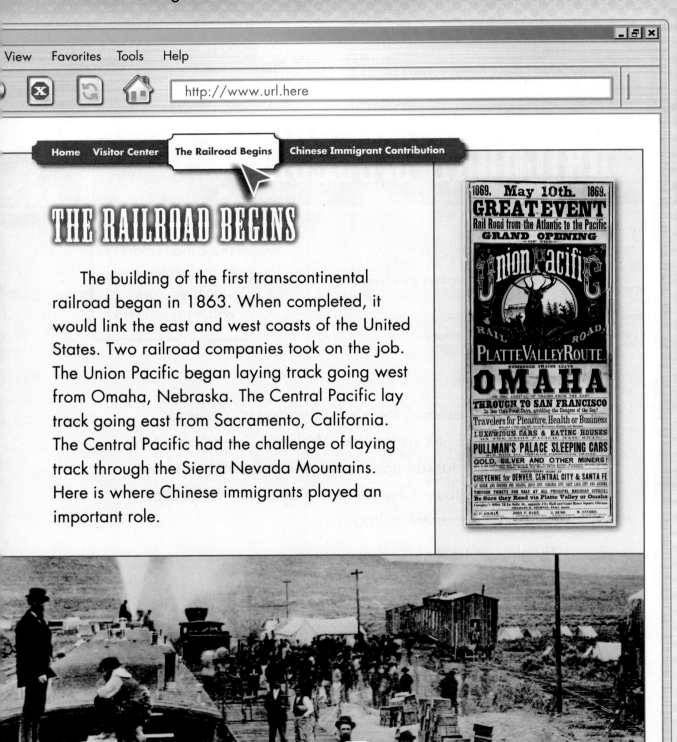

Home   Visitor Center   **The Railroad Begins**   Chinese Immigrant Contribution

THE RAILROAD BEGINS

The building of the first transcontinental railroad began in 1863. When completed, it would link the east and west coasts of the United States. Two railroad companies took on the job. The Union Pacific began laying track going west from Omaha, Nebraska. The Central Pacific lay track going east from Sacramento, California. The Central Pacific had the challenge of laying track through the Sierra Nevada Mountains. Here is where Chinese immigrants played an important role.

1869. May 10th. 1869.
GREAT EVENT
Rail Road from the Atlantic to the Pacific
GRAND OPENING
OF THE
Union Pacific
RAIL   ROAD,
PLATTE VALLEY ROUTE.
PASSENGER TRAINS LEAVE
OMAHA
ON THE ARRIVAL OF TRAINS FROM THE EAST
THROUGH TO SAN FRANCISCO
In less than Four Days, avoiding the Dangers of the Sea!
Travelers for Pleasure, Health or Business
LUXURIOUS CARS & EATING HOUSES
ON THE UNION PACIFIC RAIL ROAD.
PULLMAN'S PALACE SLEEPING CARS
RUN WITH ALL THROUGH PASSENGER TRAINS
GOLD, SILVER AND OTHER MINERS!
CHEYENNE for DENVER, CENTRAL CITY & SANTA FE
Be Sure they Read via Platte Valley or Omaha

CHINESE IMMIGRANT CONTRIBUTION

To do this hard work, the Central Pacific hired thousands of Chinese immigrants. These men chipped out rail bed using axes and hammers. They blasted nine tunnels through the Sierra Nevada Mountains. They worked twelve-hour days, six days a week. Each worker earned about thirty dollars a month.

The president of the Central Pacific knew how important the Chinese workers were. In 1865, he wrote, "Without them it would be impossible to complete the western portion of this great national enterprise within the time required by the acts of Congress."

On May 10, 1869, the eastward and westward tracks met in Promontory, Utah. To honor their hard work, Chinese workers were invited to place the last section of rail linking the eastern and western United States.

for more practice

Get **Online!**
www.ReadingStreet.com
Write your own e-mail to a museum.

21st Century Skills Online Activity
Log on and follow the directions to write an e-mail asking for more information about immigration.

Objectives

● Read aloud grade-level texts and understand what is read. ● Identify and explain the meaning of common adages and other sayings. ● Listen to and interpret a speaker's messages and ask questions. ● Identify the main ideas and supporting ideas in the speaker's message. ● Give organized presentations that communicate your ideas effectively. ● Participate in discussions by raising and considering suggestions from other group members.

Let's Learn It!

READING STREET ONLINE
ONLINE STUDENT EDITION
www.ReadingStreet.com

Vocabulary

Adages and Sayings

An adage is a short but memorable saying that expresses a meaningful idea. For example, "An apple a day keeps the doctor away" means that eating healthfully will keep you healthy. Other types of sayings may also hold important meanings.

Practice It! Reread *Ten Mile Day*, and think about adages and other sayings you know about hard work, or adages that could apply to the story. Work with a partner to identify and explain several adages and sayings that could apply to the story.

Fluency

Accuracy

When you read with accuracy, you read without errors or mispronunciations. Reading with accuracy allows you to better understand what you are reading.

Practice It! With your partner, practice reading aloud a page from *Ten Mile Day*. Identify and pronounce any difficult words. Then read the paragraphs aloud, taking care to be accurate. Give your partner feedback.

Get Ready For Middle School

When you give a presentation, enunciate so that your audience can understand you.

Job Advertisement

A job advertisement is a public notice that gives information about a job. The purpose of a job ad is to inform about an open job.

Practice It! With a partner, create a descriptive, detailed ad for a job with the Central Pacific Railroad Company. Discuss where to place your ad—newspaper, radio, TV, or the Internet—and explain why. Use information from *Ten Mile Day* to help you create your job advertisement.

Tips

Listening . . .

- Determine the main ideas and details in the job ad.
- Ask questions to clarify the speaker's purpose.

Speaking . . .

- Speak loudly enough so that listeners can hear you.
- Use and understand collective nouns, such as *class* and *public*.

Teamwork . . .

- When discussing the job advertisement, elicit and consider suggestions from other group members.

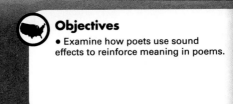

Objectives
● Examine how poets use sound
effects to reinforce meaning in poems.

Poetry

- Some poets use
  sound effects, such
  as alliteration and
  rhyme scheme, to
  reinforce meaning
  in their poems.

- Alliteration is
  the repetition of
  consonant sounds
  at the beginnings
  of words. Poets
  use alliteration to
  call attention to
  important ideas or
  to add interest to
  a poem.

- Rhyme scheme is
  the pattern of
  words that sound
  alike in a poem.
  Rhyme can draw
  attention to
  important words
  or lines.

- As you read "The
  Microscope," think
  about how sound
  effects reinforce
  meaning or add
  interest.

170

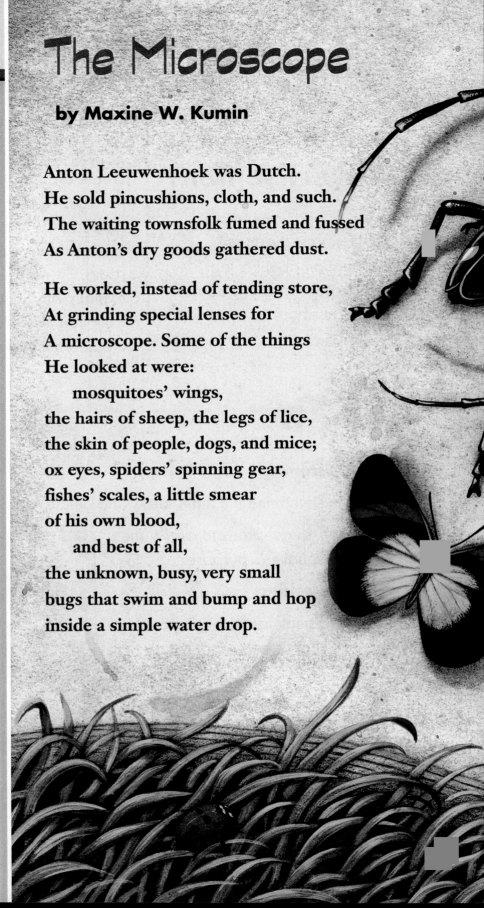

The Microscope

by Maxine W. Kumin

Anton Leeuwenhoek was Dutch.
He sold pincushions, cloth, and such.
The waiting townsfolk fumed and fussed
As Anton's dry goods gathered dust.

He worked, instead of tending store,
At grinding special lenses for
A microscope. Some of the things
He looked at were:
    mosquitoes' wings,
the hairs of sheep, the legs of lice,
the skin of people, dogs, and mice;
ox eyes, spiders' spinning gear,
fishes' scales, a little smear
of his own blood,
    and best of all,
the unknown, busy, very small
bugs that swim and bump and hop
inside a simple water drop.

Impossible! Most Dutchmen said.
This Anton's crazy in the head.
We ought to ship him off to Spain.
He says he's seen a housefly's brain.
He says the water that we drink
Is full of bugs. He's mad, we think!

They called him *dumkopf*, which means dope.
That's how we got the microscope.

Let's **Think** About...

How does the alliteration in lines 12 and 13 add interest to the poem?

Let's **Think** About...

Does the rhyme scheme reinforce meaning in the poem or make the poem fun to read? Is the poet successful?

Full Day

by Naomi Shihab Nye

The pilot on the plane says:
in one minute and fifty seconds
we're going as far
as the covered wagon went
in a full day.

172

We look down
on clouds,
mountains of froth and foam.
We eat a neat
and subdivided lunch.

How was it for the people in
the covered wagon?
They bumped and jostled.
Their wheels broke.
Their biscuits were tough.
They got hot and cold and old.
Their shirts tore on the branches
they passed.

But they saw the pebbles
and the long grass
and the sweet shine of evening
settling on the fields.
They knew the ruts and the rocks.
They threw their furniture out
to make the wagons lighter.
They carried their treasures
in a crooked box.

Doing the Right Thing

What makes people want to do the right thing?

Reading Street Online

www.ReadingStreet.com
- Big Question Video
- eSelections
- Envision It! Animations
- Story Sort

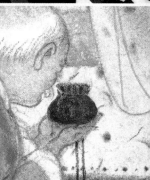

Objectives
- Listen to and interpret a speaker's messages and ask questions.
- Identify the main ideas and supporting ideas in the speaker's message.

Oral Vocabulary

Let's Talk About

Honesty

- Share opinions about the importance of being honest.

- Listen to a classmate's ideas about honesty.

- Determine your classmates' main and supporting ideas about honesty.

READING STREET ONLINE
CONCEPT TALK VIDEO
www.ReadingStreet.com

You've learned

0 5 0

Amazing Words

so far this year!

177

Objectives

• Evaluate the effects of sensory details, imagery, and figurative language in literary text.

Envision It! | Skill Strategy

Skill

Strategy

READING STREET ONLINE
ENVISION IT! ANIMATIONS
www.ReadingStreet.com

Comprehension Skill

🎯 Compare and Contrast

• When writers compare and contrast, they tell how things are alike or different.

• Words such as *same, unlike, but,* and *although* are clues that sometimes show comparisons and contrasts.

• Sometimes writers do not use clue words when they compare and contrast things.

• Use a graphic organizer like the one below to compare and contrast Ryan's actions.

Responsible	Not Responsible

Comprehension Strategy

🎯 Visualize

Active readers look for sensory details to create pictures in their minds as they read. The sights and smells described by the author help you visualize the story. As you read, think about the impact sensory details and imagery have on the story.

Ryan & Jonah

Ryan was babysitting his brother, Jonah. He started a movie, set Jonah down, and told him to stay put. Then he began sorting his baseball cards. After a while, he looked up. Where was Jonah? Ryan dashed around the living room and then through the whole house. Usually Jonah liked to sit and watch a whole movie, but now he wasn't there.

Skill What contrast is signaled by the word *but*?

Then he noticed the open back door and ran outside. Just then, Jonah fell in the swimming pool. Ryan ran over and pulled him out. As the boys hurried into the house, Ryan said, "Don't tell Mom what happened. Let's get you some dry clothes."

Just then, the boys' mom walked in and asked why Jonah was soaked. "He got his clothes dirty, and I tried to clean them," said Ryan. Mom took off Jonah's wet clothes and shoes. She wrapped a towel around the shaking little boy. Ryan looked at Jonah's wet shoes and said, "I wasn't watching, and Jonah fell into the pool. I pulled him out, but we were scared to tell you."

Skill Ryan gives his mother two explanations. In what ways are the explanations alike? In what ways are they different?

Strategy How do the imagery and sensory details in this story affect your understanding of the story?

Mom hugged each of the boys. "Jonah could have drowned! Thank goodness you found him in time, and everyone is OK."

Your Turn!

Need a Review? See the *Envision It! Handbook* for help with comparing, contrasting, and visualizing.

Let's Think About...

Ready to Try It? Use what you've learned as you read *At the Beach*.

Objectives

● Determine the meanings of unfamiliar words or multiple-meaning words by using the context of the sentence.

Envision It! | Words to Know

driftwood

hammocks

tweezers

algae

concealed

lamented

sea urchins

sternly

READING STREET ONLINE
VOCABULARY ACTIVITIES
www.ReadingStreet.com

Vocabulary Strategy for

◎ Unfamiliar Words

Context Clues As you read, you may see a word you don't know. Often you can use context to determine the meaning of a new word. *Context* means "the words and sentences near an unfamiliar word or words."

Choose one of the *Words to Know* and follow these steps.

1. Reread the sentence with the unfamiliar word. The author may include a synonym or other context clue to the word's meaning.

2. If you need help, read the surrounding sentences for context clues.

3. Think about the clues and then decide on the meaning of the word.

4. Check to see that this meaning makes sense in the sentence.

Read "My Special Island" on page 181. Use context clues to help you determine the meanings of unfamiliar words.

Words to Write Reread "My Special Island." Imagine you are at the beach. Write a paragraph about what you see, hear, taste, smell, and touch. Use words from the *Words to Know* list.

My Special Island

I like to daydream about my special island. It has the most beautiful beach for exploring. I walk along the sand and admire the wild driftwood shapes, polished by the waves and sun. I pause beside a tidal pool and watch crabs, sea urchins, and other strange animals.

Standing in the water, I look at a forest of algae stretching as far as I can see. I wonder what strange and beautiful creatures lie concealed in that underwater forest. In my dream I am a world-famous scientist. Armed with my microscope, tweezers, and diving equipment, I learn all the secrets of the ocean world.

After a long day of amazing discoveries, I head for one of the hammocks under the palm trees. There I store my treasures and lie down, letting a gentle breeze rock me to sleep.

"Martin!" Ms. Smith says sternly. "Wake up and get to work!" Oh, well. Back to arithmetic. I have often lamented my bad habit of daydreaming during classes!

Your Turn!

⏸ **Need a Review?** For additional help with using context clues to determine the meanings of unfamiliar words, see *Words!*

▶ **Ready to Try It?** Read *At the Beach* on pp. 182–193.

181

At The Beach

Abuelito's Story

by Lulu Delacre
paintings by Michael Sterinagle

Genre

Realistic fiction deals with characters and actions that seem real but come from the author's imagination. As you read, notice how the author uses words to paint a realistic picture of Guanabo Beach.

Question of the Week

Why is honesty important?

Let's

Think

About

Reading!

I remember those evenings well when I was a young boy in Cuba, those balmy island nights before a trip to Guanabo Beach. The spicy aroma of *tortilla española* that Mami had left to cool would waft through the house as I lay in my bed. But I was always too excited to sleep. All I could think about was the soft white sand, the warm foamy water, and Mami's delicious tortilla. Ahhh. A day at the beach. It was full of possibilities.

One Saturday in May, I was awakened at the crack of dawn by sounds of laughter. My aunts, Rosa and Olga, had arrived with hammocks, blankets, and an iron kettle filled with Aunt Rosa's steaming *congrí*. And best of all, they had arrived with my cousins: Luisa, Mari, and little Javi. Uncle Toni had come too.

Let's **Think** About...

From what you have read so far, visualize Cuba, the setting. Is this like or unlike where you live?

◉ **Visualize**

When we were ready to leave, Papi, the only one in the family who owned a car, packed his Ford woody wagon with the nine of us. No one cared that we children had to squeeze into the back along with the clutter of pots and plates, food and bags, towels and blankets and hammocks. Soon the engine turned, and the car rumbled down the road into the rising sun.

Along the way, we drove past sugarcane fields and roadside markets. My cousins and I shouted warnings to the barking dogs and laughed at the frightened hens that scurried in every direction at the sight of our car. It seemed like a long time until the cool morning breeze that blew into the windows turned warm. And the growing heat made the aroma of Mami's tortilla all the more tempting.

"Lick your skin, Fernando," my older cousin Luisa told me. "If it tastes salty, that means we'll be there any time now."

She was right. My skin tasted salty. And soon—almost magically—the turquoise ocean appeared as we rounded a bend in the road. Papi pulled into the familiar dirt lot and parked under the pine trees. While the grown-ups unloaded the car, we eagerly jumped out and ran toward the sea, peeling off our clothes along the way.

Let's Think About...

Who do you think is telling the story? What do you know about this character and the other characters?
Inferring

185

"Remember, don't go too far!" Mami and Aunt Olga warned us sternly from the distance. I turned to see them picking up our scattered clothing.

When we reached the edge of the ocean, the water felt cold. I waded farther in and went under to warm up quickly. When I emerged I saw Luisa, Mari, and little Javi, all standing still in the clear water. They were watching the schools of tiny gold-and-black striped fish rush between their legs. Then they swam over to join me, and together we rode the big waves.

Later, Uncle Toni came in to play shark with us. We splashed and swallowed the stinging seawater as he chased us above and under the waves. But after a while, we tired him out, and he went back to sit with the grown-ups.

I was getting very hungry, and for a moment I thought of returning with him to sneak a bite of Mami's tortilla. But then I had a better idea.

"Let's explore the reef!" I said.

"¡Sí!" everyone agreed. "Let's go!"

We all splashed out of the water and ran, dripping wet, across the sand. High above, the sun beat down on us.

When we got to the marbled rocks, Luisa looked concerned. "Our moms told us not to come this far," she said.

"I know the way well," I replied. "Besides, nobody will notice. They're too busy talking."

I looked in the distance and saw Mami and my two aunts in the shady spot they had picked. They had set up a nice camp. The hammocks were tied to the pine trees; the blankets were spread over the fine sand. Papi and Uncle Toni played dominoes, while they sipped coffee and shared the *cucurucho de maní* they had purchased from the peanut vendor. They were having fun. No one would miss us for a long time.

Let's Think About...

Why do you think Mami and Aunt Olga warned the children not to go too far? **Inferring**

"Watch out for sea urchins!" I warned as I led the group on our climb. The spiny black sea urchins hid inside the crevices and crannies of the rough boulders. It was very painful if you stepped on one. Luisa and Mari followed behind me. They were careful to only step on the rocks I stepped on. Little Javi came last. He stopped constantly to look at the *cobitos,* the tiny hermit crabs that scurried around on the rocks, and at the iridescent tropical fish that were concealed in the deepest tide pools. I had to keep checking behind me to make sure he didn't stray from our path.

Just then, I turned around to watch helplessly as Javi slipped on an algae-covered rock. *"¡Cuidado!"* I warned. But it was too late.

Let's Think About...

Picture the children playing on the rocks. Why do you think Javi stopped so often to look at the crabs and fish?

Visualize

"*¡Ay!*" he shrieked, and then began to cry uncontrollably.

Cautiously, we all hurried back to help Javi. Luisa and Mari crouched down to examine his foot.

"He stepped on a sea urchin!" Mari cried. "Now what are we going to do?"

"We should have never followed you," Luisa lamented. "We'll all be punished."

At that moment I did not want to think of what the punishment would be. What if we couldn't have any of Mami's tortilla? All I knew was that we had to help Javi right away. I looked around and found a piece of driftwood.

"Luisa," I ordered. "Hold his leg still while I remove the urchin from his foot."

Let's **Think** About...

What's happened to Javi and the cousins so far?
Summarize

Luisa held Javi's leg still as Mari held his hand and tried to comfort him. But Javi's desperate cries were now drowning out the sound of the sea.

I pulled and tugged, but the urchin wouldn't budge. It was stuck to Javi's foot by the tips of its spines. Javi was scared and in pain. And we were too far from our parents to ask for help. What if we couldn't get Javi back? I struggled relentlessly until I was finally able to remove the spiny creature from his foot.

Gently, Luisa poured some seawater over Javi's foot. That was when she noticed there was still a piece of the sea urchin's spine lodged in it. Javi wasn't going to be able to walk back, and he was much too heavy for us to carry. We had to remove that piece of spine so that he could walk on his own.

The sun burnt our backs as we all took turns trying to dislodge the sea urchin's spine.

"I have an idea," said Luisa suddenly. She removed her hair barrettes and held them like tweezers. Then, with the smallest movement, she pulled the broken spine out. With that solved, we started back.

I helped Javi walk on his sore foot. He wept and limped with every step. Our walk back seemed endless. As we got closer I realized that we would have to explain how it was that we went to the reef in the first place. I would surely end up with no tortilla if we told the truth.

"What will we do now?" Mari asked.

"We'll have to tell our parents what happened," said Luisa matter-of-factly.

"No!" I said emphatically. "We'll be punished for sure."

We walked the rest of the way in silence. The sound of crashing waves, children playing, and seagulls' calls became a background drone to Javi's cries.

When we finally reached our parents, Javi was crying louder than ever. Aunt Olga took one look at him and gasped. *"¡Niños!* Children! What's happened to Javi?"

Mari looked at Luisa. Luisa looked at me. Javi cried even louder.

"Well...," I hesitated. By now everyone was staring at me. "We were walking along the beach looking for cockles and urchin shells," I began, "when I found a live sea urchin attached to a piece of driftwood. So I called the others. Javi came running so fast that he stepped on it by accident."

Luisa and Mari stared at me in disbelief. I didn't think they liked my story.

"Let me see your foot, Javi," Aunt Olga said, kneeling next to her son.

Let's **Think** About...

Picture the cousins walking back to the beach. How is the mood different from earlier in the day?

◉ Visualize

191

Mami and Aunt Rosa looked on as Aunt Olga examined Javi's foot closely. Then she gave him a big hug and a kiss. "He's fine," she said at last. "It looks like the children were able to pull it out."

And at this good news, Javi's tears disappeared and were replaced by a big broad smile. "I'm hungry," he said.

"Then let's have lunch," Aunt Olga suggested.

I was dumbfounded. Not only had they believed me, but we were also going to eat Mami's tortilla!

The men went back to their domino game. The women went back to their conversation as they busied themselves serving everybody. No one but me seemed to notice how quiet Luisa and Mari had grown.

Mami handed me a plate filled with my favorite foods. The tortilla smelled delicious. But I was unable to eat. I looked up at Luisa and Mari who were quietly picking at their food. I watched Mami as she served herself and sat next to my aunts. I looked at my plate again. How could I enjoy my food when I knew I had done something I wasn't supposed to do? There was only one thing I could do now. I stood up, picked up my plate, and went right over to Mami.

"What's wrong, Fernando?" Mami asked.

I looked back at Luisa and Mari and swallowed hard. Then, I handed Mami my untouched plate.

"You wouldn't have given me this if I had told you the truth," I said.

Mami looked puzzled. The whole group grew silent and watched me struggle. I was very embarrassed.

"It was my fault," Luisa said. "I should have stopped them."

"And I went along," said Mari.

"No, no, it was my idea to go to the reef," I said. Then I told everyone about our adventure at the reef. When I was finished, Mami looked at me with tear-filled eyes.

"You are right, Fernando," she said. "I should punish you for doing something you knew not to do. Somebody could have been seriously hurt."

"I know," I whispered, "and I'm sorry." But then the glimmer of a smile softened Mami's expression. She slid her arm over my shoulders as she said, "You know, Fernando, anyone can make a mistake. But not everyone has the courage to admit it. *Gracias.* Thank you for telling the truth."

That afternoon, under the shade of the pine trees, the nine of us sat down on the old blankets for lunch. We had congrí, bread, and Mami's famous tortilla española. And do you know something? That day it tasted better than it ever had before.

Let's **Think** About...

Why do you think the tortillas tasted so good to the narrator?
Inferring

Objectives

• Provide evidence from text to support understanding. • Read independently for a sustained period of time and paraphrase the reading, including the order in which events occur.

Envision It! Retell

READING STREET ONLINE
STORY SORT
www.ReadingStreet.com

Think Critically

1. Imagine that you are Fernando. How would you feel if you were responsible for someone getting hurt? Why do you think you would feel this way? **Text to Self**

2. Think about the setting of the story. Find examples to show how the author helps readers imagine the sight, feel, and taste of things at the beach. **Think Like an Author**

3. Both the grown-ups and the children are partly responsible for Javi getting hurt. Compare and contrast the ways the two groups are partly responsible.
Compare and Contrast

4. Pick the moment in the story that you remember best. Close your eyes and visualize it. Then describe it. Afterward, reread that scene to see how accurate your mental picture was. **Visualize**

5. Look Back and Write Look back at page 193. Explain in your own words what led Fernando to confess.

TEST PRACTICE Extended Response

Meet the Author

Lulu Delacre

Lulu Delacre grew up in Puerto Rico and is the daughter of two professors. Today she lives in Maryland and writes and illustrates books about Latin America.

For her story "At the Beach," Ms. Delacre says, "I wanted to write about an adventure at the beach. When I was a child, I went to the beach with my father and sister most weekends. One of my fondest memories is walking carefully on the big boulders, sidestepping sea urchins to reach the deepest pools where colorful fish hid." Like the boy in the story, Ms. Delacre has actually stepped on a sea urchin! "It is indeed very painful," she says.

"Growing up on the island was a fun-filled experience, where climbing up a *tamarindo* tree with a friend to eat its fruit was as commonplace as hunting for tiny brown lizards. I used to gently open their mouths and hang them from my earlobes as earrings!"

Here are other books by Lulu Delacre.

Salsa Stories

Arroz con Leche: Popular Songs and Rhymes from Latin America

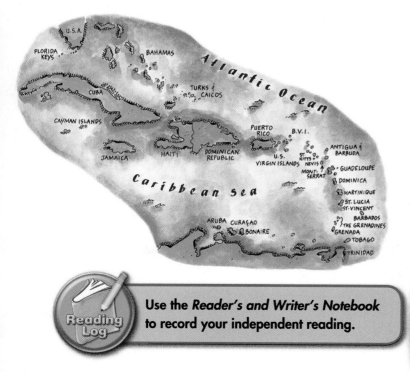

Use the *Reader's and Writer's Notebook* to record your independent reading.

Objectives
● Write a personal narrative that conveys your thoughts and feelings about an experience. ● Recognize and use commas in compound sentences. ● Recognize and use proper punctuation and spacing for quotations.

Let's Write It!

Key Features of a Description

● vivid language helps readers visualize a scene

● can be part of a longer story

● often provides details that tell what something smelled, felt, or tasted like, as well as how something looked or sounded

READING STREET ONLINE
GRAMMAR JAMMER
www.ReadingStreet.com

Narrative

Description

Descriptions are writings that describe a person, place, thing, or event. They use vivid language and details to help readers picture a subject. The student model on the next page is an example of a description.

Writing Prompt Think about a time when you learned something important. Write a description of that moment, using your sense of smell, touch, taste, sight, and hearing to make the memory vivid.

Writer's Checklist

Remember, you should . . .

☑ describe a time when you learned something valuable.

☑ include vivid details.

☑ use one or more of the five senses in your description.

☑ recognize and use proper punctuation for quotations.

Following the Rules

My mom thinks it is important to keep my room clean. I have never understood why – until this moment. She is standing in my room, holding one of my shirts. Her eyes are wide with surprise. Beside her **feet** are several beetles, crawling in and out of the pile of clothes I left on the floor.

My face grows hot as I remember my forgotten science project: watching mealworm **larvae** hatch into beetles.

Closing my eyes, I think back on how I had taken the unfinished project home to show my mom. My stomach had rumbled with hunger after school that day, so I dumped my homework and backpack on my bedroom floor before heading to the kitchen for a snack. I later forgot all about the container with the **mealworms**, which must have gotten buried underneath a pile of **clothes**.

I frown at the memory and open my eyes, but my mom speaks before I can explain the situation. "Grab a laundry basket," she says. "Do you know now why it's important to follow the rules and clean your room?"

Writing Trait Sentences
The writer uses varied sentence beginnings to add variety and interest to the passage.

Regular and irregular plural nouns are used correctly.

Genre
A **description** uses sensory details to make a memory vivid.

Conventions

Regular and Irregular Plural Nouns

Remember To make most singular nouns into plural nouns, add -s, -es, or -ies. Don't forget that some nouns have irregular plural forms, such as *person/people* or *mouse/mice.*

Objectives

● Compare and contrast the themes of works of fiction from different cultures.

Social Studies in Reading

Genre
Legend

● A legend is a fictional story. Most legends are traditional stories passed down from generation to generation.

● Legends explain how certain things came to be. They can also present certain lessons that people can use in their own lives.

● Some legends use animals as their main characters.

● Read "The Eagle and the Bat." Look for elements that make this story a legend. What does this legend explain?

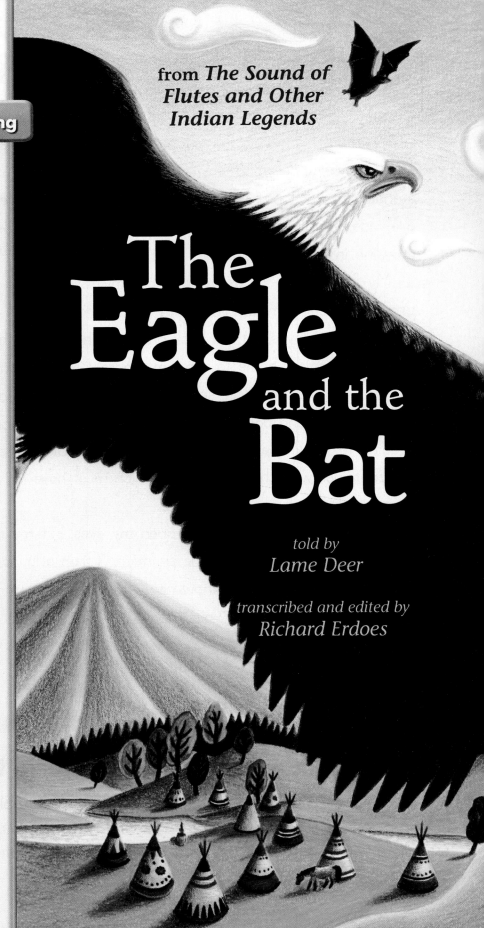

from *The Sound of Flutes and Other Indian Legends*

The Eagle and the Bat

told by
Lame Deer

transcribed and edited by
Richard Erdoes

Once all the birds came together in a big powwow. They played games to see who could fly the fastest and had other contests. At the end they said, "Now let's see which of us can fly higher than all the others." The kite, the hawk, the falcon, the wild goose, the crane—they all flew so high that they almost disappeared from sight. But then Wanblee, the eagle, spread his mighty wings and soared up into the air, higher than any other bird, almost all the way to the sun.

When Wanblee finally came down again, all the birds set up a trilling, high-pitched honoring cry, saying, "The eagle beat us all. He can fly the highest!"

But just then a little bat popped up from out of the plumes on the top of Wanblee's head, flapping its puny leather wings and yelling, "No, no, I flew higher than Wanblee, hiding myself on top of his head. Being on top of Wanblee, naturally I was higher up than he or anybody else."

For this presumption and trickery, the birds transformed the bat into a mouse, taking away his wings. "From now on," said the eagle, "you'll stay in a hole beneath the earth, and the owl will watch so that you won't dare come out of your hole until you learn how to behave yourself."

Let's Think About...

What lesson did the bat learn at the end of the story?
Legend

Let's Think About...

Reading Across Texts What can a reader learn about telling the truth from both *At the Beach* and "The Eagle and the Bat"? Compare these lessons with those of other stories you've read.

Writing Across Texts Write a paragraph explaining why honesty is the best policy.

Objectives
● Read aloud grade-level texts and understand what is read. ● Determine the meanings of unfamiliar words or multiple-meaning words by using the context of the sentence. ● Identify the point of view of media presentations. ● Give organized presentations that communicate your ideas effectively. ● Listen to and interpret a speaker's messages and ask questions.

Let's Learn It!

READING STREET ONLINE
ONLINE STUDENT EDITION
www.ReadingStreet.com

Vocabulary

Unfamiliar Words

Context Clues Words, phrases, and sentences around an unfamiliar word may give clues to the word's meaning. Use these hints to help you figure out what an unfamiliar word means.

Practice It! Reread *At the Beach* and identify any unfamiliar words in the story. For each unfamiliar word, look at the surrounding words and sentences to find clues to the word's meaning. Make a list of words in the story whose meanings you figured out by using context clues.

Fluency

Expression

Use different tones of voice to show emotion as you read. Reading with expression helps to show the suspense, concern, or excitement in a story.

Practice It! With a partner, practice reading aloud page 185 of *At the Beach*. Read with expression to show Fernando's feelings. Take turns reading and offering each other feedback.

Media Literacy

When you are a guest, tell the story from the character's point of view.

Talk Show

On a talk show, a host chats informally with guests who are knowledgeable about a subject or who have done something noteworthy. The purpose of a talk show is to inform and entertain viewers and listeners.

Practice It! With a group, conduct a talk show. Assign roles, with one student as host, and the others as guests. Choose two characters from *At the Beach* to be guests. Then discuss the story's events, and make sure to ask for each character's point of view about the events. Rehearse and then conduct your talk show in class.

Tips

Listening . . .

- Listen to the speaker's message.
- Be ready to ask questions to clarify the speaker's perspective.

Speaking . . .

- Use eye contact to communicate your ideas to others.
- Use natural gestures when you speak.

Teamwork . . .

- Elicit suggestions from other group members.
- Consider suggestions from other group members.

201

Oral Vocabulary

Let's Talk About

Taking Risks

● Share ideas about why we must take risks.

● Listen to and interpret a classmate's ideas about taking risks.

● Ask questions about taking risks.

READING STREET ONLINE
CONCEPT TALK VIDEO
www.ReadingStreet.com

Objectives
● Make inferences about a text and use evidence from the text to support understanding. ● Summarize and paraphrase information in a text.

Envision It! Skill Strategy

Skill

Strategy

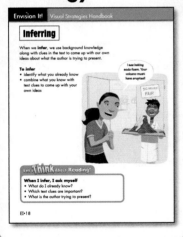

READING STREET ONLINE
ENVISION IT! ANIMATIONS
www.ReadingStreet.com

Comprehension Skill

🎯 Sequence

- The sequence of events is the order in which events take place, from first to last.

- Clue words such as *first, next, then,* and *finally* may show sequence. Other clues are dates and the times of day.

- *While* and *at the same time* are clues that events are occurring at once.

- Use a graphic organizer like the one below to put the events in sequence. Then write a summary of the events in sequence.

First Event	Second Event	Third Event	Fourth Event

Comprehension Strategy

🎯 Inferring

When you infer, you combine your own knowledge with evidence in the text to come up with an idea about what the author is presenting. Active readers often infer about the ideas, morals, and themes of a written work.

A Flag Unfurled

Do you know how many times the American flag has changed? From 1777 to 1960 Congress has changed the flag more than a dozen times!

In 1776, George Washington needed a symbol for the country. Washington had used the Grand Union during the Revolutionary War. The Grand Union flag had the British Union Jack in the upper left corner. In 1777, the Continental Congress passed the first Flag Act. The Act stated that the flag be made of 13 stripes and 13 stars.

Strategy What inference can you make about the Grand Union flag? Why was it unsuitable for the new Union?

One year earlier, Betsy Ross, a seamstress from Philadelphia, reported that she had sewed the first American flag. As the legend goes, Washington had visited her shop and showed her a flag design. The result was the first "stars and stripes" flag. It had a circle of 13 stars that represented the original 13 colonies.

The "stars and stripes" flag remained in use for several years. Then, in 1791, Vermont was added to the Union. Another star and stripe were added. After that, another star and stripe were added for every new state, until finally, in 1818, Congress decided to keep the number of stripes at 13, and allow the addition of a new star for each new state.

Skill What clue word tells you that the practice of adding stripes to the flag stopped?

Skill What is the earliest event that appears in this article?

Your Turn!

 Need a Review? See the *Envision It! Handbook* for additional help with sequence and inferring.

Ready to Try It? Use what you learned about sequence as you read *Hold the Flag High*.

205

Envision It! | **Words to Know**

canteen

glory

stallion

confederacy

quarrel

rebellion

union

READING STREET ONLINE
VOCABULARY ACTIVITIES
www.ReadingStreet.com

Vocabulary Strategy for

🎯 Unknown Words

Dictionary/Glossary When you read, you may come across a word you do not know. You can use a glossary or dictionary to find out the meaning of the word. A glossary lists and defines important words in a book. A dictionary lists all words, in alphabetical order, and gives their meanings, pronunciations, and other information.

Choose one of the *Words to Know* and follow these steps.

1. Check your book for a glossary. If there is no glossary, use a printed or electronic dictionary and find the entry for the word.

2. Read the pronunciation to yourself. Saying the word may help you recognize it.

3. Read all the meanings given for the word.

4. Choose the meaning that makes sense in your sentence.

As you read "Civil War Drummers," use the glossary or a dictionary to look up the meanings of this week's *Words to Know*.

Words to Write Reread "Civil War Drummers." Imagine you are a war drummer. Write a paragraph describing your experience. Use words from the *Words to Know* list.

Civil War DRUMMERS

In the Civil War, both the Union army and the army of the Confederacy relied on their drummers. The drummers were an essential part of their battles.

The Civil War was much more than a quarrel between the North and the South. It was a war, with fierce battles fought on the ground. For this reason, drummers were needed, and not just to play marching beats. Drummers were needed on the battlefield to alert soldiers when to retreat to safety. An officer mounted on his stallion would lean down to tell his drummer to play a drum call for a charge or some other troop movement. Off the battlefield, the drummers' beats alerted officers to planning meetings.

War drummers had to be brave. They marched onto the battlefield unarmed, carrying just their water canteens and their drums. Perhaps the drummers didn't get the glory that the soldiers did, but they performed important work for both the North and the South, as they fought during the rebellion.

Your Turn!

 **Need a Review?** For additional help with using a dictionary or glossary to find out the meanings of unknown words, see *Words!*

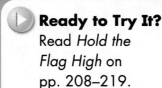 **Ready to Try It?** Read *Hold the Flag High* on pp. 208–219.

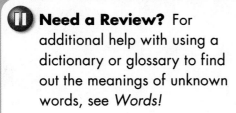

207

HOLD THE FLAG HIGH

BY CATHERINE CLINTON

ILLUSTRATED BY SHANE W. EVANS

Genre

Literary Nonfiction tells the story of a true event. As you read, notice how the author explains one man's important role in a Civil War battle.

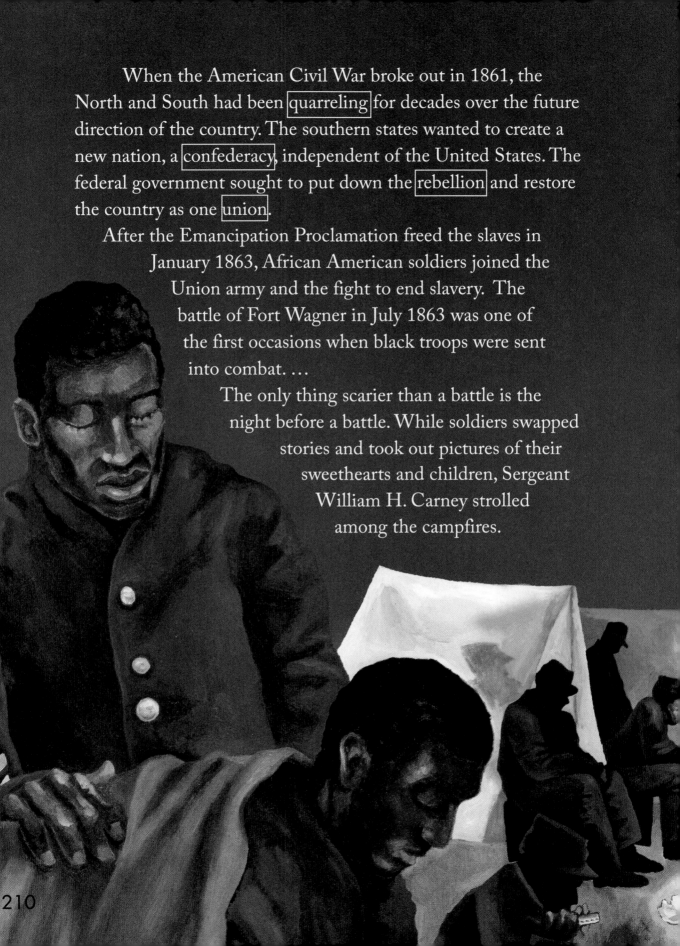

When the American Civil War broke out in 1861, the North and South had been quarreling for decades over the future direction of the country. The southern states wanted to create a new nation, a confederacy, independent of the United States. The federal government sought to put down the rebellion and restore the country as one union.

After the Emancipation Proclamation freed the slaves in January 1863, African American soldiers joined the Union army and the fight to end slavery. The battle of Fort Wagner in July 1863 was one of the first occasions when black troops were sent into combat. …

The only thing scarier than a battle is the night before a battle. While soldiers swapped stories and took out pictures of their sweethearts and children, Sergeant William H. Carney strolled among the campfires.

A homesick private played his harmonica sweet and low. Carney draped a blanket around the shoulders of Company C's drummer boy, a young slave who had run off from his master to join the fight. Carney assured him, "Tomorrow's gonna be a big day for us, Ned. You'll be drumming us to glory."

Carney was one of the few black officers in the Massachusetts Fifty-fourth, a new African American regiment formed in the spring of 1863.

Carney's men took pride in the shiny brass buttons on their uniforms and new rifles on their shoulders. Just a few weeks before, they had paraded through the streets of Boston. Ladies had waved handkerchiefs, and all had shouted hurrahs and farewells. Then the Fifty-fourth Regiment had set sail to fight in far-off South Carolina.

Once they arrived, the soldiers set up camp south of Charleston Bay. Their first battle would come tomorrow.

This was the day they had all been waiting for, the soldiers told themselves as they headed off to sleep.

Carney kicked out the fire. An owl hooted in the distance. Ned, the drummer boy, wondered if it was really an owl. Maybe it was the signal of a Confederate spy.

"Sarge, I don't know what it'll be like when the Rebs start shootin'. I'm feeling scared—and—and—" he stuttered, "and what if I get lost?"

"Son, you just play that drum, and remember what we're fighting for: Old Glory will lead the way."

"Old Glory?" Ned asked.

"Sure, son, keep your eyes on the flag," said Carney. "Like hundreds before us and thousands after, just follow those Stars and Stripes, and you can't go wrong."

"I can't go wrong," Ned murmured as Carney tucked him into his bedroll.

Then the sergeant said a little prayer, hoping it would be true.

Long before the sun rose, the men of the Fifty-fourth awoke to prepare for the battle. They checked and rechecked their rifles, making sure the flints were dry and the bayonets sharp and shined. Ned worked hard, filling canteens with water.

After a breakfast of hardtack and coffee, each soldier had his name pinned onto the back of his uniform. This way soldiers who did not survive the battle could be identified. Soldiers who could write helped those who couldn't.

Carney tipped his hat at the color-bearer. He was the soldier who carried the regiment's flag into battle on a short flagpole, called a staff. "We're all counting on you, brother."

The wind whipped the banner, held aloft on its staff: back and forth; then again, back and forth.

Soldiers bristled with anticipation.

Ned could see their commanding officer, Robert Gould Shaw, approaching on horseback. As he galloped up, spurs gleaming on his heels and a fringed silk sash across his chest, the colonel seemed to own the day.

But when Shaw dismounted, Ned noticed that his pale face was nearly as white as his stallion. Ned wondered, *Could he be scared, too?*

Maybe Shaw *was* a bit afraid; he had already been wounded in battle once. But his speech to his troops betrayed no fears. Shaw fired up his men for battle. The Fifty-fourth had been picked to lead the charge against Fort Wagner—the Confederate outpost guarding Charleston. Chests swollen with pride, these soldiers could hardly wait. They would gladly follow Shaw to the ends of the Earth, eager to prove their courage under fire.

The artillery shelled all day, but finally the generals were ready to send in the infantry. "Forward, march!" the order rang out.

An endless line of men in blue snaked along the sand. They headed for the fortress towering on the horizon.

Ned solemnly drummed on the beat—footfalls and drumsticks in syncopation. He glanced at the flag snapping in the stiff breeze. The gulls gently swooped, as waves lapped the shore. …

In a split second, everything tilted. Cannonballs pounded the ground. Bullets pelted helter-skelter. A greenish-yellow glow of smoke rose at the same time bodies began to fall. Streams of blood flowed into the foam, washing out to sea. The metallic taste in Carney's mouth mixed with the fear rising in his throat.

Ned could barely hear the drum over the roar. Then a shell exploded behind him, and he fell to his knees. His heartbeat pounded in his ears as he tried to get his bearings. Uninjured but dazed, Ned scanned the horizon.

Far above, he could see Colonel Shaw lit by the firelight from exploding shells. He was mounting a rampart, saber in hand, shouting: "Forward, Fifty-fourth," as he disappeared into the breach. But where was the flag?

Carney felt a burning sensation as a bullet tore through his flesh. Just ahead, the soldier carrying Old Glory staggered to a halt, shot dead by a Confederate sharpshooter. As he sank toward the ground, Carney plunged forward to catch the falling flag. He lifted the banner above his head and two more shots slammed into him.

Fighting the pain, the sergeant triumphantly raised the Stars and Stripes over Fort Wagner's ramparts. The flag would show Ned and the others the way.

Many hours later, when the Union bugler finally sounded retreat, the federal soldiers struggled away from the fort, defeated. Yet Carney carried the flag safely back behind Union lines before he collapsed. Ned and other members of the Fifty-fourth Regiment surrounded their wounded sergeant's cot. They congratulated him as Carney murmured, "The old flag never touched the ground." Those who survived the battle of Fort Wagner would never forget their brave Sergeant Carney, who showed the way by holding the flag high.

EPILOGUE:

Confederate troops held their position and declared victory at Fort Wagner on July 19, 1863. However, the Massachusetts Fifty-fourth Regiment took great pride in their performance, tested in battle.

Long after the Civil War had ended, Sergeant Carney appeared in Boston in 1897 at an unveiling ceremony. A monument for Colonel Robert Gould Shaw, who lost his life at Fort Wagner, was being dedicated. Carney and other members of the Fifty-fourth had contributed funds to erect an impressive bronze memorial honoring their fallen leader. At this solemn occasion, Carney received a standing ovation. His courageous act to preserve the flag was a tribute to those who died to defend it.

William H. Carney was eventually awarded the Congressional Medal of Honor—the first African American to earn this tribute.

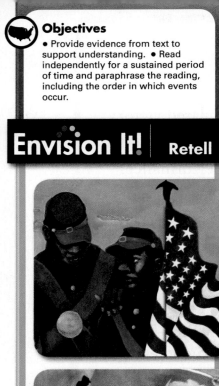

Objectives
- Provide evidence from text to support understanding. • Read independently for a sustained period of time and paraphrase the reading, including the order in which events occur.

Envision It! Retell

Think Critically

1. In the United States, a Flag Code was established to regulate the use of the American flag. One of the code laws states that the flag should never touch the ground. Why would it be important that the flag never touch the ground? What makes a flag such an important symbol for a country?
Text to World

2. How does Sergeant William H. Carney treat Ned, the drummer boy? Why might the author have included the drummer boy in the story? **Author's Purpose**

3. In your own words, describe what happens to Sergeant Carney on pages 212–216. Make sure the events you describe are in chronological order. **Sequence of Events**

4. Reread pages 212–214. Where are the Confederate troops positioned? How did the Confederate troops have a strategic advantage over the Union troops? **Inferring**

5. Look Back and Write Look back at the Epilogue on page 219. Why was William H. Carney awarded the Congressional Medal of Honor? Why was this a special achievement?

TEST PRACTICE Extended Response

CATHERINE CLINTON

Catherine Clinton has written many historical books for children and adults. In college, Ms. Clinton studied African American Studies. Eventually, she became a professor of history and taught for many years at various universities, such as Brown University, Harvard University, and Queen's University in Ireland.

Ms. Clinton became interested in children's literature when she had children of her own. In order to have more time for her family, she interrupted her busy teaching career. She began consulting and writing for elementary school textbooks. She also started to sketch out ideas for children's books about historical topics that she thought were important, but had not yet been written about.

Many of Catherine's books are based on heroes in African American history, such as Phillis Wheatley and Harriet Tubman. Her books help bring these key figures to life.

Here is another book by Catherine Clinton.

When Harriet Met Sojourner

Reading Log

Use the *Reader's and Writer's Notebook* to record your independent reading.

Objectives

● Write letters that communicate ideas, include important information, contain a conclusion, and use the correct format and style.

Let's Write It!

Key Features of an Informal Letter

- contains a date, greeting, and closing

- has a casual tone

- is usually written to someone you know well

READING STREET ONLINE
GRAMMAR JAMMER
www.ReadingStreet.com

Expository

Informal Letter

An **informal letter** is a casual letter. It uses informal language and has a relaxed tone. The student model on the next page is an example of an informal letter.

Writing Prompt Think of a time when you or someone you know acted bravely. Write a letter to a friend or family member, describing the event.

Writer's Checklist

Remember, you should . . .

☑ write informally as you express ideas.

☑ include important information as you describe the event.

☑ use appropriate conventions, including date, salutation, and closing.

☑ demonstrate a sense of closure.

June 10, 20_ _

Dear Ronny,

You won't believe what happened last weekend. My dog Harold and I saved my little sister Lisa's life!

Some friends came to my house Saturday. We were playing catch on the front lawn. You know how Lisa likes to follow me around? She's so annoying. She kept riding her tricycle around us, and then up and down the driveway.

But then, all of a sudden, I heard Harold's barking and Lisa's loud cries. I ran over to see what was going on. I heard a "ssss" sound! There was a huge rattlesnake in the corner of the garage! Harold had tried to warn us.

I was scared, but I knew I had to be brave. I grabbed an empty box in the corner of the garage and threw it over the snake. Then Mom called Animal Control to take the rattlesnake away. Can you believe it?

I can't wait to tell you more details! Let's hang out soon.

Your friend,

Enrique

Writing Trait Voice The letter reveals the writer's personality.

Possessive nouns are used correctly.

Genre An **informal letter** is a casual way to communicate with someone.

Conventions

Possessive Nouns

Remember To form a **singular possessive noun,** add an apostrophe and s *(dog's)*. For a **plural possessive noun** ending in *-s*, add only an apostrophe *(musicians')*.

223

Objectives
● Analyze whether Web sites and other digital media are formal or informal.

21st Century Skills
INTERNET GUY

Want to quickly find information at a **Web site**? Type Control and F. Then type the information you are looking for. Hit return. A great trick!

● Web sites contain information about a topic or topics.

● Web sites contain links to other information.

● Sites use formal or informal language, depending on the writer and the topic. For example, a Web site about an historical event might use more formal language than one about cartoons.

● Read "How to Fold the American Flag." Analyze whether the site uses formal or informal language.

How to Fold the American Flag

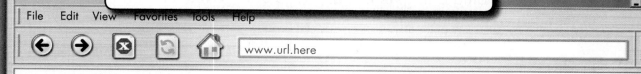
When you open your web browser, type the URL for the site here.

File   Edit   View   Favorites   Tools   Help

www.url.here

The United States Flag

The American flag is a symbol of our country. That is why we treat the flag with respect. There is a proper way to fold the American flag. Click on the links below to find out how to fold the flag

History of the American flag

Symbolism of the American flag

How to fold the American flag

You click your mouse on the link for *How to fold the American flag*, and a new page pops up.

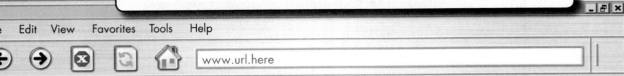

On this new page, you read about the procedure for folding a flag. Is the language used formal or informal?

☆How to Fold the American Flag☆

1. It takes two people to fold the flag. Each person should hold two of the rectangular corners of the flag. They should stand apart until they are holding the flag flat.

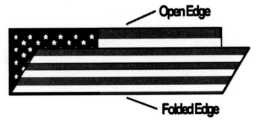

2. Then, fold the flag in half so that the striped section covers the stars section.

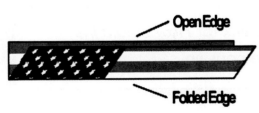

3. Next, fold the flag one more time. Now, the stars should be on top.

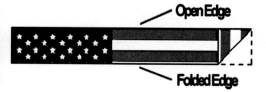

Open Edge

Folded Edge

4. Take the striped corner of the flag. Fold it back in the shape of a triangle.

5. Keep folding the flag in triangular folds. Do this until you come to the end of the flag.

6. Make your last triangular fold. Now the flag should be folded into a small triangle. Only the star section should be showing.

The flag is now folded correctly. It should be stored in a safe place.

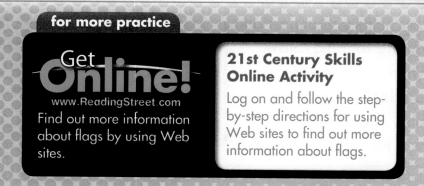

for more practice

Get **Online!**
www.ReadingStreet.com
Find out more information about flags by using Web sites.

21st Century Skills Online Activity
Log on and follow the step-by-step directions for using Web sites to find out more information about flags.

Objectives

● Read aloud grade-level texts and understand what is read. ● Use a dictionary, a glossary, or a thesaurus to locate information about words.
● Listen to and interpret a speaker's messages and ask questions.
● Give organized presentations that communicate your ideas effectively.
● Participate in discussions by raising and considering suggestions from other group members and by identifying points of agreement and disagreement.

Let's Learn It!

READING STREET ONLINE
ONLINE STUDENT EDITION
www.ReadingStreet.com

Vocabulary

Unknown Words

Dictionary/Glossary When you can't determine the meaning of a word from context clues, look up the word in a dictionary or glossary. Dictionaries provide definitions as well as other important information about words.

Practice It! Look through *Hold the Flag High* or another text. Choose at least three words whose meanings you are unsure of. Use a dictionary or glossary to look up the words. Write each word, its definition, and its part of speech. Use the pronunciation to silently pronounce each word to yourself.

Fluency

Accuracy

Partner Reading Reading accurately helps you understand what you are reading. Slow down when you come to a word you don't know. Read it carefully. Then read the sentence again with meaning.

Practice It! With your partner, practice reading aloud a page from *Hold the Flag High*. Preview the words on the page to make sure you understand them and know how to pronounce them.

Listening and Speaking

Get Ready For Middle School

When you speak in front of a group, be sure to make eye contact with your audience.

Informational Speech

In a speech, a speaker gives a formal talk to an audience for a specific purpose. The purpose of an informational speech is to provide listeners with facts about a topic.

Practice It! Prepare an informational speech about a Civil War battle. Research the battle, including noteworthy facts and details. Rehearse your speech with a partner. Then deliver your speech to the class.

Tips

Listening . . .

- Pay attention and listen to what the speaker is saying.

- Ask questions to clarify the speaker's purpose or perspective.

Speaking . . .

- Speak with volume.

- Use natural gestures to help communicate your ideas.

Teamwork . . .

- Discuss why you agree and disagree with others.

- Obtain suggestions from other students.

Objectives
● Listen to and interpret a speaker's messages and ask questions.
● Identify the main ideas and supporting ideas in the speaker's message.

Oral Vocabulary

Let's Talk About

Helping Others

● Share ideas about how to help others.

● Listen to and interpret a classmate's ideas about helping others.

● Determine classmates' main and supporting ideas about helping others.

READING STREET ONLINE
CONCEPT TALK VIDEO
www.ReadingStreet.com

You've learned
0 7 0
Amazing Words
so far this year!

231

Objectives

• Describe specific events in the story or novel that result in or hint at future events.

Envision It! | Skill Strategy

Skill

Strategy

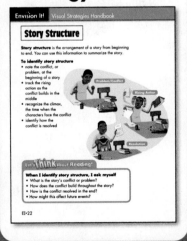

READING STREET ONLINE
ENVISION IT! ANIMATIONS
www.ReadingStreet.com

Comprehension Skill

🎯 Compare and Contrast

- When you compare and contrast things, you tell how they are alike or different.

- Sometimes clue words point out comparisons and contrasts, but not always.

- You can compare and contrast things within a story, or one story with another.

- Use a graphic organizer like the one below to help you write a folk tale. Include ideas that are similar to and different from "Ah Tcha's Leaves."

Similarities in Text	Differences in Text	Compare with What I Know

Comprehension Strategy

🎯 Story Structure

Active readers pay attention to story structure. Generally, authors identify the problem of the main character at the start. They work through the problem as the action rises in the middle, and then solve it with the climax and outcome. Authors also use story incidents to foreshadow or give rise to future events.

Ah Tcha's Leaves

Ah Tcha was a wealthy man. He owned seven farms and seven rice mills in China. He paid his workers in gold, but some grumbled about the hard work. An old woman, Nu Wu, complained the most.

One night, Ah Tcha found mice eating his rice. A cat slept nearby. Ah Tcha threw a giant sack at the cat to wake her. Poof! The cat changed into Nu Wu. She was angry with Ah Tcha. She cried, "You will sleep eleven hours out of every twelve!"

Skill How is Ah Tcha's current situation different from his situation at the beginning of the story?

Ah Tcha slept nearly every day and night. He lost everything and became poor. One night, Nu Wu pounded on Ah Tcha's door, waking him. She wanted food. Ah Tcha had only leaves from a bush by his house, so he tossed them into hot water. Nu Wu grumbled, but drank her cup and left.

Skill Find two times Nu Wu changed Ah Tcha's life. How were those times alike? How were they different?

Ah Tcha drank a cup. He did not fall asleep! He smiled. "Nu Wu thanked me by charming the leaves to banish my sleepiness."

Strategy How do the events in the story give rise to the ending?

Ah Tcha sold the leaves. He planted extra bushes and became rich. Throughout China, people asked for the "drink of Ah Tcha" or "Tcha." In time, *Tcha* became *Tay*, and finally *tea*.

Your Turn!

⏸ **Need a Review?** See the *Envision It! Handbook* for help with comparing, contrasting, and story structure.

▶ **Ready to Try It?** As you read *The Ch'i-lin Purse*, look for story incidents that foreshadow or give rise to future events.

The Ch'i-lin Purse

233

Objectives
● Determine the meaning of English words with roots from Greek, Latin, and other languages.

Envision It! | Words to Know

astonished

gratitude

procession

behavior

benefactor

distribution

recommend

sacred

traditions

READING STREET ONLINE
VOCABULARY ACTIVITIES
www.ReadingStreet.com

Vocabulary Strategy for

🎯 Greek and Latin Roots

Word Structure When you come to an unknown word, particularly an academic vocabulary word, look for a root within the word. For example, the Latin root *bene-* means "well" or "good," as in *benefit* and *benefactor*. The Greek root *myth-* means "fable" or "legend," as in *myth* and *mythology*. You can use roots to figure out the meaning of an unknown word.

1. Find a root in the word. Think about other words you know that also have this root.

2. Do the words you know give you clues about the meaning of the unknown word?

3. Check to see if the meaning makes sense in the sentence.

Read "The Meaning of Tales" on page 235. Look for roots to help you figure out the meanings of this week's *Words to Know* or words such as *mysterious, triumph,* or *celebrate.*

Words to Write Reread "The Meaning of Tales." Write a myth or tale of your own that explains something or teaches a lesson about life. Use words from the *Words to Know* list.

The Meaning of Tales

Myths, fairy tales, and folk tales are time-honored traditions in many countries. Before people could write, they told stories to make each other laugh, cry, or shake with fear. These stories do more than just entertain. They preserve the earliest ideas and history of a people. A myth may explain why something happens in nature. It may tell what causes the seasons, for example. A tale may show us the rewards for our behavior and teach us a lesson. Often, both myths and tales are tied to what people in earlier times found sacred and mysterious.

Fairy tales reach into the world of fancy. A poor girl finds a benefactor, such as a fairy godmother. A handsome prince discovers the girl and is astonished by her beauty. They fall in love. Someone evil tears them apart, and they suffer great misery. A magic being helps them defeat the evil. They feel a joyful gratitude. They celebrate their triumph in a grand procession through the kingdom. The distribution of these stories all over the world shows how important they are to all people. Do you want to understand the nature of people? I recommend that you study tales.

Your Turn!

❚❚ Need a Review? For additional help with Greek and Latin roots, see *Words!*

▶ Ready to Try It? Read *The Ch'i-lin Purse* on pp. 236–249.

The Ch'i-lin Purse

retold by Linda Fang
illustrated by Ed Young

Genre

Folk tales are stories or legends that are told over and over from one generation to the next. As you read, imagine that someone is sitting next to you telling you the story.

Question of the Week

What are the rewards in helping others?

237

It is said that many years ago in China, in a small town called Teng-chou, there lived a wealthy widow, Mrs. Hsüeh. She had only one daughter, Hsüeh Hsiang-ling. Hsiang-ling was beautiful and intelligent, and her mother loved her dearly. But since everything Hsiang-ling wanted was given to her, she became rather spoiled.

When Hsiang-ling was sixteen years old, her mother decided that it was time for her to marry. Through a matchmaker, Hsiang-ling was engaged to a young man from a wealthy family in a neighboring town.

Mrs. Hsüeh wanted to prepare a dowry for Hsiang-ling that no girl in town could match. But Hsiang-ling was hard to please. Almost everything her mother bought for her was returned or exchanged at least two or three times.

When the dowry was finally complete, Mrs. Hsüeh decided to add one more item to it. It was the Ch'i-lin Purse, a red satin bag embroidered on both sides with a *ch'i-lin*, a legendary animal from ancient times. The *ch'i-lin* had scales all over its body and a single horn on its head. In the old Chinese tradition, the *ch'i-lin* is the symbol of a promising male offspring. Mrs. Hsüeh wanted to give Hsiang-ling the purse because she hoped that her daughter would give birth to a talented son.

When the purse Mrs. Hsüeh had ordered was ready, a family servant brought it home. But Hsiang-ling was not satisfied at all. "I don't like the pattern, take it back!" she said.

The servant returned to the store and ordered another. But when it was brought home, Hsiang-ling merely glanced at it and said, "The colors of the *ch'i-lin* are too dark, take it back!"

The servant went to place another order, but the new purse still did not please her. This time the servant broke down in tears.

"I won't go back again, young mistress. The people in the store laugh at me. They say I am hard to please. This is not true. You are the one who is hard to please. If you don't want this purse, I am going to leave you and work for someone else."

Although Hsiang-ling was spoiled, she was not a mean-spirited person. She somehow began to feel sorry for the old man, who had been with her family for more than forty years. So she looked at the purse and said, "All right, I will have this one. You may go and pay for it." The servant went back to the store, paid for the purse, and gave it to Mrs. Hsüeh.

Hsiang-ling's wedding fell on the eighteenth day of the sixth month according to the lunar calendar. It was the day Hsiang-ling had longed for since her engagement. She was very excited and yet a bit sad, because she knew she was leaving her mother and the home she had lived in for sixteen years.

Hsiang-ling wore a red silk dress and a red silk veil over her head. As she sat in her *hua-chiao*, a sedan chair draped with red satin, and waited to be carried to her new home, her mother came to present her with the Ch'i-lin Purse.

"My dear child," she said as she lifted up the satin curtain in front, "this is your *ta-hsi-jih-tzu*, your big, happy day. I am delighted to see you get married even though I will miss you terribly. Here is the Ch'i-lin Purse. I have put some wonderful things in it. But don't open it now. Wait until you are in your new home, and you will feel that I am with you."

Hsiang-ling was hardly listening. She was thinking about the wedding and wondering about her husband-to-be, whom she had never met. She took the purse and laid it on her lap. A few minutes later, four footmen came. Picking up the *hua-chiao*, they placed it on their shoulders, and the wedding procession began.

As the procession reached the road, it started to rain. Soon it was pouring so heavily that the footmen could not see well enough to continue. The wedding procession came to a halt, and the *hua-chiao* was carried into a pavilion that stood alongside the road.

There was another *hua-chiao* in the pavilion. It was shabby, with holes in the drapes. Hsiang-ling could hear a girl sobbing inside. This annoyed her, because she believed that a person crying on her wedding day could bring bad luck. So she told her maid to go and find out what was wrong.

"The bride is very sad," the maid said when she returned. "She is poor and has nothing to take to her new home."

Hsiang-ling couldn't help feeling sorry for the girl. Then her eyes fell on the Ch'i-lin Purse in her lap. She realized that she was lucky to have so many things, while this girl had nothing. Since she wasn't carrying any money with her, she handed the Ch'i-lin Purse to her maid. "Give this to the girl, but don't mention my name."

So the maid went over and gave the purse to the other bride. The girl stopped crying at once. Hsiang-ling had given away her mother's wedding gift without ever finding out what was inside.

A few minutes later, the rain stopped, the footmen picked up Hsiang-ling's *hua-chiao*, and the procession continued on its way. In an hour, Hsiang-ling arrived at her new home. She was happily married that evening, and to her delight she found her husband to be a wonderful and handsome young man. In a year's time, when she became the mother of a little boy, she felt she was the happiest woman in the world.

But six years later, there came a terrible flood. Hsiang-ling and her family lost their home and everything they owned. When they were fleeing their town, Hsiang-ling became separated from her husband and young son in the crowds of other townspeople. After searching for them in vain, Hsiang-ling followed a group of people to another town called Lai-chou. She had given up hope that she would ever see her husband and child again.

As Hsiang-ling sat, exhausted and alone, at the side of the road leading to Lai-chou, a woman came up to her and said, "You must be hungry. Don't you know that a *li* (one-third of a mile) down the road there is a food-distribution shack? Yüan-wai Lu has opened it to help the flood victims. Talk to his butler. I am sure you can get something to eat there."

Hsiang-ling thanked the woman, followed her directions, and found the place. A long line of people with bowls in their hands was waiting to get a ration of porridge. Hsiang-ling had never done such a thing in her life. As she stood in line holding a bowl and waiting her turn, she felt distraught enough to cry, but she forced herself to hold back the tears.

Finally, when it was her turn, Yüan-wai Lu's butler scooped the last portion of porridge into her bowl and said to the rest of the people in line, "Sorry, no more porridge left. Come back early tomorrow."

The person behind Hsiang-ling began to sob. Hsiang-ling turned around and saw a woman who reminded her of her mother, except that she was much older. Without a word, she emptied her porridge into the woman's bowl and walked away.

The butler was surprised at what Hsiang-ling had done. Just as she had made her way back to the road, he caught up with her and said, "Young lady, I don't understand. Why did you give away your porridge—are you not hungry?"

"I am hungry," said Hsiang-ling, "but I am young and I can stand hunger a bit longer."

"You are very unselfish," said the man. "I would like to help you. My master, Yüan-wai Lu, is looking for someone to take care of his little boy. If you are interested, I would be happy to recommend you."

Hsiang-ling gratefully accepted his offer and was brought to the house where Yüan-wai Lu and his wife lived.

Yüan-wai Lu, a man in his early thirties, was impressed by Hsiang-ling's graceful bearing, and he agreed to hire her. "My wife's health is very delicate and she seldom leaves her room. Your job is to take care of our son. You may play with him anywhere in the garden, but there is one place you must never go. That is the Pearl Hall, the house that stands by itself on the east side of the garden. It is a sacred place, and if you ever go in there, you will be dismissed immediately."

So Hsiang-ling began her life as a governess. The little boy in her care was very spoiled. Whenever he wanted anything, he wanted it right away, and if he didn't get it, he would cry and cry until he got it. Hsiang-ling was saddened by his behavior; it reminded her of how spoiled she had been as a child.

One day, Hsiang-ling and the little boy were in the garden. Suddenly, the ball they were playing with disappeared through the window of the Pearl Hall. The boy began to wail, "I want my ball, I want my ball! Go and get my ball."

"Young Master, I cannot go into the Pearl Hall," said Hsiang-ling. "Your father doesn't allow it. I will be dismissed if I do."

But the little boy only cried louder, and finally Hsiang-ling decided that she had no choice. She walked over to the east side of the garden and looked around. No one was in sight. She quickly walked up the steps that led to the Pearl Hall and again made sure that no one was watching. Then she opened the door and stepped in.

She found herself standing in front of an altar, where two candles and some incense sticks were burning. But in the place where people usually put the wooden name-tablets of their ancestors was a Ch'i-lin Purse! Instantly she recalled the events of her wedding day and how happy she had been. She thought of her wonderful husband and her own son and how much she missed them. She had everything then, and now she had nothing! Hsiang-ling burst into tears.

Suddenly, she felt a hand on her shoulder. When she turned around she found herself face-to-face with Mrs. Lu, her mistress, and a young maid.

"What are you doing here?" Mrs. Lu asked angrily.

"Young Master told me to come here and pick up his ball," Hsiang-ling replied.

"Then why are you weeping at the altar?"

"Because I saw the purse which once belonged to me."

Mrs. Lu looked startled. "Where are you from?" she asked, as she took the purse from the altar and sat down on a chair that leaned against a long table. There was a tremble in her voice.

"I am from Teng-chou."

"Bring her a stool," said Mrs. Lu, motioning to her maid. Not wanting to wait on another servant, the maid grudgingly brought a stool and put it to Mrs. Lu's right. "You may sit down," said Mrs. Lu. Somewhat confused, Hsiang-ling sat down.

"What was your maiden name?"

"Hsüeh Hsiang-ling."

"When were you married?"

"On the eighteenth day of the sixth moon, six years ago."

"Bring her a chair and put it to my left," Mrs. Lu ordered the maid. Hsiang-ling was told to move to the chair. She was surprised to see herself treated as a guest of honor.

"Tell me how you lost the purse," said Mrs. Lu.

"It was a gift from my mother. My wedding procession was stopped on the road because of a storm, and my *hua-chiao* was carried into a pavilion. There was another *hua-chiao* in it, and the bride was crying."

"Move her chair to the middle and move mine to the right side," ordered Mrs. Lu. The chairs were switched, and once again Hsiang-ling was told to sit down. She was astonished to find herself sitting in the middle seat—the place of the highest honor.

"Please continue," said Mrs. Lu.

"I gave the bride my purse. I never saw it again, and I have no idea how it got here."

Mrs. Lu dropped to her knees in front of Hsiang-ling and cried, "You are my benefactor! All these years I have been praying here for your well-being. When I got to my new home, I opened the purse and found it full of valuables, including this." She opened the purse and took out a piece of jade. "My husband and I were able to pawn it for a large sum of money. Using the money, we started a business and have now become very wealthy. So I reclaimed the jade and have kept it here in the purse since. We also built the Pearl Hall to house the purse and to honor you.

"I knew that you lived in the Teng-chou area, so when I heard about the flood I prayed day and night in that direction, begging Buddha to protect you from harm. I was hoping that one day I would find you and show you my gratitude. And here you are, taking care of my son! I know what we must do. We shall divide our property and give you half of it. That will make us all very happy."

Hsiang-ling was speechless as Mrs. Lu placed the purse in her hands. That same day, Yüan-wai Lu sent out servants in all directions to look for Hsiang-ling's husband and son. Soon they were found, in a village not far from Teng-chou.

A great friendship developed between the two families. Later, whenever Hsiang-ling told people about her purse, she would always end the tale by saying, "If you have a chance to do something good, be sure to do it. Happiness will come back to you."

Objectives
● Provide evidence from text to support understanding. ● Write responses to literary or expository texts and provide evidence from the text to show that you understand the text.

Envision It! Retell

READING STREET ONLINE
STORY SORT
www.ReadingStreet.com

Think Critically

1. Both Fernando in *At the Beach* and Hsiang-ling in *The Ch'i-lin Purse* "do the right thing" when the time comes. Compare Fernando's decision to tell the truth to Mami and Hsiang-ling's decision to give her purse away. How are their motivations the same? How are they different? **Text to Text**

2. In ancient times, someone told, wrote, or painted this story. Then it was handed down for generations. Why? What makes *The Ch'i-lin Purse* an important story to pass down? **Think Like an Author**

3. Look back at pages 240–241 and 248–249. Compare and contrast what the two women did for each other and why they did it. **Compare and Contrast**

4. When is it revealed that Hsiang-ling's decision to give away her purse was a good one? **Story Structure**

5. **Look Back and Write** Look back at the question on page 237. How does the story *The Ch'i-lin Purse* show that one good deed deserves another?

TEST PRACTICE Extended Response

250

Meet the Author

Linda Fang

As a ten-year-old girl living in Shanghai, China, Linda Fang was too shy to speak up in class. So one day her teacher handed her a picture book, told her to read it that night, and said, "Come back tomorrow and see if you can tell it to me." The teacher's goal was to help her student overcome her shyness.

The teacher's plan must have worked, because today Ms. Fang is a professional storyteller and the winner of the 1998 Storyteller of the Year Award.

She credits the start of her professional career, however, to good luck. She was working for a television station in Washington, D.C., in 1987. "They had a storytelling show. I saw that they didn't have Chinese stories, so I sent them one. The station liked the story, but they didn't have the right person to tell it. They tried me on camera and thought I did well."

Fang first heard *The Ch'i-lin Purse* from her mother. As a little girl, she was fascinated that you could do something that might change someone's life without your ever knowing it.

More Chinese stories:

Fa Mulan by Robert D. San Souci

Da Wei's Treasure: A Chinese Tale by Margaret and Raymond Chang

Use the *Reader's and Writer's Notebook* to record your independent reading.

Objectives
● Write poems using techniques such as alliteration and onomatopoeia.
● Write poems using figurative language.

Let's Write It!

Key Features of a Poem

● uses verse to communicate ideas

● may rhyme or use poetic techniques

● often includes sensory details or vivid language

READING STREET ONLINE
GRAMMAR JAMMER
www.ReadingStreet.com

Narrative

Poem

A **poem** is a piece of writing that often has a particular rhythm or rhyme. The student model on the next page is an example of a poem.

Writing Prompt Write a poem about an important event in your life, or in the life of someone you know.

Writer's Checklist

Remember, you should . . .

☑ write a poem about an important event.

☑ use poetic techniques, such as alliteration, onomatopoeia, or assonance.

☑ use vivid language to express thoughts and feelings.

252

New Baby Brother

I **was** sitting in school
when I heard the news.
"Your baby brother **is** born,
and wants to see you!"

Dad got me from school,
and to the hospital with no delay.
Hurrying on our journey,
he almost forgot the way!

My brother's hands **were** tiny,
and wrinkly soft, like a prune.
After he **smiled** at me,
Mom said, "He'll come home soon!"

Everyone "oohing" and "aahing,"
they say "He is so sweet,
and one day he'll walk around on those little baby feet!"

Writing Trait Organization
This poem is structured into stanzas, or separate groups of lines.

Action and linking verbs are used correctly.

Genre Poems use verse to express ideas and feelings.

Conventions

Action and Linking Verbs

Remember An **action verb** tells what the subject does. A **linking verb** connects the subject with the predicate and tells what the subject is or is like *(is, am, are, was)*.

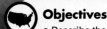

Objectives

● Describe the phenomena explained in origin myths from various cultures. ● Make connections between and among texts.

Social Studies in Reading

Genre
Myth

● A myth is an ancient story that is handed down by word of mouth for generations.

● Some myths are known as origin myths because they describe how phenomena in the natural world came to be. Natural phenomena are things that happen in nature.

● There are different kinds of origin myths that come from various cultures.

● Read "The Story of Phan Ku." Look for elements that make this selection a myth. According to this myth, how was the earth separated from the sky?

The Story of
Phan Ku
a Chinese origin myth

In the beginning there was nothing but a large egg. The egg floated for thousands of years, until one day—*crack!* The egg popped open and out stepped a giant. The giant's name was Phan Ku.

Phan Ku was known as the Great Creator. His body was covered with coarse, thick hair. Horns grew from the top of his head. Two sharp tusks sprouted from his jaw.

When the egg had hatched, the bottom half of the shell fell downward and became the earth. This "earth" was called *yin*. The top half of the egg drifted upward and became the sky. This "sky" was called *yang*. Between the yin and yang stood Phan Ku.

Phan Ku walked along the earth and smoothed out all the rough edges with his hands and feet. He stomped his heavy feet and packed down all the loose dirt and clay. Then he turned his attention to the sky and pushed it farther away from the earth. Phan Ku grew ten feet a day and lived for tens of thousands of years. As Phan Ku continued to grow, the distance between the earth and sky also grew larger.

Phan Ku looked up into the heavens. He took the sun and placed it in the daytime sky. Then he took the stars and the moon and placed them in the night sky. He told the sun and moon they must take turns sharing the heavens.

There was more to be done. Phan Ku had a chisel. He used this chisel to carve out rivers, streams, and lakes. He also used his chisel to scoop out large chunks of dirt from the earth. He called these places valleys and canyons. Then Phan Ku pushed dirt and rocks into piles. The smaller piles he called hills. The larger piles he called mountains.

After thousands of years, Phan Ku was very tired. He lay down and started to cry. His tears filled the rivers, streams, and lakes. Finally, Phan Ku rested forever. His bones became rocks while his hair became forests and plants. His voice became the sound of thunder. His breaths became the wind, storms, and clouds.

At last, Phan Ku became part of the earth, never to be seen again. As people began to roam the earth, they knew that Phan Ku was gone. They were lonely without Phan Ku, who created the world for them.

Let's **Think** About...

According to this myth, how were rivers and mountains formed? **Myth**

Let's **Think** About...

Reading Across Texts Phan Ku and Hsiang-ling both make sacrifices. How are their sacrifices similar and different?

Writing Across Texts Write a short paragraph describing the lessons you learned from the sacrifices made by Phan Ku and Hsiang-ling.

Objectives

● Read aloud grade-level texts and understand what is read. ● Determine the meaning of English words with roots from Greek, Latin, and other languages. ● Listen to and interpret a speaker's messages and ask questions. ● Participate in discussions by raising and considering suggestions from other group members and by identifying points of agreement and disagreement.

Let's Learn It!

**READING STREET ONLINE
ONLINE STUDENT EDITION**
www.ReadingStreet.com

Vocabulary

Greek and Latin Roots

Word Structure Many English words contain Greek or Latin roots and affixes. You can use these roots to help you find the meanings of English words.

 The Latin root *bene* means "good" or "well," and *sacr* means "holy." The Greek root *derm* means "skin." The Greek prefix *anti-* means "against." Look through stories you've read this year, and list and define as many words as you can that are formed using these roots and affixes.

Fluency

Expression

Partner Reading When you read with expression, you bring the characters in a story to life. Change your tone of voice as you read to reflect each character's feelings or personality.

Practice It! With a partner, practice reading aloud a page from *The Ch'i-Lin Purse*. Adjust your tone of voice to represent the emotions of the characters.

Listening and Speaking

Get Ready For Middle School

When you participate in a performance, make eye contact with others.

Readers' Theater

In Readers' Theater, actors read from a script to present a story as a drama without a stage or costumes.

Practice It! With a group, choose a scene from *The Ch'i-lin Purse*. Use the scene to create a script. Assign roles, and use details from the story to find clues about how to speak each character's dialogue. Then perform for the class.

Tips

Listening . . .

- Listen carefully to each speaker.
- Interpret what each speaker says.

Speaking . . .

- Use volume to make sure your listeners can hear you.
- Speak clearly and vary your speaking rate.

Teamwork . . .

- Identify points of agreement and disagreement.
- Consider suggestions from other group members.

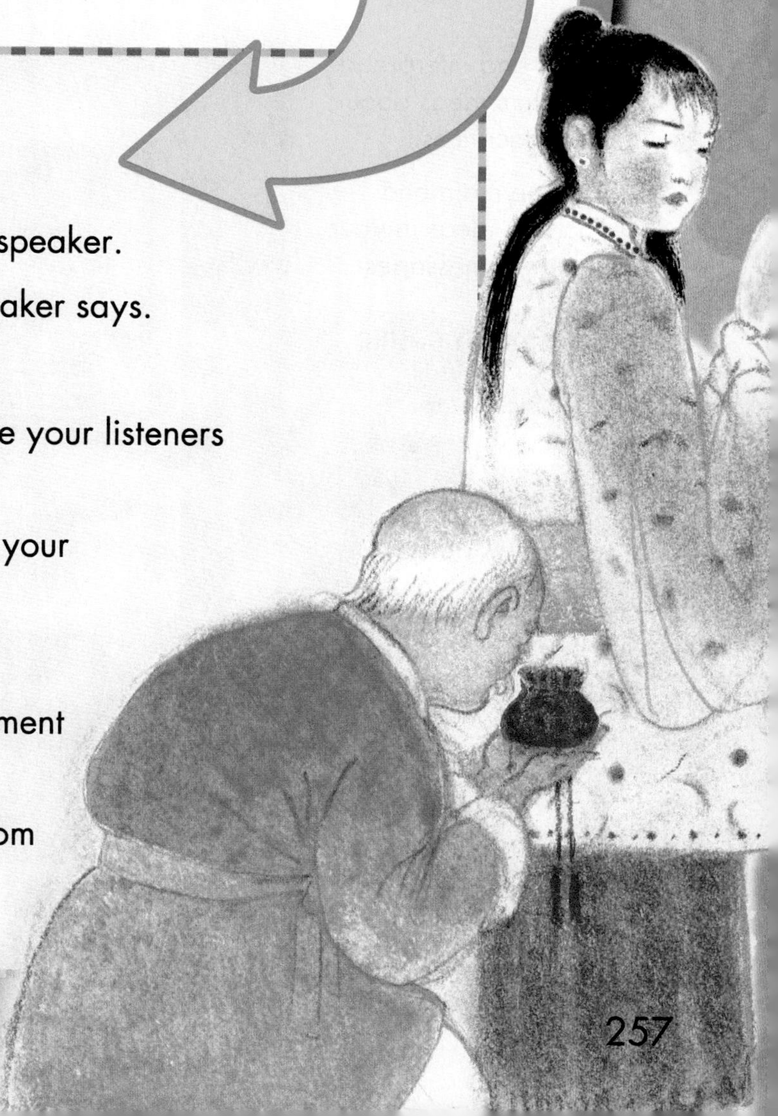

Objectives
● Listen to and interpret a speaker's messages and ask questions.
● Identify the main ideas and supporting ideas in the speaker's message.

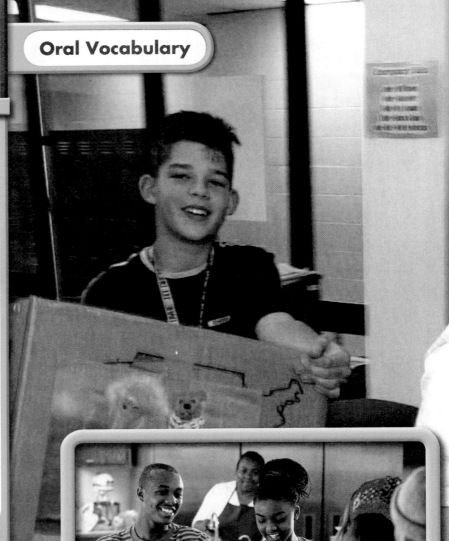

Oral Vocabulary

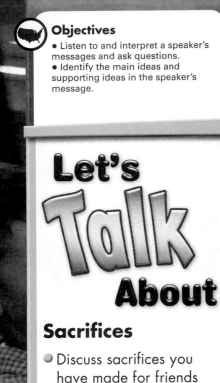

Let's Talk About

Sacrifices

● Discuss sacrifices you have made for friends or family.

● Listen to and interpret a classmate's ideas about making sacrifices.

● Determine main and supporting ideas in your classmates' messages.

READING STREET ONLINE
CONCEPT TALK VIDEO
www.ReadingStreet.com

You've learned
0 8 0
Amazing Words
so far this year!

259

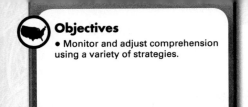

Objectives
- Monitor and adjust comprehension using a variety of strategies.

Envision It! | Skill Strategy

Skill

Strategy

READING STREET ONLINE
ENVISION IT! ANIMATIONS
www.ReadingStreet.com

Comprehension Skill

🎯 Author's Purpose

- The author's purpose is the main reason an author has for writing a selection.

- The author may wish to persuade, to entertain, to inform, or to express feelings or ideas.

- What the author says and the details he or she gives help you figure out the author's purpose.

- Use a graphic organizer like the one below to fill in the details the author provides that give clues to the purpose the author had for writing.

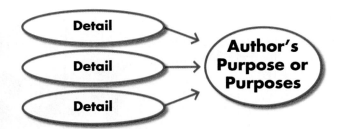

Comprehension Strategy

🎯 Monitor and Clarify

Good readers check, or monitor, their understanding as they read. As you read "The Trading Post," monitor your understanding by slowing down and reading a passage aloud.

The Trading Post

Imagine you are a Navajo living in the Southwest in the 1800s. Where would you go to catch up with friends *and* buy food and clothing? The mall? No! You would go to the trading post.

In those days, the Navajo would pack up their woven woolen blankets and rugs and jewelry, and travel several hours to the trading post. They would trade goods and talk with friends. Often these were the only times they saw neighbors.

Today these trading posts act mainly as banks and safes for the special needs of the Navajo. For example, where banks will not accept a sheep to secure a loan, a trading post will. The trading post understands that animals are a vital source of income for a Navajo family.

Other goods, such as ceremonial skins and baskets, are given to the trading post to store. These items are considered "live pawn" and are kept in the back of the store until the Navajo owner needs them. Tourists can't buy these items, but they can view them to learn about Navajo traditions. In this way, trading posts still act as the cultural hubs they were in the past.

Skill What do you think is the author's purpose? Is the author writing to entertain, express, or inform?

Strategy Pause here to monitor your comprehension. Reread the paragraph to clarify your understanding.

Skill Do you know more about trading posts now than you did before reading? Did the author achieve his or her purpose?

Your Turn!

Need a Review? See the *Envision It! Handbook* for help with author's purpose and monitoring and clarifying.

Ready to Try It? Use what you've learned about author's purpose as you read *A Summer's Trade*.

Objectives

● Determine the meanings of unfamiliar words by using the context of the sentence.

Envision It! | **Words to Know**

hogan

mesa

turquoise

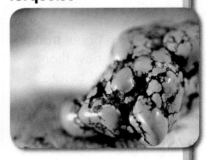

bandana

bracelet

jostled

Navajo

READING STREET ONLINE
VOCABULARY ACTIVITIES
www.ReadingStreet.com

Vocabulary Strategy for

🎯 Unfamiliar Words

Context Clues As you read, you may see a word you do not know. Often the author will give clues to determine and clarify the meaning of an unfamiliar word. Check the context—the words and sentences around the unfamiliar word—for these clues.

1. Reread the sentence where the unfamiliar word appears.

2. Is there a specific clue to the word's meaning?

3. For more help, read the sentences around the sentence with the unfamiliar word. Look for words or phrases that suggest a reasonable meaning.

4. Try the meaning in the sentence with the unfamiliar word. Does it make sense?

Read "At the Navajo Nation Fair." Use context clues to help you figure out the meanings of this week's *Words to Know.*

Words to Write Reread "At the Navajo Nation Fair." Imagine that you are writing an advertisement for things you can do and buy at the fair. Use words from the *Words to Know* in your advertisement.

At the Navajo Nation Fair

"I'm too old to go to the fair," I told my granddaughter, Yolanda.

"Aw, come on, Ami," Yolanda said. "Rikki and I really want to go, and Mami is too busy with the horses to come."

Yolanda looked up at me, smiling hopefully over the red bandana she wore as a scarf around her neck. How could I say no?

I had not left the hogan where I lived for quite some time. I spent many days there working diligently to make woven rugs to sell at the fair. I was going to give them to my son, Ed, to take, but he was taking care of his ill wife.

The trip to the fair was a long, bumpy ride across the desert floor and past several large mesas. When we got to the fairground gate, Yolanda and Rikki jumped out and disappeared with cries of "Thank you, Ami!" hanging in the air.

The hordes of people at the Navajo fair bumped and jostled me. To get out of the way, I walked over to a booth selling jewelry with inlaid turquoise stones. I started to slip a bracelet over my wrist, but what really caught my eye was a lovely silver necklace. Suddenly Yolanda appeared at my side.

"Don't buy it, Ami!" she said. "Rikki and I bought you a present for bringing us to the fair." And there in the palm of her hand was the necklace's twin. "Let's go see the rest of the fair together, Ami," Yolanda said happily.

Your Turn!

⏸ **Need a Review?** See *Words!* for additional support.

▶ **Ready to Try It?** Read *A Summer's Trade* on pp. 264–277.

Genre

Realistic fiction tells a story about characters and situations that seem real but come from the author's imagination. As you read, notice how the story's events give rise to the ending.

A Summer's Trade

by Deborah W. Trotter illustrated by Irving Toddy

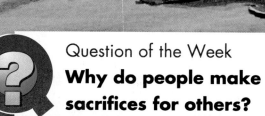

Question of the Week
Why do people make sacrifices for others?

265

A dusty pickup bounced along the rutted, dirt road on the Navajo Indian Reservation outside of Gallup, New Mexico. The early morning sun brought out deep red hues in nearby rocks, and yellows and purples on distant mesas. In the passenger seat, Tony barely noticed how the ride jostled him. He had made this long trip to Gallup with his mother many times.

This morning, Tony daydreamed about spending some of his summer days at home on the reservation instead of going into Gallup. He would ride with his father, helping to tend the family's roaming flocks of sheep and goats. But Tony needed a saddle before he could sit for hours on the back of a pony.

In the Trading Post next door to the restaurant where his mother was a waitress, Tony had discovered a beautiful, used saddle for sale. Its dark leather was worn smooth, and there were small nuggets of turquoise laced into the rawhide braid wrapped around the horn. Mr. Hilson, the owner of the Trading Post, invited Tony to help out around the store. In payment, Mr. Hilson put twenty dollars a week into an account for him. As soon as he earned enough money, Tony wanted to buy that saddle. He hoped no one else bought it first.

"Here we are," said his mother, as she parked in front of the Trading Post. Tony got out and slammed the truck door. The high desert wind fluttered the bandana covering his straight, black hair. "Come see me at lunchtime," his mother said. Tony waved as she walked toward the restaurant.

The bell on the door jingled as Tony walked into the Trading Post. "Good morning, Tony," said Mr. Hilson. "Today, I need you to unpack some canned goods and stack them carefully on the store shelves. Then you can sweep out the storage area. It's really dusty back there."

"Okay, Mr. Hilson."

The Trading Post did a lot of business. Tourists came to buy Indian-made goods, such as baskets, pottery, turquoise jewelry, and colorful, woven rugs. Regular customers could buy or trade for just about anything they needed.

Navajos could trade or "pawn" their jewelry in exchange for cash. Some did it because they needed money. Many did it because they wanted their turquoise jewelry to be safe in the Trading Post vault until they needed it for ceremonial wear.

Tony worked hard. There was almost always sweeping to do. Unpacking boxes and stacking things on shelves was a regular job too. If Mr. Hilson was busy, Tony could help customers. He knew where to find everything that was stocked in the Trading Post.

At lunchtime, Tony went next door as usual. He sat on a tall stool at the counter. Clattering dishes, chattering voices, and cooking aromas filled the air. Merl's Diner was always busy.

As customers ate, Navajo craftsmen took turns coming in from their vendor stands outside to move among the tables, offering their jewelry and art for sale. Sometimes Tony's grandmother did that too. One day a week, she came to Gallup with him and his mother to see his aunt's handcrafted silver necklaces and rings, set with turquoise and coral stones.

After lunch, Tony returned to the Trading Post. The first thing he saw was a skinny man in worn denims and a black hat looking at saddles. The man picked up the saddle Tony wanted. "How much for this, Mr. Hilson?" he called out.

"That's one seventy-five," Mr. Hilson answered.

The man put the saddle down, but kept rubbing its smooth leather. Tony held his breath. Finally, the man moved away.

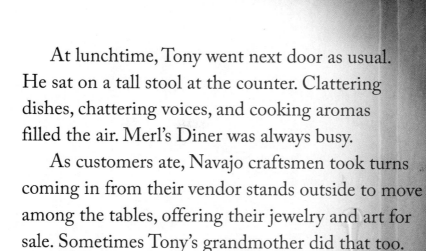

That afternoon, Tony spent some time straightening the traditional Navajo rugs displayed on wooden rods in the Trading Post. With their complex patterns, the rugs took months to design and complete. Tony's grandmother wove rugs and had a loom outside her hogan.

When he was younger, Tony had spent many days at Grandmother's side watching her work. While she wove, she told Tony stories about the ancient days of the Navajo People, or Diné. He learned about the sacredness of the Turquoise Mountain, towering in the sky to the east. He learned about Changing Woman and how her twin sons killed many monsters to save the People. He loved the story of how Sun Bearer first brought horses to the People.

On the drive home after work, they passed Tony's aunt's trailer and Grandmother's nearby hogan.

"Look. My uncle is home early," said Tony. "There's his truck."

"I wonder what that's about," said his mother. "I guess we'll find out tomorrow when we pick up Grandmother." Tony's uncle worked many miles away in Chinle, Arizona. His job was driving tourists through Canyon de Chelly to visit the many ancient Anasazi ruins there.

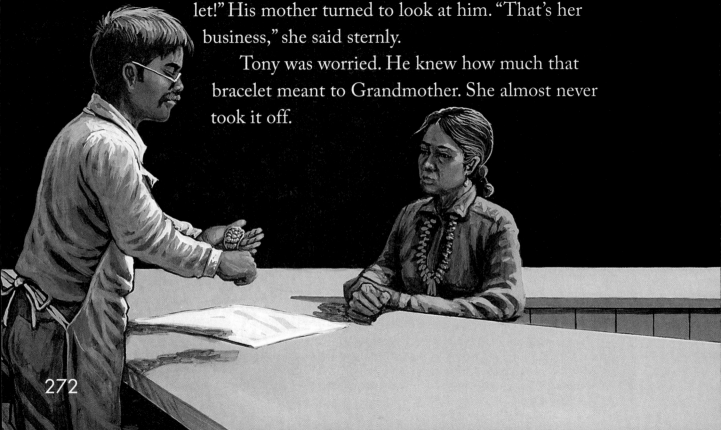

let!" His mother turned to look at him. "That's her business," she said sternly.

Tony was worried. He knew how much that bracelet meant to Grandmother. She almost never took it off.

The next week, when they stopped to pick up Grandmother for the drive to Gallup, Tony's aunt came out to the truck, followed by Tony's two young cousins. "Grandmother is not well," she said. "She hasn't come out of her hogan for a couple days. It may be time to call the medicine man."

"I'll talk to my husband about it," Tony's mother said.

Tony crossed his arms and lowered his chin. He knew what Grandmother needed.

"By the way," said Tony's aunt, "she gave me some cash to help with expenses while my husband isn't working. Wouldn't say where she got it."

That day, the drive to Gallup seemed endless. When they got to Merl's, Tony ran to the Trading Post and went straight to the pawn counter. "Mr. Hilson," he said. "I have to buy back my grandmother's bracelet."

"You know the rules, Tony. Pawn can't be sold except to the owner for at least six months," said Mr. Hilson.

"But it's for her," Tony's voice quavered. "She's sick. She needs it back."

"Well, since you're family, I guess it might be all right." Mr. Hilson hesitated. "Should I take the money out of your account?"

Tony stood up straighter and nodded. "Yes, please. Today."

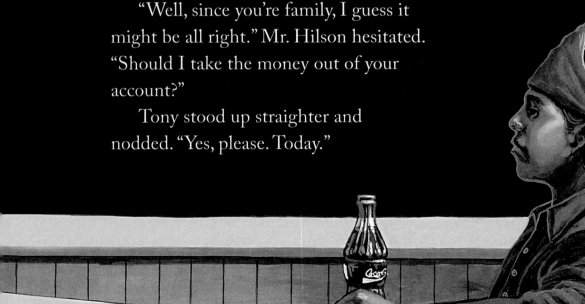

273

On the drive home, Tony said, "We need to stop at Grandmother's. I have something for her."

His mother said nothing, but she turned off the main road and stopped in front of Grandmother's hogan. Tony got out and quietly entered. Grandmother was lying, down, her eyes closed.

"My grandmother," Tony whispered. He held out her turquoise bracelet. She opened her eyes and nodded slightly. Tony approached and carefully lifted her wrist. Then he slipped the bracelet back on where it belonged. Grandmother closed her eyes again, and Tony left the hogan.

That night, Tony's father drove over to see Grandmother and talk with his sister about arranging for a healing ceremony. He returned in a happy mood. "Grandmother is better," he reported. Tony closed his eyes and smiled.

The following week, Grandmother went with Tony and his mother to Gallup. When they arrived at Merl's, Tony dragged his feet toward the Trading Post. He had to start all over again, saving for a saddle. He kicked a few bottle caps along the sidewalk and finally went inside.

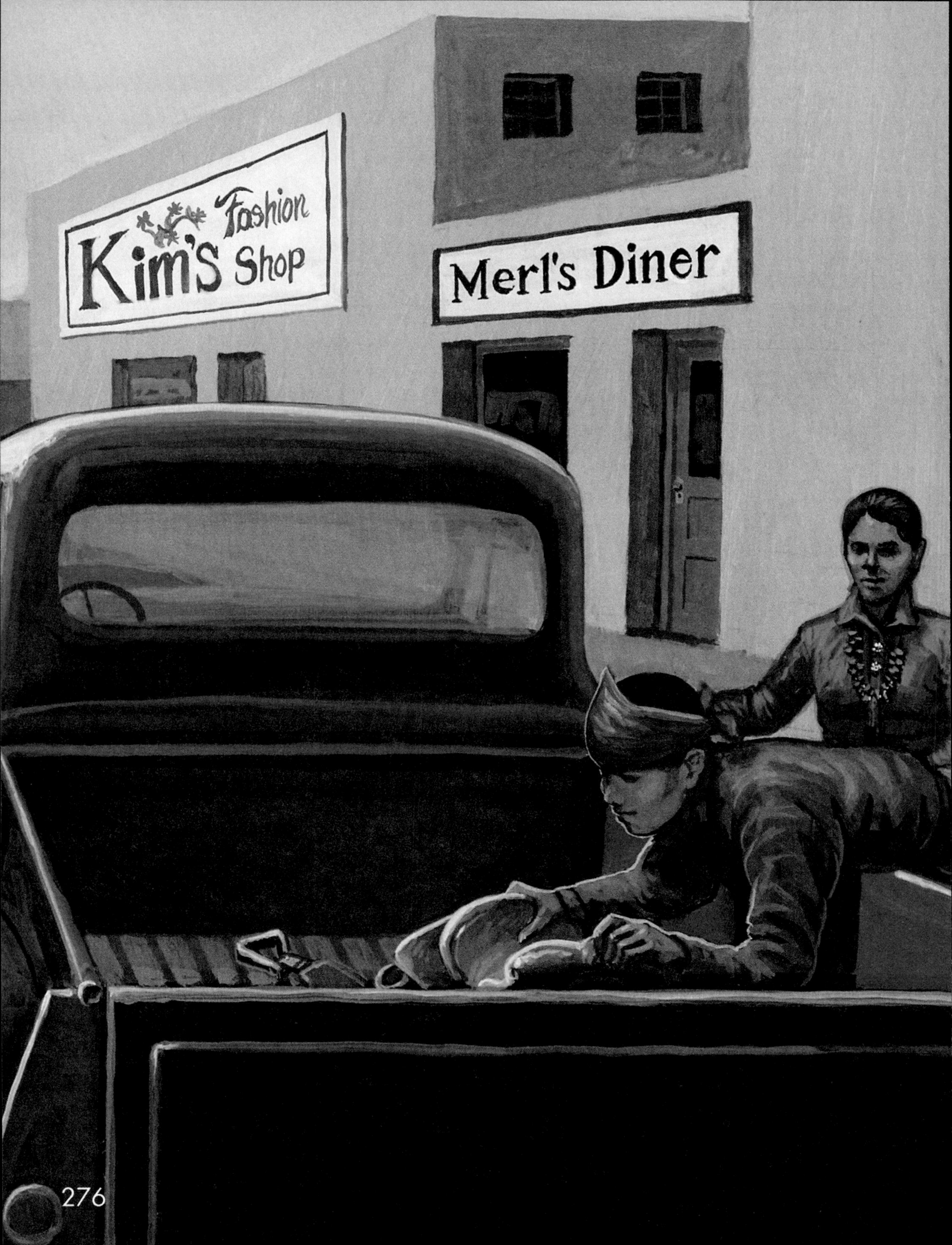
Kim's Fashion Shop
Merl's Diner

Grandmother was talking with Mr. Hilson. Tony went to look at the saddle. There was an empty space on the sawhorse where it used to sit. Someone had bought it.

Tony hid from Grandmother as she left the store so she wouldn't see his sad face. Somehow, he made it through the day without anyone asking him what was wrong.

When it was time to go home, he went out to the truck. His mother said, "You got your saddle, my son."

He looked at her in confusion and shook his head. He didn't know what to say. She pointed to the back of the truck.

Tony hopped up and leaned on his forearms, feet dangling, to see into the truck bed. He couldn't believe it. There it was . . . his beautiful saddle. His mother smiled and climbed into the truck.

Tony felt Grandmother touch his shoulder. He turned, and she nodded slowly, her wrinkled, brown face not quite hiding a smile. "Mr. Hilson traded your saddle against my next rug," she said. "Now, let's go home."

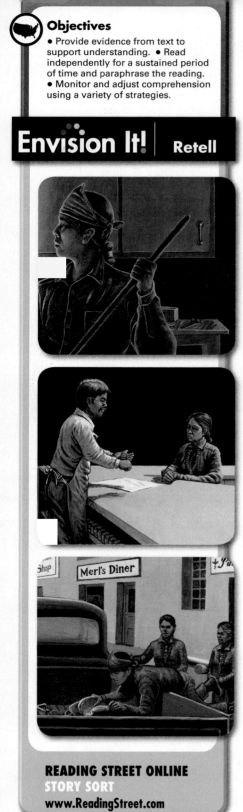

Objectives
● Provide evidence from text to support understanding. ● Read independently for a sustained period of time and paraphrase the reading. ● Monitor and adjust comprehension using a variety of strategies.

Envision It! Retell

READING STREET ONLINE
STORY SORT
www.ReadingStreet.com

Think Critically

1. Both the Navajo story *A Summer's Trade* and the Chinese folk tale *The Ch'i-lin Purse* involve a person making a sacrifice for another person. How are the stories' themes or moral lessons similar or different? Compare and contrast the themes from those two stories with the themes of other stories you've read. **Text to Text**

2. Tony is both humble and proud. How does the author show that he has these traits? Use examples from the text. **Think Like an Author**

3. Is the author's purpose to entertain, inform, persuade, or something else? Find examples from the text to justify your answer. Remember, an author may have more than one purpose.
   Author's Purpose

4. Reread pages 272–273. Why did Tony's grandmother sell her cherished bracelet? Reread these pages aloud to help you understand Tony's grandmother's reason.
   Monitor and Clarify

5. **Look Back and Write** Look back at the last page of the story. How does the grandmother's trade of the saddle for a rug that she will make *in the future* add to Tony's good deed?
   TEST PRACTICE Extended Response

Deborah W. Trotter

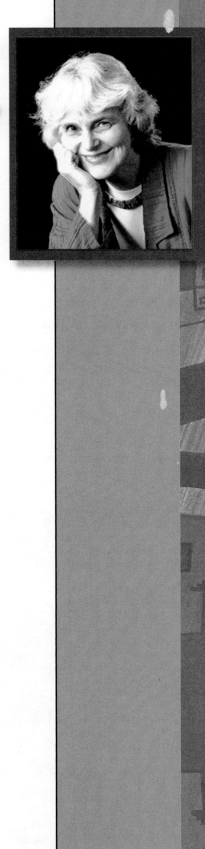

Deborah Trotter has always loved to read. She grew up in a small town in California with no TV or computer in the house, so she spent a lot of time reading books. Reading is one of the pleasures she thinks of when recalling her childhood days. She also remembers riding her bike to the library and having her parents read books aloud to her and her siblings.

After graduating from college, Deborah went on to obtain a law degree and practiced law until after her first child was born. It wasn't until years later, after the birth of her fourth child, that she began writing. She has written two books for children, focusing on the importance of family.

Deborah W. Trotter now lives in Moraga, California, and hopes to write more books. She says, "I hope to continue writing and having my books published and enjoyed by many."

Reading Log

Use the *Reader's and Writer's Notebook* to record your independent reading.

Objectives
- Write a personal narrative that conveys your thoughts and feelings about an experience.

Let's Write It!

Key Features of a Personal Narrative

- uses the first-person point of view (I, me)
- tells a story about a real event in your life
- shares thoughts and feelings about an event or time

READING STREET ONLINE
GRAMMAR JAMMER
www.ReadingStreet.com

Personal Narrative

A **personal narrative** uses personal thoughts and descriptive details to tell about something you have experienced.

Writing Prompt In *A Summer's Trade*, a character is faced with a difficult decision. Think about a time when you struggled to do the right thing. Now, write a personal narrative about that experience.

Writer's Checklist

Remember, you should . . .

✓ tell a true story about an experience you have had.

✓ communicate thoughts and feelings about the experience.

✓ include details to engage the reader.

280

Doing the Right Thing

Doing the right thing is not always easy. It always seems easy to my dad, though. Many weekends he works at a homeless shelter making suppers or organizing events.

Every year the shelter tries to raise money to host a big Thanksgiving dinner. This year, my dad told me I could bake cookies and have my own table at the bake sale.

I eagerly displayed my cookies on red dishes and made a sign for them: $1 a cookie. Mrs. David came by first and bought four cookies. Then my neighbor, Mrs. Cole, came by.

Mrs. Cole is old and has trouble seeing. When she reached into her purse to get a dollar, a twenty-dollar bill fell out onto the floor. She walked away without noticing.

The twenty-dollar bill would have been easy to slip into my pocket. No one was looking. As I crumpled it up in my palm, I dreamed about the new shirt I could buy. But then I thought how Mrs. Cole needed a new pair of glasses. I knew I shouldn't take the money. I hurried over to her and returned the bill. My dad had never been more proud!

Genre
A **personal narrative** tells about an experience in the writer's life.

Main and helping verbs are used correctly.

Writing Trait Word Choice
Descriptive words make the passage interesting.

Conventions

Main and Helping Verbs

Remember A **main verb** shows action (He *ran*). A **helping verb** helps tell the time of the action (We *should have* run). Some common helping verbs are *has, have, had, am, is, are, was, were, be, been, do, does, did, can, could,* and *would.*

Objectives
● Describe the phenomena explained in origin myths from various cultures. ● Explain the roles and functions of characters, including their relationships and conflicts.

Myth

Genre
Myth

- A myth is an ancient story that is handed down for generations. Myths, including origin myths, can be found in various cultures.

- Some myths are known as origin myths because they describe how natural phenomena, or things that happen in nature, came to be.

- Read "Thunderbird and Killer Whale." As you read, look for elements that make this story a myth. What two types of natural phenomena does the myth explain?

THUNDERBIRD and KILLER WHALE

adapted from a Quillayute myth
by Helen Morton

Thunderbird was immense. His wings were so long that when he flapped them, they made great gusts of wind and the sound of thunder.

Thunderbird made lightning too. Whenever Thunderbird blinked, lightning appeared.

Whenever there was a storm with thunder and lightning, Thunderbird was there, flying around, flapping his wings and blinking his eyes.

When Thunderbird got tired and flew back to his home on a mountain, the storm would come to an end. Thunderbird lived in a cave high on a mountaintop. Thunderbird liked his privacy. He did not want any visitors.

Once, a group of hunters approached his cave. Thunderbird was angry that anyone would dare approach his home. He flapped his wings to make the sound of thunder. Then he rolled ice out of his cave so that it would roll down the mountain and break into a million pieces. The hunters ran away. They were terrified of Thunderbird.

Thunderbird had a big appetite. His favorite food was whale. To catch it, Thunderbird flew over the ocean. When he saw a whale come up for air, Thunderbird swooped down. Thunderbird was so big that he could snatch a whale with his gigantic claws. He would fly back to his cave, carrying the whale in his claws. He ate happily.

Some whales were more difficult to catch than others. Killer Whale, in particular, always gave Thunderbird a very hard time. Every time Thunderbird caught Killer Whale and tried to carry him to his cave, Killer Whale would get away and go back into the water.

This made Thunderbird very angry. He flapped his wings, making huge sounds of thunder! He blinked his eyes, making great flashes of lightning!

But no matter how hard Thunderbird tried to catch him, Killer Whale always escaped Thunderbird's grasp.

Thunderbird was determined. "I will catch and eat Killer Whale!" he said.

To achieve his goal, Thunderbird flew over the ocean all day long. He was waiting for Killer Whale to come up for air.

Let's **Think** About...

How does Killer Whale create a conflict for Thunderbird? **Myth**

Describe the relationship between Thunderbird and Killer Whale.
Myth

How does this myth compare and contrast with other origin myths you've read? **Myth**

But Killer Whale was very, very clever. Killer Whale swam under the surface of the ocean for long periods of time. Sometimes Killer Whale would pop up for air many miles from where he had last been seen. That made it difficult for Thunderbird to know where to look for him. "The ocean is wide," thought Thunderbird. "Big as I am, I can't be above every part of it all the time."

So Thunderbird devised a plan. "Killer Whale swims just below the surface of the ocean. The next time Killer Whale escapes my grasp, I will fly just above the surface of the water. Wherever I see Killer Whale go, I shall follow. Then, when Killer Whale comes up for air, I will be right above him. I will have him in my clutches. I will take him back to my cave and eat him. It is the perfect plan!"

Meanwhile, as he swam, Killer Whale was also talking to himself.

"This is exhausting," Killer Whale admitted. "Thunderbird is always swooping down on me. How many times can I escape Thunderbird? Sooner or later, Thunderbird is going to manage to take me back to his cave, and that will be the end of me! I can't let that happen. But how can I get away from Thunderbird when he is flying right above me all the time?"

Suddenly Killer Whale had an idea. "What if I live in the deepest part of the ocean? That way, Thunderbird will never be able to spot me."

284

So Killer Whale tried it out. Killer Whale swam to the deepest part of the ocean. He swam so deep that he could not even see the rays of light that came from the sun. The deep ocean was dark and cool and safe. "I like it here," Killer Whale said. "I especially like that down here Thunderbird will never bother me again."

Up above, Thunderbird flew around and around and around.

"Where is Killer Whale?" Thunderbird asked angrily. "I am so hungry, and he is nowhere to be seen!"

Several days passed by and Thunderbird still saw no sign of Killer Whale. Thunderbird became so hungry that he had to find other whales to eat. After many weeks passed, Thunderbird said, "Well, I guess I won't be eating Killer Whale."

Ever since that time, Thunderbird has never bothered Killer Whale, and Killer Whale has lived safe and sound in the deep, dark ocean.

Let's **Think** About...

Reading Across Texts In *A Summer's Trade*, Tony enjoyed when his grandmother told Navajo myths. Do you think he would enjoy listening to "Thunderbird and Killer Whale"? List your reasons why.

Writing Across Texts Write a journal entry for Tony that explains his reasons for enjoying origin myths, both from his own culture and from other cultures.

Objectives

● Read aloud grade-level texts and understand what is read. ● Identify and explain the meaning of common adages and sayings. ● Identify the main ideas and supporting ideas in the speaker's message.
● Participate in discussions by raising and considering suggestions from other group members and by identifying points of agreement and disagreement.

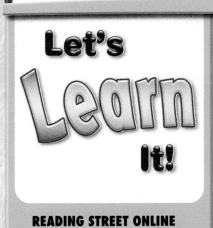

READING STREET ONLINE
ONLINE STUDENT EDITION
www.ReadingStreet.com

Vocabulary

Adages and Sayings

An adage is a short but memorable saying that expresses a meaningful idea. For example, "The early bird gets the worm" means that if you prepare for something in advance, you are more likely to succeed. Other types of sayings may hold meaning.

Practice It! Think about what you read in *A Summer's Trade*. Do you know any adages or other sayings that apply to the story's theme? Identify and explain adages and sayings that may apply to the story.

Fluency

Appropriate Phrasing

Partner Reading When you use appropriate phrasing, you group words together as you read so that you better understand the sentences.

Practice It! With your partner, practice reading aloud a page from *A Summer's Trade*. Try to group related words together in phrases as you read. Then listen as your partner reads, and offer feedback.

Listening and Speaking

Get Ready For Middle School

When you participate in a discussion, ask questions to clarify the speaker's purpose.

Panel Discussion

In a panel discussion, a group of experts shares ideas and information about a topic.

Practice It! Work with a group to present a panel discussion about making sacrifices. Assign roles, with one student acting as moderator and the others as experts on the topic. Use information from *A Summer's Trade* in your discussion.

Tips

Listening . . .

- Determine the speaker's main and supporting ideas.

Speaking . . .

- Speak loudly and enunciate.
- Make eye contact when answering questions.

Teamwork . . .

- Identify points of agreement and disagreement.
- Consider suggestions from other group members.

287

Objectives
• Listen to and interpret a speaker's messages and ask questions.
• Identify the main ideas and supporting ideas in the speaker's message.

Oral Vocabulary

Let's Talk About

Promoting Freedom

● Share ideas about how to promote freedom.

● Listen to and interpret a classmate's ideas about promoting freedom.

● Determine main and supporting ideas in your classmates' messages.

READING STREET ONLINE
CONCEPT TALK VIDEO
www.ReadingStreet.com

288

Objectives
- Draw conclusions about texts and evaluate how well the author achieves his or her purpose.

Skill

Strategy

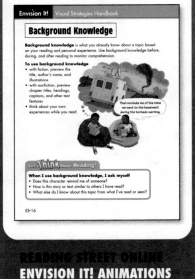

READING STREET ONLINE
ENVISION IT! ANIMATIONS
www.ReadingStreet.com

Comprehension Skill

◎ Author's Purpose

- The author's purpose is the reason or reasons an author has for writing. Most selections have one main purpose.

- An author may write to persuade you, to inform you, to entertain you, or to express ideas or feelings.

- Use a graphic organizer like the one below to decide on the author's purpose for writing "Before the Midnight Ride." Then think about how well the author achieved that purpose.

Kinds of ideas	→	**Author's Purpose(s):** persuade inform entertain express
Ways ideas are stated		

Comprehension Strategy

◎ Background Knowledge

Active readers use what they already know to understand what they read. As you read, think about what you already know about people and events from your own life that are similar to those in the story. Making these types of connections will help you become a more active reader.

Before the Midnight Ride

Strategy Preview the title. What specific kind of knowledge would you need to understand what this selection will be about?

Paul Revere was born in December 1734 in Boston, Massachusetts. His childhood was much like that of other boys at the time.

When Paul was a teenager, he was paid to ring the bells at a church. At the same time, his father was teaching him to work with silver. Revere was a silversmith until he joined the army in 1756. After his army service, Revere married Sarah Orne and returned to his work.

In the 1760s and 1770s, trouble arose between the colonies and England. Revere joined a group called the Sons of Liberty. They believed the colonies should be free from England. In December 1773 he helped throw tea into Boston Harbor as a protest because the tea was taxed by England. This protest became known as the Boston Tea Party.

Skill What is the author's purpose for writing this selection?

After that, Revere became an express rider for the Massachusetts government. He rode a horse to bring news from Boston to the other colonies. He was at this job on that day in 1775, when his most famous ride took place.

Skill What does the author include in this selection that helped you determine the purpose for writing?

Your Turn!

Need a Review?
See the *Envision It! Handbook* for help with author's purpose and background knowledge.

Ready to Try It?
Use what you've learned about author's purpose as you read *The Midnight Ride of Paul Revere*.

Envision It! | **Words to Know**

fearless

glimmer

somber

fate

lingers

magnified

steed

**READING STREET ONLINE
VOCABULARY ACTIVITIES**
www.ReadingStreet.com

Vocabulary Strategy for

◎ Endings *-s, -ed, -ing*

Word Structure The endings *-s*, *-ed*, and *-ing* come from Old English and may be added to a verb to change the tense, person, or usage of the verb. You can use these endings to help you figure out the meanings of *lingers* and *magnified*.

1. Cover the ending and read the base form of the word.

2. Reread the sentence and make sure the word is a verb. (Nouns can also end in *-s*.)

3. Now look in the sentence for clues about what the word may mean.

4. See if your meaning makes sense in the sentence.

Read "War Heroes in Stone" on page 293. Look for verbs that end with *-s*, *-ed*, or *-ing*. Think about the endings and the way the words are used to help you figure out the words' meanings.

Words to Write Reread "War Heroes in Stone." Write a paragraph describing a statue you've seen. Describe what it looks like and what it represents. Use words from the *Words to Know* list in your writing.

War Heroes in Stone

Monuments to war heroes have a noble feeling. Artists who make statues to honor the war dead seem to understand their job. Soldiers who died in battle gave their lives for their country and for freedom. The somber job of the artist is to honor these heroes. Artists also want us to feel proud of what these heroes did. The artists' work is one way of giving thanks to those who met their fate on the field of battle.

Often the statue shows a general sitting on his steed, sword raised overhead. The marble forms are beautiful, powerful, and larger than life. In addition, the statue sits high on a pedestal so that visitors must look up. Both horse and man are a study in fearless forward motion. In this way, their bravery and patriotism are magnified and set in stone.

Have you ever seen such a statue at night? Imagine the white stone looming in the dark. Then a glimmer of moonlight brings it to life. The effect is strange to see. You feel you can almost hear the tread of troops marching down a dusty road. The distant sound of marching lingers in the air. You send a silent word of thanks to those who fought to keep your country free.

Your Turn!

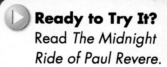

Need a Review?
For additional help with verb endings, see *Words!*

Ready to Try It?
Read *The Midnight Ride of Paul Revere.*

Genre

A **poem** is a composition arranged in lines. Some poems have rhyme, some have rhythm, and some have both. As you read this narrative poem—a long poem that tells a story—notice how the rhyme and rhythm reinforce the story's meaning.

THE MIDNIGHT RIDE OF
PAUL REVERE

by

**Henry
Wadsworth
Longfellow**

graved and painted by

Christopher Bing

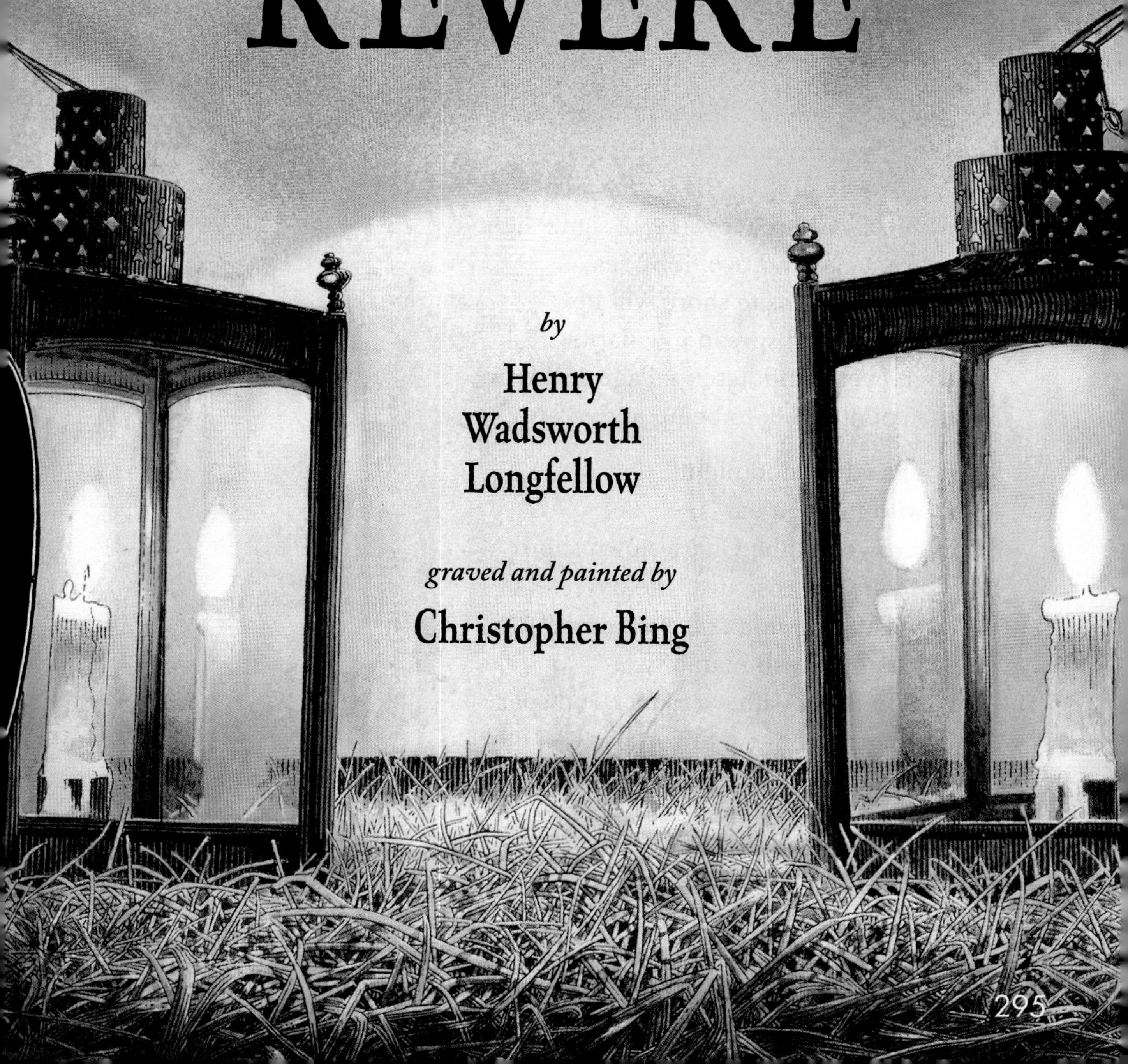

LISTEN, MY CHILDREN, AND YOU SHALL HEAR

Of the midnight ride of Paul Revere,

On the eighteenth of April, in Seventy-Five,
Hardly a man is now alive
Who remembers that famous day and year.

He said to his friend, "If the British march
By land or sea from the town tonight,
Hang a lantern aloft in the belfry arch
Of the North Church tower as a signal light—
One, if by land, and two, if by sea;
And I on the opposite shore will be,
Ready to ride and spread the alarm
Through every Middlesex village and farm,
For the country folk to be up and to arm."

Then he said, "Good night!"
  and with muffled oar
Silently rowed to the Charlestown shore,
Just as the moon rose over the bay,
Where swinging wide at her moorings lay
The *Somerset,* British man-of-war;
A phantom ship, with each mast and spar
Across the moon like a prison bar,
And a huge black hulk, that was magnified
By its own reflection in the tide.

Meanwhile, his friend, through alley and street,
Wanders and watches, with eager ears,
Till in the silence around him he hears
The muster of men at the barrack door,
The sound of arms, and the tramp of feet,
And the measured tread of the grenadiers,
Marching down to their boats on the shore.

Then he climbed the tower
   of the Old North Church,
By the wooden stairs, with stealthy tread,
To the belfry-chamber overhead,
And startled the pigeons from their perch
On the somber rafters, that round him made
Masses and moving shapes of shade—
By the trembling ladder, steep and tall,
To the highest window in the wall,
Where he paused to listen and look down
A moment on the roofs of the town,
And the moonlight flowing over all.

Beneath in the churchyard, lay the dead,
In their night-encampment on the hill,
Wrapped in silence so deep and still
That he could hear, like a sentinel's tread,
The watchful night-wind, as it went
Creeping along from tent to tent,
And seeming to whisper, "All is well!"
A moment only he feels the spell
Of the place and the hour, the secret dread
Of the lonely belfry and the dead;
For suddenly all his thoughts are bent
On a shadowy something far away,

Where the river widens to meet the bay—
A line of black that bends and floats
On the rising tide, like a bridge of boats.

Meanwhile, impatient to mount and ride,
Booted and spurred, with a heavy stride
On the opposite shore walked Paul Revere.
Now he patted his horse's side,
Now gazed on the landscape far and near,
Then, impetuous, stamped the earth,
And turned and tightened his saddle girth;
But mostly he watched with eager search
The belfry tower of the Old North Church,
As it rose above the graves on the hill,
Lonely and spectral and somber and still.

And lo! as he looks, on the belfry's height
A glimmer, and then a gleam of light!
He springs to the saddle, the bridle he turns,
But lingers and gazes, till full on his sight
A second lamp in the belfry burns!

A hurry of hoofs in a village street,
A shape in the moonlight, a bulk in the dark,
And beneath, from the pebbles,
   in passing, a spark
Struck out by a steed flying fearless and fleet:
That was all! And yet,
   through the gloom and the light,
The fate of a nation was riding that night;
And the spark struck out
   by that steed, in his flight,
Kindled the land into flame with its heat.

He has left the village and mounted the steep,
And beneath him, tranquil and broad and deep,
Is the Mystic, meeting the ocean tides;
And under the alders that skirt its edge,
Now soft on the sand, now loud on the ledge,
Is heard the tramp of his steed as he rides.

It was twelve by the village clock,
When he crossed the bridge
   into Medford town.
He heard the crowing of the cock,
And the barking of the farmer's dog,
And felt the damp of the river fog,
That rises after the sun goes down.

It was one by the village clock,
When he galloped into Lexington.
He saw the gilded weathercock
Swim in the moonlight as he passed,
And the meeting-house windows,
   blank and bare,
Gaze at him with a spectral glare,
As if they already stood aghast
At the bloody work they would look upon.

It was two by the village clock,
When he came to the bridge in Concord town.
He heard the bleating of the flock,
And the twitter of birds among the trees,
And felt the breath of the morning breeze
Blowing over the meadows brown.
And one was safe and asleep in his bed
Who at the bridge would be first to fall,
Who that day would be lying dead,
Pierced by a British musket-ball.

You know the rest. In the books you have read
How the British Regulars fired and fled—
How the farmers gave them ball for ball,
From behind each fence and farmyard wall,
Chasing the red-coats down the lane,
Then crossing the fields to emerge again
Under the trees at the turn of the road
And only pausing to fire and load.

So through the night rode Paul Revere,
And so through the night went his cry of alarm
To every Middlesex village and farm—
A cry of defiance and not of fear,
A voice in the darkness, a knock at the door,
And a word that shall echo for evermore!
For, borne on the night-wind of the Past,
Through all our history, to the last,
In the hour of darkness and peril and need,
The people will waken and listen to hear
The hurrying hoof-beats of that steed,
And the midnight message of Paul Revere.

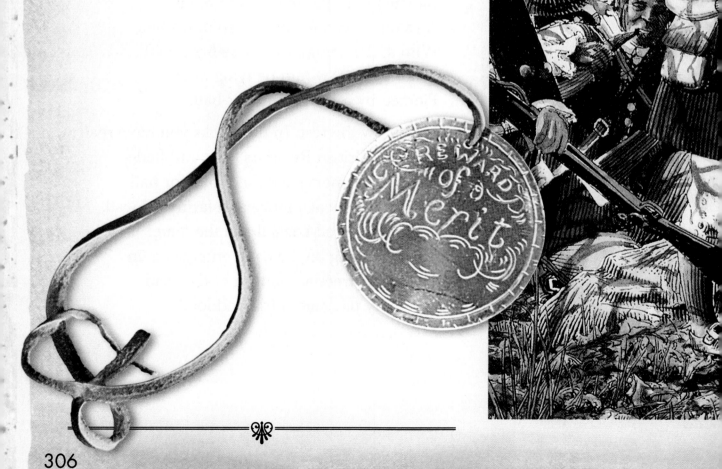

Objectives

• Provide evidence from text to support understanding. • Read independently for a sustained period of time and paraphrase the reading, including the order in which events occur.

Envision It! | Retell

Think Critically

1. Longfellow's poem *The Midnight Ride of Paul Revere* was published shortly before the Civil War in 1861. His poem inspired feelings of patriotism in Americans. Why do you think it is important to feel patriotic about your country? **Text to World**

2. Read your favorite stanza aloud. Get the gallop into the rhythm as you read. Make the spoken words reveal the scene.
   Think Like an Author

3. Longfellow includes vibrant descriptions. Why would he include these descriptions? How do they add to the story of the poem?
   Author's Purpose

4. On page 305, Longfellow writes "You know the rest." What is the "rest" he is referring to? **Background Knowledge**

5. **Look Back and Write** Look back at pages 300–305. How did Paul Revere feel before and during his ride? Use evidence from the text to support your answer.

   TEST PRACTICE Extended Response

Henry Wadsworth Longfellow and Christopher Bing

Here are other books by Christopher Bing and Henry Wadsworth Longfellow.

Casey at the Bat: A Ballad of the Republic Sung in the Year 1888 by Ernest L. Thayer, illustrated by Christopher Bing

Henry Wadsworth Longfellow became the most popular poet of his day. Longfellow was one of the first American poets to write about people, traditions, and events with American themes.

Longfellow climbed the steps of the Old North Church and visited an inn in New England. These experiences probably inspired him to write *The Midnight Ride of Paul Revere.*

Paul Revere's Ride by Henry Wadsworth Longfellow, illustrated by Ted Rand

Christopher Bing has said, "When people pick up one of my books, I want them to become absorbed into the work and feel like they are experiencing the time and the period of the event that they're looking at or reading about." He uses maps and re-created documents to make characters and settings come alive.

In the illustrations for *The Midnight Ride of Paul Revere*, Mr. Bing used a pen, ink, and a brush on white scratchboard to create the look of an old book. Mr. Bing has contributed editorial and political cartoons to *The New York Times*, *The Washington Post*, and other newspapers. His illustrations for *Casey at the Bat* won a Caldecott Honor Book award.

Use the *Reader's and Writer's Notebook* to record your independent reading.

Narrative

Historical Fiction

Let's Write It!

Key Features of Historical Fiction

● takes place during a real time in history

● uses realistic details to describe the past

● can include real historical figures or events

READING STREET ONLINE
GRAMMAR JAMMER
www.ReadingStreet.com

Historical fiction tells a story that takes place at a certain point in history. The story and characters may be made up, but often the story includes some real historical people and events.

Writing Prompt Imagine you were living in a past era. Write a narrative story about your experiences.

Writer's Checklist

Remember, you should . . .

☑ create a believable historical setting.

☑ have characters act and talk as people might have.

☑ use descriptive details to make the story seem real.

☑ research the time period, if possible.

☑ have subject-verb agreement.

310

My Friend, Susan B. Anthony

Yesterday, Susan and I met for afternoon tea, and she told me some interesting news.

She said that she had decided to travel across the United States giving speeches about suffrage and equality.

"It is 1852," she said, "and many people in our country still do not have the right to vote."

Susan put down her teacup and folded her hands in her lap. Her eyes were bright. "I hope that people will understand the message about equality for all people."

I felt proud of my friend Susan, but was also worried about how hard it might be to journey such long distances, fighting for the right to vote.

"How long do you think you'll be traveling and writing speeches?" I asked her, though I was pretty sure what her answer would be.

"I will travel and fight for equality for as long as there are people in this country who live without it," she replied.

"I'm going to give all that I have."

Genre Historical fiction tells a story that is set in the past.

Writing Trait Word Choice Sensory words make the story seem real.

Subjects and verbs agree in number.

Conventions

Subject-Verb Agreement

Remember The subjects and verbs in your sentences must agree in number. A singular subject needs a singular verb (Sophia **is** laughing), while a plural subject needs a plural verb (Sophia and Marco **are** laughing).

311

Social Studies in Reading

Genre
Drama

- A drama is a story that is to be acted out. It usually includes dialogue, or lines that the characters speak to one another.

- A drama will also include descriptions of settings. This will let readers know where and when the drama takes place.

- A drama may include stage directions, or specific instructions about how to perform.

- Read *The Heroic Paul Revere*. While reading, think about ways this drama is similar to and different from the original poem.

312

THE HEROIC
Paul Revere

adapted from the poem *The Midnight Ride of Paul Revere*
a play written by Charles Blair

CAST

Henry Wadsworth Longfellow,
as LONGFELLOW

PAUL REVERE	BRITISH SOLDIER 1
COLONIST	BRITISH SOLDIER 2

NOTE: *This play includes a scene where the character of Paul Revere rides a horse. The horse does not need to be a real horse. The actor can either pretend to ride a horse or a simple prop, such as a toy horse, can be used.*

SCENE I

THE SETTING: *Colonial Boston in 1775, night. PAUL REVERE and a COLONIST stand before a church. On the stage is a small house and a fence. HENRY WADSWORTH LONGFELLOW enters.*

LONGFELLOW: Listen, my children, and you shall hear of the midnight ride of Paul Revere. What's that? You don't know the tale? Well, allow me to set the stage for you. The date is April 18, 1775. The American colonies and England are on the brink of war. Paul Revere speaks to his friend, a colonist.

REVERE: If the British march by land or sea from Boston tonight, hang a lantern aloft in the belfry arch of the North Church tower — one if by land, two if by sea.

COLONIST: Yes, sir.

REVERE: I will be on the opposite shore, ready to ride my horse and spread the alarm. Do you understand?

COLONIST: Yes, sir.

(The two men shake hands.)

REVERE: Good night, my friend. And good luck.

(PAUL REVERE exits the stage.)

COLONIST: What a brave man! But I mustn't waste time. I must find out what the British are up to!

LONGFELLOW: The colonist wandered through the streets, listening for British soldiers. He didn't have to wait long.

(Several BRITISH SOLDIERS exit the house, yelling loudly. The COLONIST hides behind the fence.)

BRITISH SOLDIER 1: The time has come to teach these rebels a lesson.

BRITISH SOLDIER 2: To the boats!

COLONIST: Listen to that! The British soldiers are on the move! And they are marching down to their boats on the shore. I must warn Mr. Revere!

END OF SCENE I.

Let's **Think** About...

How is the structure of this play different from that of the poem? **Drama**

SCENE II

The COLONIST *is standing inside the church's belfry.*
He places one lantern on the belfry. PAUL REVERE *enters*
from the opposite side of the stage.

REVERE: Look! It's a light! One light!

(The COLONIST *places another lantern.)*

Let's **Think** About...

What parts of the play are similar to the original text you just read? **Drama**

314

REVERE: A second light! The British are coming by sea! I must get my horse ready! We must ride and warn the colonists!

LONGFELLOW: With a hurry of hoofs Paul Revere rode off. Just imagine the sight! A shape in the moonlight, a bulk in the dark. The fate of a nation was riding that night.

REVERE: *(yelling from offstage)* Ride, my friend! Faster!

(PAUL REVERE enters the stage, riding a horse.)

LONGFELLOW: At twelve o'clock he crossed the bridge into Medford town! At one o'clock he galloped into Lexington! At two o'clock he rode into Concord. The people, safe and asleep in their beds, heard him exclaim . . .

REVERE: The British are coming! The British are coming!

LONGFELLOW: So through the night rode Paul Revere. He cried the alarm to every village and farm, a cry of defiance and not of fear. His voice called in a voice that shall echo forevermore—

REVERE: The British are coming!

LONGFELLOW: And the people fought bravely. Thus ends our tale. Now if anyone asks you what it means to be a hero, you can tell them about the midnight ride of Paul Revere.

THE END

Let's **Think** About...

Reading Across Texts Both *The Midnight Ride of Paul Revere* and *The Heroic Paul Revere* tell the story of the most famous ride in American history. Make a chart to compare and contrast these two versions.

Writing Across Texts Write a paragraph that compares and contrasts the two selections.

Objectives

● Read aloud grade-level texts and understand what is read. ● Determine the meaning of English words with roots from Greek, Latin, and other languages. ● Identify the point of view of media presentations. ● Show agreement between subjects and verbs in simple and compound sentences. ● Give organized presentations that communicate your ideas effectively. ● Explain how different messages in various forms of media are presented.

Let's **Learn** It!

READING STREET ONLINE
ONLINE STUDENT EDITION
www.ReadingStreet.com

Vocabulary

Endings -s, -ed, -ing

Word Structure You can use the structure of words to help you understand a word's meaning. The endings -ed, -ing, and -s come from Old English. The ending -ing shows that an action is happening now or continuing to happen. The ending -ed on a verb shows that an action happened in the past. The ending -s on a verb shows that an action is happening now.

Practice It! Find three verbs in *The Midnight Ride of Paul Revere* that end with -ing, -ed, and -s. How does understanding the endings help you understand these words?

Fluency

Rate

When you read poetry, use the line breaks and the rhythm of the poem itself to help you determine the rate that will help you understand the poem. Some poems have a slow internal rhythm and are meant to be read slowly. Other poems can be read more quickly.

Practice It! With a partner, practice reading aloud a page from *The Midnight Ride of Paul Revere*. Notice the words that rhyme in each stanza. Pay attention to the similar rhythms of the stanzas. Read the poem at a measured rate, and make sure you understand each line.

Media Literacy

Get Ready For Middle School

When you give a presentation, speak with volume, and enunciate your words.

Documentary

A documentary is a film or TV show that tells a true story about real people and events. Usually, a documentary contains interviews with the people who lived through an event, or with experts on the subject. In some documentaries, narrators provide background information and describe what is happening.

Practice It! Work with a team to write a proposal for a documentary about a day in the life of a student at your school. Think of whom you will interview and what information is most important. Present your proposal to the class. Then discuss ways documentaries differ from news shows and commercials.

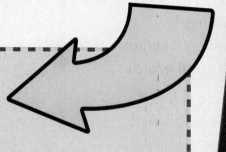

Tips

Listening . . .

• Listen to the speaker's message.

• Ask questions to identify the documentary's point of view.

Speaking . . .

• Use and understand complete simple and compound sentences with correct subject-verb agreement.

• Speak with volume and enunciation.

Teamwork . . .

• Consider suggestions from others.

• Identify points of agreement and disagreement.

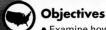

Poetry

● Poets use sound effects, such as internal rhyme and rhyme scheme, to add meaning to a poem.

● Internal rhyme occurs within the lines of a poem. Internal rhyme reinforces a poem's meaning by drawing attention to important words.

● Rhyme scheme is the pattern of words that sound alike in a poem. Rhyme scheme can draw attention to important words or lines.

● As you read the poems, consider how internal rhymes or rhyme scheme draws attention to certain words and adds to meaning.

For Peace Sake
by Cedric McClester

For peace sake
we need to do our best.
For peace sake
let's put the hate to rest.
For peace sake
it never is too late.
For peace sake
let's rid our lives
  of hate.
I believe that we can
build a bridge to
  understand,
we're all in this together.
It never ever is too late,
together let's rid our
  lives of hate.
Let's do it for peace
  sake.
For peace sake
we need to do our best.
For peace sake
let's put love to the test.

Love is really what we
  need;
together we can plant
  the seed.
For peace sake let's
  work in harmony.
For peace sake,
for love and happiness,
for peace sake
and for all the rest.
I believe that we can
build a bridge to
  understand,
we're all in this
  together.
It never ever is too late,
together let's rid our
  lives of hate.
Let's do it, let's do it
for peace sake.
For peace sake
we can make it right.
For peace sake
it can happen
  overnight.

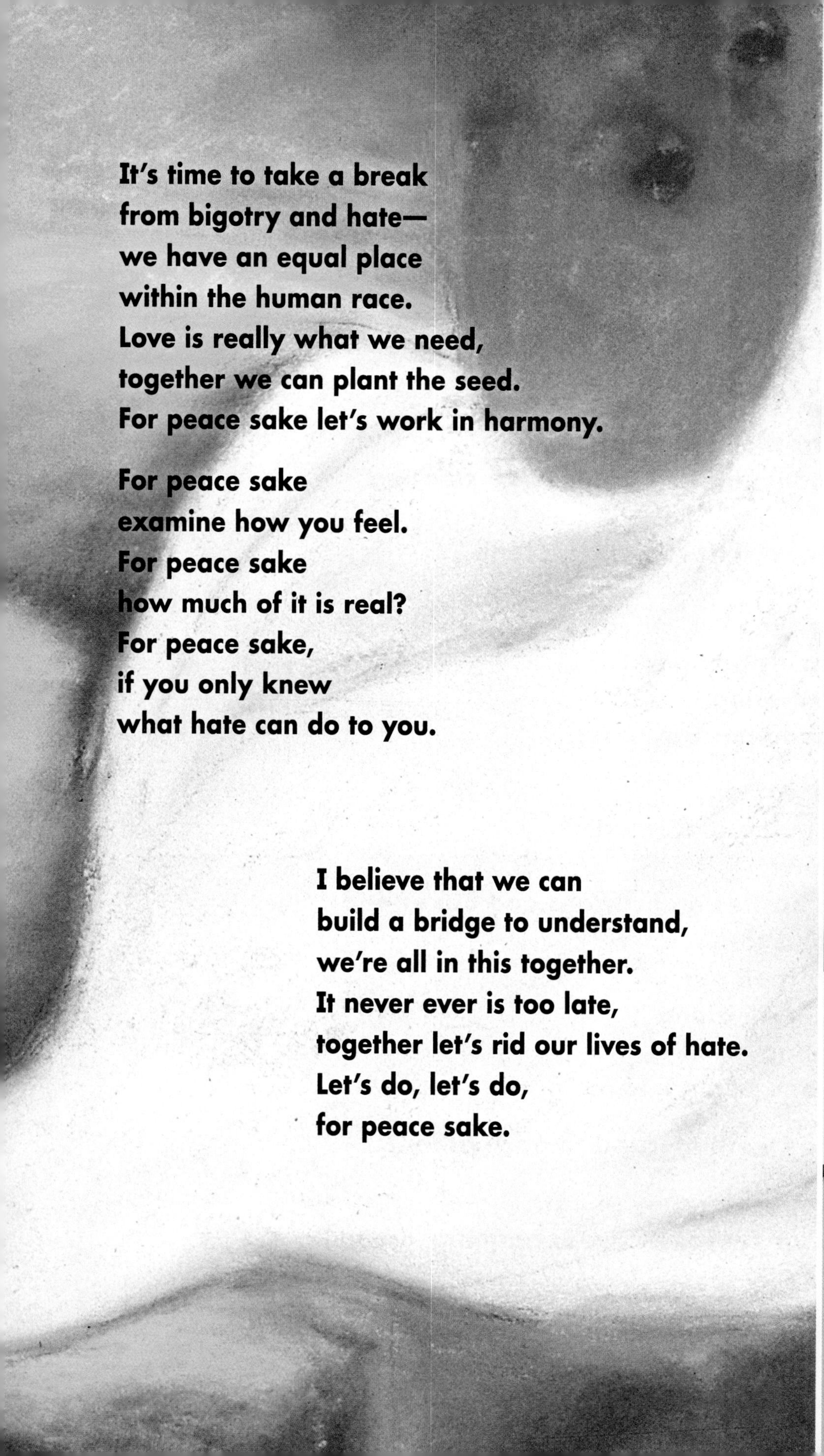

It's time to take a break
from bigotry and hate—
we have an equal place
within the human race.
Love is really what we need,
together we can plant the seed.
For peace sake let's work in harmony.

For peace sake
examine how you feel.
For peace sake
how much of it is real?
For peace sake,
if you only knew
what hate can do to you.

I believe that we can
build a bridge to understand,
we're all in this together.
It never ever is too late,
together let's rid our lives of hate.
Let's do, let's do,
for peace sake.

Let's **Think** About...

What words rhyme in the poem? How does this rhyme scheme reinforce the poem's meaning?

Let's **Think** About...

How does the internal rhyme in the fourth line of this stanza call attention to important words or ideas?

319

Two People I Want to Be Like

by Eve Merriam

That man
stuck in traffic
not pounding his fists against the steering
wheel
not trying to shift to the next lane
just
using the time
for a slow steady grin
of remembering
all the good unstuck times

and that woman
clerking in the supermarket
at rush hour
bagging bottles and cartons and boxes and
    jars and cans
punching it all out
slapping it all along
and leveling a smile
at everyone in the line.

I wish they were married to each other.

Maybe it's better they're not,
so they can pass their sweet harmony around.

Not in Vain

by Emily Dickinson

If I can stop one heart from breaking,
I shall not live in vain:
If I can ease one life the aching,
Or cool one pain,
Or help one fainting robin
Unto his nest again,
I shall not live in vain.

STRANGERS

by Janet S. Wong

Sometimes strangers talk so fast,
                    so rough,
                    so big—
you wonder if it's just a bluff.

They can make you feel so weak,
                    so small,
                    so dumb—
you wonder if they know it all.

But maybe they're the ones who need
someone to follow. Take the lead.

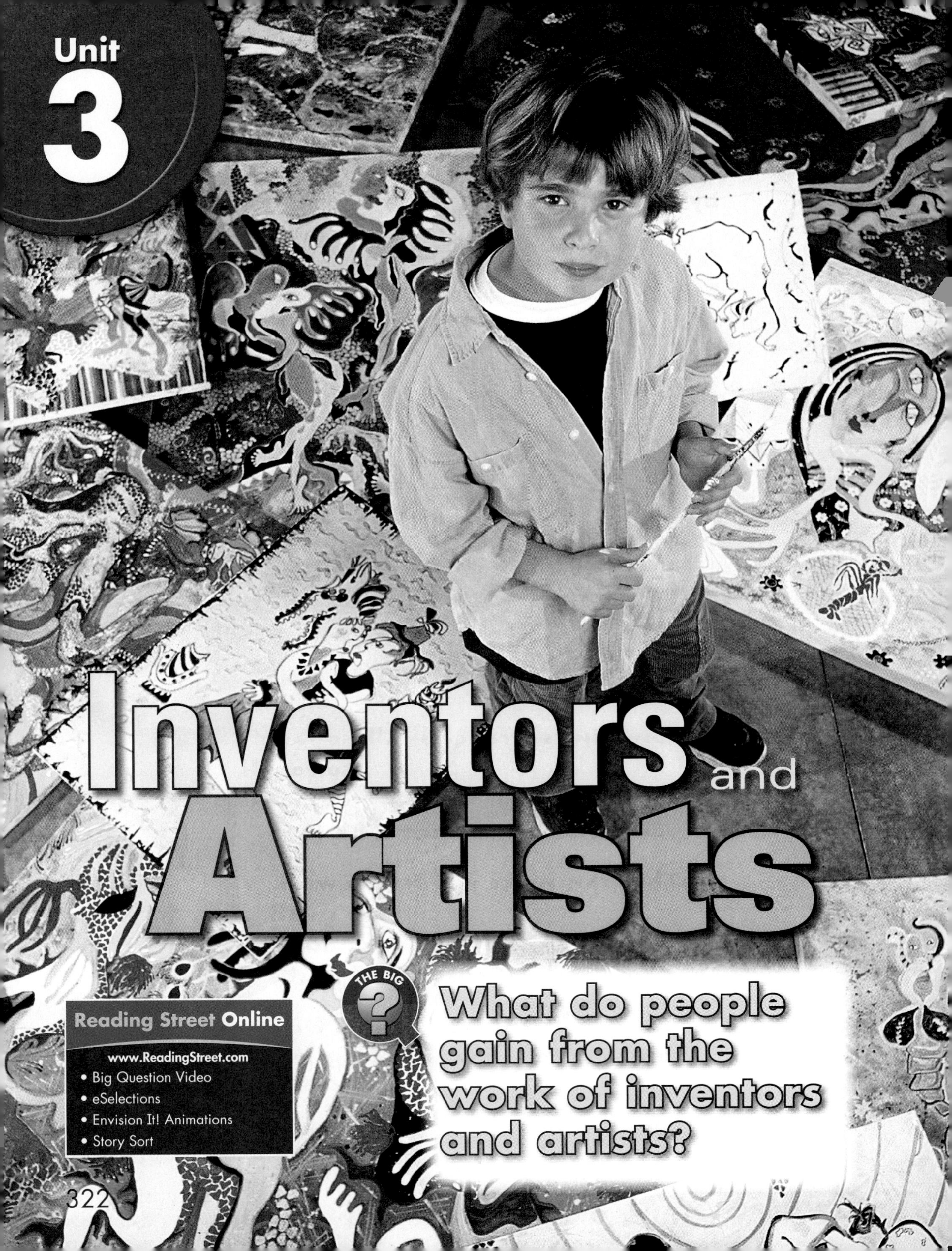

Unit 3

Inventors and Artists

THE BIG ?

What do people gain from the work of inventors and artists?

Reading Street Online

www.ReadingStreet.com

- Big Question Video
- eSelections
- Envision It! Animations
- Story Sort

Objectives
• Listen to and interpret a speaker's messages and ask questions.
• Identify the main ideas and supporting ideas in the speaker's message.

Let's Talk About

Inventors and Their Inventions

- Share opinions about favorite inventors or inventions.

- Listen to a classmate's opinions about inventions.

- Determine your classmates' main and supporting ideas about inventions.

READING STREET ONLINE
CONCEPT TALK VIDEO
www.ReadingStreet.com

Objectives
● Summarize and paraphrase information in a text. ● Analyze how the organization of a text affects the way ideas are related.

Envision It! | Skill Strategy

Skill

Strategy

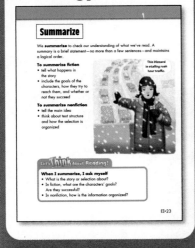

READING STREET ONLINE
ENVISION IT! ANIMATIONS
www.ReadingStreet.com

Comprehension Skill

🎯 Sequence

- The sequence of events is the order in which they take place, from first to last.

- Clue words such as *first, next,* and *then* may show sequence in a story or an article, but not always. Other clues are dates and times.

- Two events can happen at the same time. *While* and *at the same time* are clue words that indicate this.

- Use a graphic organizer like the one below to chart the sequence of events in "Kid Inventor." Then think about how the sequence influences the relationships among ideas in the text.

First Event	→	Second Event	→	Third Event	→	Fourth Event

Comprehension Strategy

🎯 Summarize

Active readers summarize to check their understanding of a selection. As you read "Kid Inventor," summarize to maintain meaning by stating main ideas and leaving out unimportant details. Summarizing helps you make sure you understand and remember what you read. A good summary should be brief and use a reader's own words.

Kid Inventor

Some of the most amazing inventions have not come from expensive laboratories. They have come from children your age!

Strategy What are one or two of the main ideas of this article that you could use in a summary?

One of the most delicious inventions in the world came from an eleven-year-old named Frank Epperson, who in 1905 created the frozen fruit bar. First, Epperson made a fruit drink for himself. Instead of finishing it, he left his drink outside overnight with a stick in it. Then, temperatures in San Francisco dropped to below freezing, and the drink froze. The next morning he discovered that he liked the taste of the frozen fruit drink.

Skill What is the last thing that Epperson did with his invention?

Epperson couldn't apply for a patent to claim ownership of the invention until much later, because at the time he was too young. He waited many years, until he was an adult, to patent the treat. Later, Epperson sold the idea to a company, which then produced the treats that you find in the store today.

Skill Which words in this paragraph tell you about the sequence of events?

Your Turn!

⏸ **Need a Review?** See the *Envision It! Handbook* for help with sequence and summarizing.

Let's Think About..

▶ **Ready to Try It?** Talk about sequence as you read *The Fabulous Perpetual Motion Machine*.

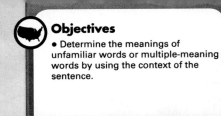

Objectives

• Determine the meanings of unfamiliar words or multiple-meaning words by using the context of the sentence.

applauds

inspecting

project

browsing

fabulous

READING STREET ONLINE
VOCABULARY ACTIVITIES
www.ReadingStreet.com

Vocabulary Strategy for

Multiple-Meaning Words

Context Clues Some words have more than one meaning. Use words and sentences around the word with multiple meanings to figure out which meaning the author is using.

1. When you find a multiple-meaning word, read the context clues around it.

2. Think about the different meanings the word has. For example, the word *crop* can mean "a product grown for food" or "to cut short."

3. Reread the sentence, replacing the word with one of the meanings.

4. If this meaning does not work, try another meaning of the word.

Read "The Play's the Thing" on page 329. Use context clues to help you determine and clarify the meanings of multiple-meaning words.

Words to Write Reread "The Play's the Thing." Write a note to a friend explaining why you would like to see a play. Use words from the *Words to Know* list in your note.

The Play's the Thing

Writing a play is hard work. But it can also be an enjoyable project for an author—and the audience. An author creates a whole new world, and then fills it with people who do what he or she wishes. The author can use them to tell realistic stories, or send them off on fabulous adventures.

The next time you are browsing in the library, look for famous plays. Notice the way that authors describe their characters. How do they look and sound? Look at the stage directions. They tell you how the characters will move and what will be around them.

If you get a chance, go to a play. It can be lots of fun. Inspecting the stage before the play starts will tell you something about the mood the author wants to create. When the actors come on stage, this fantasy world comes alive.

As the play ends and the audience applauds, the author often feels a real sense of joy. So does the crowd. They were able to escape—even for a little while—to a different world.

Your Turn!

Need a Review? For additional help with using context clues to determine and clarify the meaning of multiple-meaning words, see *Words!*

Ready to Try It? Read *The Fabulous Perpetual Motion Machine* on pp. 330–343.

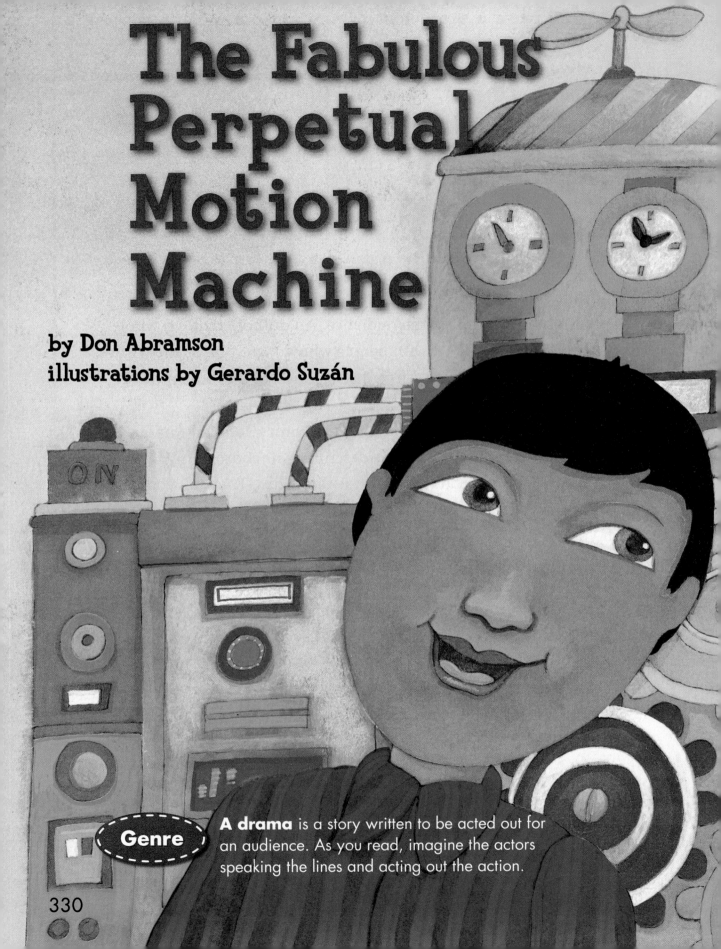

The Fabulous Perpetual Motion Machine

by Don Abramson
illustrations by Gerardo Suzán

Genre

A drama is a story written to be acted out for an audience. As you read, imagine the actors speaking the lines and acting out the action.

Question of the Week

How do inventors inspire our imaginations?

Let's
Think
About
Reading!

Characters

CARLOS PÉREZ

LILY PÉREZ

LARRY SAND
a friend

EFFIE BROWNING
a friend

JOYCE REARDON
a friend

MRS. PÉREZ

MR. PÉREZ

DOMINGO PÉREZ
their older brother

LEE COMER
a reporter

Scene 1

Let's **Think** About...

How does the dialogue between the characters help you visualize the feeling, or mood, in the rec room?
Visualizing

SETTING: *A basement rec room, filled with well-worn furniture. Upstage center is a large, mysterious object draped with a sheet. LILY, CARLOS, EFFIE, and LARRY are on stage.*

LARRY: Okay, Lily, Carlos, what's this about?

EFFIE: Yeah, you wanted to show us something?

LILY: Just be patient, Effie.

CARLOS: We're waiting till—

LILY: Joyce gets here.

LARRY: What, you're going to have some big unveiling?

CARLOS: Sure are, Larry.

LILY: You know we were thinking about a project—

CARLOS: For the Science Fair.

332

EFFIE: We were all trying to come up with something that hadn't been done to death.

LARRY: That wasn't so easy. I'm doing a dinosaur diorama.

EFFIE: Done to death.

LARRY: I said it wasn't easy.

EFFIE: Carlos, Lily, you're driving us crazy here.

LARRY: Yeah, give us a little hint!

CARLOS: All right. Prepare to be blown away.

LILY: This year, first prize at the Science Fair—

CARLOS: Will be awarded to—

LILY: The fabulous Pérez Twins! Take a bow, Carlos. *(She applauds as he bows.)*

Let's **Think** About...

What can you infer about Effie's personality?
Inferring

Let's **Think** About...

What details help you summarize the story and determine the main idea so far?
Summarize

CARLOS: And Lily. Yea-a-a! *(He applauds as she bows; then turns to EFFIE and LARRY.)* You're not getting into the spirit, you two.

LARRY: We haven't seen anything yet.

EFFIE: And you're really going to have to be fabulous to win first prize at that Science Fair.

LARRY: It's usually somebody from Higgins School. They've got that hot-shot science teacher.

LILY: Well, not this year. This year the Mary Dimity Witherspoon Elementary School—

CARLOS: Will go down in history!

LARRY: Enough, already! What is this project?

LILY: Well, Carlos was browsing the Internet—

CARLOS: Looking for failed inventions.

EFFIE: Hey, you can't take your science project off the Internet!

CARLOS: We found the idea, not the plan.

LILY: People have been playing around with this for years—

CARLOS: For centuries! But until now, nobody's done it. Until us, the fabulous—

LILY: Pérez Twins! Yea-a-a! *(CARLOS and LILY both cheer, applaud, and bow. She turns to LARRY and EFFIE.)* C'mon, guys!

MRS. PÉREZ *(entering):* And just what is it the fabulous Pérez Twins have achieved to warrant a spontaneous round of applause?

CARLOS: Hi, Mom. We were just telling Effie and Larry—

MRS. PÉREZ: Well, tell Joyce too. She just got here.

Let's **Think** About...

What do you know about the Internet that helps explain Effie's surprise?
Background Knowledge

Let's **Think** About...

What important details can you use to summarize the events on this page?
Summarize

JOYCE *(entering):* Hi, guys. *(Everyone adlibs greetings.)* What's up? Is this your Science Fair idea?

LILY: Yes, and I tell you—

MRS. PÉREZ: Aha! So that's what you've been banging around down here about.

CARLOS: We're going to win the—

LARRY: We've heard this already!

MRS. PÉREZ: If you're finally going to disclose this big secret, do you mind if your mother sits in? *(to the others)* They've been driving the whole family crazy.

LILY: Sure, Mom.

CARLOS: Sit over here.

JOYCE *(inspecting the draped thing):* Is this it?

LILY: Yes! But first let us tell you—

(JOYCE has tugged at a corner of the sheet, which falls away, revealing a contraption with dials, levers, pulleys, etc.)

Let's **Think** About...

What do Mrs. Perez's comments tell about the kind of person she is? **Inferring**

335

EFFIE: Wow!

MRS. PÉREZ: You really have been busy!

LARRY: But what is it? What does it do?

JOYCE (*inspecting it from all sides*): Does it plug in . . . or what? I don't see a cord.

CARLOS: No. That's the point.

EFFIE: It runs on batteries?

LILY: No. It doesn't have a power source. But once we start it up—

CARLOS: It'll keep running forever.

LARRY (*after a moment's silence*): Did you say "forever"?

LILY: Yep!

CARLOS: It's a perpetual—

LILY: Motion—

CARLOS: Machine!

MRS. PÉREZ: That's something all right.

EFFIE: If you're right—oh, wow!

JOYCE: Have you tried it out yet?

LILY: No, we wanted you all here—

CARLOS: For the demonstration. Lily, will you kindly do the honors?

LILY: I'd be honored to do the honors. Thank you, Carlos.

(*She flips a switch on the front. Slowly, the machine comes to life. Wheels spin, dials shift, levers move up and down. Ratchet noises are heard.* CARLOS *and* LILY *bow. The others applaud.*)

LARRY: I'm impressed. I'm really impressed!

MRS. PÉREZ: Lily, Carlos, I'm so proud of you!

EFFIE: This is fabulous!

Let's **Think** About...

Why does the author include a moment of silence before Larry speaks? **Inferring**

Let's **Think** About...

What details would you include to briefly describe the machine?  **Summarize**

Let's **Think** About...

What can you do to help remember all the characters? **Monitor and Clarify**

337

Let's **Think** About...

How does the author use descriptions to set the scene?
Story Structure

About three hours later. LILY, CARLOS, EFFIE, LARRY, and JOYCE sit watching the machine, which is still running merrily along. They each have an almost-finished glass of lemonade.

LARRY: Well, it's better than watching paint dry. At least you've got some things that go round and round.

EFFIE: And some things that go up and down.

LARRY: But why are we sitting here watching things go round and round and up and down?

LILY: We have to make sure it's perpetual. That it keeps going.

JOYCE: But what does it do?

CARLOS: You've got to think big, Joyce.

LILY: We can attach stuff to it.

CARLOS: Run other machines, lots of them.

LILY: Just think—free power for everybody!

CARLOS: We're going to be rich!

EFFIE: How are you going to get rich if it's free power?

LILY: Somebody has to build the machines.

LARRY: But how does it work?

CARLOS: Oh, we can't disclose its secrets—

LILY: Until we apply for our patents.

EFFIE: Hmm. How long is it now?

LARRY: Must be nearly three hours. *(He looks at his watch and then shakes it.)* That's funny. My watch must be running slow.

Let's **Think** About...

What details help you to summarize how the characters feel about the machine?
Summarize

EFFIE *(finishing her lemonade):* I should be getting home.

JOYCE: Yeah, I should go too. Thanks for the lemonade.

DOMINGO *(entering):* So, what's going on down here? Mom said you've got a special science project.

LILY: Domingo, come look!

DOMINGO: Yow! What on Earth is that?

CARLOS: It's a perpetual motion machine.

LILY: That means it runs forever.

DOMINGO: I know what that means. Well, I'll be darned. Wait a minute, where's the power?

LILY: There isn't any. That's what we're telling you.

CARLOS: It just keeps running and running.

DOMINGO: It's impossible. Perpetual motion. Can't work.

CARLOS: But look at it!

DOMINGO: Okay, look, I know there's something wrong with this. I don't know what, but I'm going to find out!

Let's **Think** About...

How does the author use dialogue to set up the problem?
Story Structure

339

(He leaves.)

EFFIE: Well, see you, Lily, Carlos. Good work! I think you're right about that first prize.

MR. PÉREZ *(offstage):* It's just down here, Lee. Watch your step. *(He enters, followed by LEE, who carries a camera.)* What's this about first prize?

CARLOS: At the Science Fair, Dad.

MR. PÉREZ: If this thing really works, they'll have to make up a special prize just for you! Lee, you remember my kids.

LEE: I sure do. Hi, Lily, Carlos.

LILY: Hello, Mrs. Comer. Um—these are our friends.

MR. PÉREZ: When your mother called me at work about this, I thought, hey, what luck we've got a friend who's a newspaper reporter. This is some real

Let's **Think** About...

What can you do to help understand the scene so far? **Monitor and Clarify**

340

news. *(He approaches the machine.)* This it? Come see this, Lee. *(LEE joins him. They inspect the machine from all sides.)* Perpetual motion. The dream of ages. How long has it been running, kids?

CARLOS: About three hours.

LARRY: We lost track. My watch stopped.

JOYCE *(looking):* Funny, mine too.

MRS. PÉREZ *(entering with a tray with a pitcher and glasses):* Are you going to make my children famous, Lee?

LEE: I'd say they did that themselves. All I can do is report it.

MRS. PÉREZ: Funniest thing. I've had some chicken in the oven for the last hour, but it's not cooking at all. Here, I brought you some lemonade. *(She sets down the tray.)*

LEE: Thanks.

MR. PÉREZ: Well, what do you think, Lee?

LEE: I'll take some pictures first and then do an interview. We'll get one with Lily and Carlos beside the machine—tinkering—and maybe another one with their friends looking on in admiration. *(EFFIE, LARRY, and JOYCE perk up and start fixing their hair and clothes.)*

MR. PÉREZ: Sounds good. Where do you want the kids now?

LEE: One on either side, I think. Where's Domingo? Did he have anything to do with this?

LILY: He did not. He said it wouldn't work.

CARLOS: But it's been going for three hours.

LEE: Hold it! *(She presses the shutter, but there's no flash.)* That's funny.

DOMINGO *(entering, waving an encyclopedia):* I knew it,

Let's **Think** About...

How would you describe Mr. Perez's opinion of the machine?
🔄 **Summarize**

Let's **Think** About...

Why do you think so many different things have stopped working?
Questioning

341

I told you! My computer sort of crashed, but we still have these encyclopedias—and I found it!

LILY: Dom, not now!

MRS. PÉREZ: What are you talking about, Domingo?

DOMINGO: The laws of thermodynamics. We'd studied them in science, but I couldn't remember for sure.

MR. PÉREZ: Well, what about them?

DOMINGO: Listen! *(Reading)* "The First Law of Thermodynamics. Energy can be converted from one form to another, but it cannot be created or destroyed."

EFFIE: So?

DOMINGO: Energy cannot be created! Don't you see?

MRS. PÉREZ: Uh-oh. I think I understand.

DOMINGO: So that machine can't work!

LARRY: But there it is, round and round and up and down and *chhht!* (He imitates the ratchet noise.)

DOMINGO: But it's not really a perpetual motion machine. *(The lights flicker; they all notice.)*

LEE: Wait a minute. If it's not a perpetual motion machine, where's the perpetual motion coming from?

What do you know about encyclopedias? How does it help you understand Domingo's conclusion?
Background Knowledge

DOMINGO: I don't know, but it's not creating its own energy. It can't. *(The lights flicker again and go to half power.)*

CARLOS: It's borrowing.

MR. PÉREZ: What?

MRS. PÉREZ: From where?

CARLOS: From all the other energy sources around here.

LILY: The lights, the oven, your watches.

DOMINGO: My computer!

JOYCE: But what happens now?

CARLOS: Only one thing. *(He and LILY look sadly at each other.)*

LILY: You or me? *(CARLOS shrugs.)* I will. *(She turns off the switch. The machine sputters to a halt. The lights start to come back up.)*

EFFIE: Rats! I thought we were making history.

LEE: We were. Well, some kind of history got made here today.

DOMINGO: Sorry about that!

MRS. PÉREZ: Carlos, Lily, are you disappointed?

CARLOS: Sure.

LILY: Who wouldn't be?

LARRY: Yeah. Now you need a new science project.

EFFIE: Just don't do another diorama. *(LARRY scowls at her.)*

LILY: Oh, we'll come up with something.

CARLOS: Yeah. You know, I was thinking the other day . . .

Blackout

Let's **Think** About...

What details would you include in an explanation of the machine's source of energy?

Summarize

Let's **Think** About...

Why does the author end with the word *Blackout* in the illustration?

Questioning

343

Envision It! | Retell

Think Critically

1. Think about how Lily and Carlos created their invention together. Then think about a time when you and a partner worked together to create something. How does the way you worked compare to the way Lily and Carlos worked? **Text to Self**

2. The author presents Lily and Carlos as a sister and brother who are close. How does he do this? **Think Like an Author**

3. Reread Scene 2. In your own words, describe the sequence of events that occurs when the Perez twins demonstrate the perpetual motion machine to their friends and family. Be sure to use sequence words, such as *first, then*, and *next*. **Sequence**

4. Summarize the events that occur when Carlos and Lily reveal the perpetual motion machine in Scene 1. **Summarize**

5. Look Back and Write Look through the play. What goals do Lily and Carlos have for inventing their machine other than winning the prize at the science fair? Are these the goals you would have if you invented such a machine? Provide evidence to support your answer.

TEST PRACTICE | **Extended Response**

344

Don Abramson

Don Abramson became involved in theater as a high school freshman. Since then, he has directed and acted in plays and designed and built theatrical sets. Several of his plays have been published in textbooks. One of his works (a collection of poetry) was staged in Phoenix, Chicago, New York, and London. Mr. Abramson has also written books and lyrics for musical theater. His children's musical *The Well of the Guelphs* was produced in Iowa and Nebraska.

Recently, he had fun doing research on Cinderella. Do you know there are hundreds of Cinderella stories from countries all around the world? He read dozens of these stories and then chose four—from China, India, the Philippines, and America—to combine into one musical entitled *Who Is Cinderella?*

Reading Log

Use the *Reader's and Writer's Notebook* to record your independent reading.

Objectives
● Write creative stories with dialogue. ● Write creative stories that include a clear focus, plot, and point of view.

Let's Write It!

Key Features of a Play

● includes a list of characters

● tells the setting, time, or place

● has characters that often speak or act distinctly

READING STREET ONLINE
GRAMMAR JAMMER
www.ReadingStreet.com

Play

A **play** is a story that is written to be performed. It is often acted out on a stage, and uses dialogue and stage directions to help tell the story. The student model on the next page is an example of a short play.

Writing Prompt In *The Fabulous Perpetual Motion Machine,* young inventors create a special machine. Think about something that could be invented. Now write a short play based on your ideas.

Writer's Checklist

Remember, you should . . .

☑ provide a list of characters.

☑ include dialogue to develop the story.

☑ put stage directions in parentheses.

☑ consider how your play will sound out loud.

The Best Design

Characters: Mona (age 15), Freddy (age 14)

Setting: Modern day. In the kitchen of Mona's house.

Freddy (at kitchen table): I know—we should design a time machine that takes people back in time. We can see stuff from history, such as how ancient people **lived**!

Mona: Time machines aren't real, and we're supposed to design something real. How about an improved parachute? We could test our designs using raw eggs until we find the best one.

Freddy: An egg parachute? Who **cares**? I want to visit ancient Greece and watch people who **raced** chariots!

Mona: Yeah—right! We only have until tomorrow to design something. (Mona opens the refrigerator.) What a mess!

Freddy: That's it! **We will** design a better system for finding snacks in a refrigerator. I **think** the shelves need to swing outward, and the bins need to be see-through.

Mona: Freddy, you **are** a genius! Who knows better than teens how to use refrigerators?

Genre
A **play** tells a story that is meant to be performed.

Writing Trait Word Choice
Descriptive words make the dialogue interesting.

Past, Present, and Future Tenses are used correctly.

Conventions

Past, Present, and Future Tenses

Remember For **present tense,** use the basic verb form (I *jump*). Simple **past tense** shows that action has already happened, and often ends in *-ed* (I *jumped*). For the simple **future tense,** use the word *will* and the basic verb form (I *will jump*).

Objectives
- Identify the author's viewpoint or position and explain the relationship among ideas in the argument.
- Recognize exaggerated, contradictory, or misleading statements in text.

Science in Reading

Genre
Persuasive Text

- Persuasive text tries to convince the reader to do or think something. An advertisement is an example of persuasive text because it tries to convince someone to buy something.

- The author of a persuasive text has a distinct viewpoint and position.

- Persuasive text may contain exaggerated, misleading, or contradictory statements.

- Read the advertisement "The Toy Space Shuttle Is Here!" As you read, look for elements that make this selection a persuasive text. What is the author's viewpoint and position?

You just read a story about a fictional invention, The Fabulous Perpetual Motion Machine. *Now read an advertisement for another fictional invention, the Toy Space Shuttle.*

THE TOY SPACE SHUTTLE IS HERE!

You've seen the launch of a space shuttle on TV. Now launch one in your backyard!

That's right. The Toy Space Shuttle is an exact replica of a NASA space shuttle. Only it measures just one foot tall and four inches across.

But here's the really big news. The Toy Space Shuttle can do everything that a real space shuttle can do. When you launch the Toy Space Shuttle, it rockets up, up, up into the sky. It keeps soaring until it disappears from sight. That's when you run upstairs to your bedroom. The Toy Space Shuttle comes with its own Mission Control Center, just like the one at the NASA Johnson Space Center in Houston, Texas. It is small enough to fit on your desk, but powerful enough to let you track your Toy Space Shuttle while it is in orbit!

You read that correctly. The Toy Space Shuttle can orbit around the Earth!

How do you play with a toy that is so far away? It's easy.

Put on your Mission Control Center headphones. Key in your password. Now that you've logged in, you can see and hear everything that your Toy Space Shuttle is doing. You can even direct your Toy Space Shuttle to take photos of the Earth. It's truly amazing!

Let's  About...

Are there any exaggerated statements in this advertisement?
Persuasive Text

349

Ever wondered what Iceland looks like? Direct your Toy Space Shuttle to fly above it. Punch in the code to tell your Toy Space Shuttle to take some pictures of Iceland. Then download the photos to your computer. Whatever fun you've ever had in your life, there is no way it compares to this!

It's even better if your friend also has a Toy Space Shuttle. Then, you can view each other's shuttle missions. You can even arrange for your Toy Space Shuttles to meet up in orbit! How cool is that?

When you're ready to have your Toy Space Shuttle come back, simply key in the code for HOME. This tells the Toy Space Shuttle to head on home. You can monitor your shuttle's progress from your Mission Control Center. You can even program the Toy Space Shuttle to fly into your bedroom window. Just be sure to leave your window open!

Here's what one happy customer had to say about the Toy Space Shuttle:

"Ever since I got the Toy Space Shuttle, I have been smiling twenty-four hours a day. I rush home from school in order to check in at Mission Control. Will my shuttle be flying near Asia today? or Australia? I can't wait to find out. Because of the Toy Space Shuttle, I have become really interested in space travel. I think I may want to become an astronaut. And I owe it all to this remarkable invention."

Parents will love the Toy Space Shuttle too. One parent who bought it said, "We used to get

Let's **Think** About...

Why does the Toy Space Shuttle make the customer happy?
Persuasive Text

Let's **Think** About...

How does the author use comparison in this argument?
Persuasive Text

350

our children all these fancy toys, which they would misplace or lose. But with the Toy Space Shuttle, we know exactly where that toy is. All we have to do is look at the Mission Control Center."

There is something wonderful about having a toy that can go into orbit. Every time your Toy Space Shuttle comes home, you can give it a hug. It's pretty amazing to have a toy that has flown so high!

In short, if you want to have fun, if you want to learn about space, if you want to be happy, you should run out and buy the Toy Space Shuttle. It is more exciting than any video game. It is more educational than any book about space travel. It is the invention of the century.

So get your Toy Space Shuttle now before they're all gone! For a special price of just $10,000, you will agree that this fabulous and amazing toy is well worth the money.

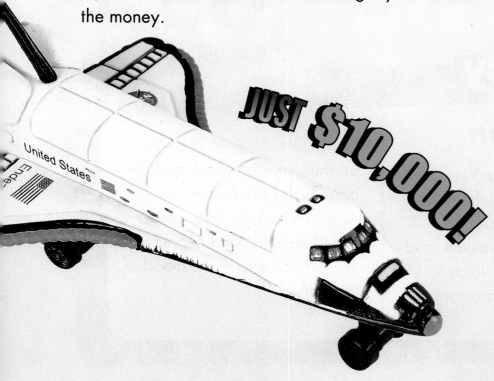

JUST $10,000!

United States

Let's **Think** About...

What is misleading or contradictory about the paragraphs on this page?
Persuasive Text

Let's **Think** About...

Reading Across Texts Look back at *The Fabulous Perpetual Motion Machine* and "The Toy Space Shuttle Is Here!" Why do you think inventions are so useful to people? List your reasons.

Writing Across Texts Create your own invention and write about it. Why would your invention be useful to people?

Objectives

● Read aloud grade-level texts and understand what is read. ● Identify and explain the meaning of common adages and sayings. ● Listen to and interpret a speaker's messages and ask questions. ● Give organized presentations that communicate your ideas effectively. ● Participate in discussions by raising and considering suggestions from other group members and by identifying points of agreement and disagreement.

Let's **Learn** It!

READING STREET ONLINE
ONLINE STUDENT EDITION
www.ReadingStreet.com

Vocabulary

Adages and Sayings

An adage is a short but memorable saying that expresses a meaningful idea. For example, "One bad apple spoils the bunch" means that people often remember bad things instead of good things. Other sayings you know may also have meanings.

Practice It! Reread *Perpetual Motion Machine* and think about adages and other sayings you know that could apply to the play's theme or to what it takes to make an invention. Identify and explain each adage and saying that you come up with.

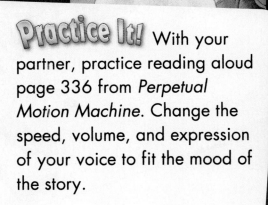

Fluency

Expression

Partner Reading You can use your voice to differentiate the speakers as you read. Change the tone, volume, and expression of your voice to reflect different characters.

Practice It! With your partner, practice reading aloud page 336 from *Perpetual Motion Machine*. Change the speed, volume, and expression of your voice to fit the mood of the story.

352

Listening and Speaking

Listen closely to determine the main and supporting ideas in a speaker's message.

Play Review

A play review offers an opinion of a drama, and makes a recommendation about it.

Practice It! Prepare a review of *The Fabulous Perpetual Motion Machine*. Give your opinion of the play, and tell whether classmates should see it or read it. Support your opinion with details from the play. Then present your review to the class.

Tips

Listening . . .

- Interpret a speaker's message.
- Ask questions to clarify a speaker's opinion of the play.

Speaking . . .

- Use speaking rate to communicate with the audience.
- Make eye contact with your listeners.

Teamwork . . .

- Ask for suggestions from others.
- Talk about what you agree and disagree on.

Oral Vocabulary

Let's Talk About

Art and Artists

● Share opinions about art and artists.

● Listen to a classmate's ideas about art.

● Ask a classmate questions about art.

READING STREET ONLINE
CONCEPT TALK VIDEO
www.ReadingStreet.com

Objectives
- Summarize the main ideas and supporting details in a text.
- Evaluate the effects of sensory details, imagery, and figurative language in literary text.

Envision It! | **Skill Strategy**

Skill

Strategy

READING STREET ONLINE
ENVISION IT! ANIMATIONS
www.ReadingStreet.com

Comprehension Skill

Main Idea and Details

- The main idea is the most important idea about a topic. Details are small pieces of information that tell more about the main idea.

- Sometimes the author states the main idea of a paragraph or an entire article in a single sentence at the beginning, middle, or end.

- Use a graphic organizer like the one below to help you summarize and maintain the meanings of main ideas and supporting details from "Bronze" on page 357. Be sure to keep the ideas and details in logical order.

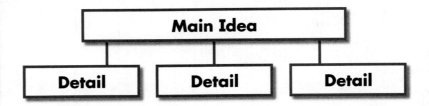

Comprehension Strategy

Visualize

Active readers visualize as they read. They use the details from the text to make pictures in their minds. For example, when you read nonfiction text, visualizing some of the supporting details can help you understand information. As you read, evaluate the impact the sensory details and imagery have on the story.

356

Bronze

People have used bronze for thousands of years to make many things. Bronze is a soft metal made from copper and tin. It cannot be hammered or bent, so it is not a good material for making tools. However, in molten or liquid form, it can be shaped into things such as statues, pots, and bowls.

Skill What is the main idea of this paragraph?

Thousands of years ago, bronze was shaped using the "lost-wax method." In this method, a model was made using plaster or clay. Then it was coated in wax followed by another layer of plaster or clay. When heated, the wax melted away, leaving a space. The bronze was melted and poured into the space. When the bronze cooled, the plaster or clay was taken off. Using this method, only one item could be made from the model.

Strategy As you read the details in this paragraph, what pictures or images do you visualize? How does this help you understand the information presented?

In time, molds were formed out of other materials, such as wood. A wooden mold could be used again and again. It was pressed into sand, and when it was removed, the impression was left in the sand. Bronze was poured into the sand. Later, the bronze was removed, and the surface was smoothed.

Skill Write the main idea of this paragraph in your own words.

Bronze is still used today. You may even have some items made from bronze in your home!

Your Turn!

‖ Need a Review? See the *Envision It! Handbook* for help with main idea and visualizing.

▷ Ready to Try It? Use what you've learned about main idea and visualizing as you read *Leonardo's Horse*.

Objectives

● Determine the meaning of English words with roots from Greek, Latin, and other languages.

Envision It! | Words to Know

architect

bronze

cannon

achieved

depressed

fashioned

midst

philosopher

rival

READING STREET ONLINE
VOCABULARY ACTIVITIES
www.ReadingStreet.com

Vocabulary Strategy for

🎯 Greek and Latin Roots

Word Structure Many words in English, particularly academic vocabulary words, are based on Greek and Latin roots. For example, the Greek root *bio* means "life." The Latin word *canna* means "reed or tube." When you see a longer word you do not understand, look for a root that can help you figure out the meaning.

1. Look at the word. Try to identify its root.

2. Think of words you know where this same root appears, and then try to determine a meaning for the word.

3. Try the meaning in place of the unfamiliar word and see if it makes sense in the sentence.

Read "They Called It the Renaissance." Use your knowledge of Greek and Latin roots to help you determine the meanings of words such as *architect*, *philosopher*, or *achieved*.

Words to Write Reread "They Called It the Renaissance." Look at the illustrations in *Leonardo's Horse*. Write a paragraph about what you think he achieved. Use words from the *Words to Know* list in your writing.

They Called It the RENAISSANCE

The Middle Ages ran from about 500 A.D. to about 1450 A.D. This was a time that might have depressed anyone. People in Europe looked back at the past instead of forward to the future.

But by 1450, people had stopped thinking only about the past and started looking ahead to what might be achieved in the future. This new age was known as the Renaissance.

Inventors started coming up with exciting new inventions. The title *philosopher* became important again, as thinkers explored new ways to enrich people's lives. The architect became an important figure as beautiful new buildings took shape in cities and towns across Europe. Artists fashioned powerful sculptures and painted vivid paintings that looked natural and real.

In the midst of all this growth and change, of course, there was still fighting. Art was the glory of the age, but war was the harsh reality. Bronze might be used to make a beautiful statue or a deadly cannon. People were sailing off to find new lands. A nation might become a rival of another nation, fighting for land in the Americas. In so many ways, people in the Renaissance were preparing for the modern world.

Your Turn!

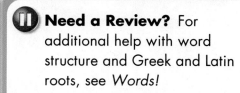

Need a Review? For additional help with word structure and Greek and Latin roots, see *Words!*

Ready to Try It? Read *Leonardo's Horse* on pp. 360–377.

BY JEAN FRITZ

ILLUSTRATED BY HUDSON TALBOTT

LEONARDO'S HORSE

Question of the Week
**How do artists inspire
future generations?**

Genre

A **biography** is a story of a person's life
written by another person. As you read, notice
all the major events in Leonardo da Vinci's life.

361

ANYONE who watched the young Leonardo wander the countryside around his home in Vinci might have guessed that he would be an artist. He stopped to examine everything. He looked at the landscape as if he were memorizing it. So it was no surprise when his father took him as a young teenager to Florence to study art.

363

People noticed that Leonardo was different.

He dressed differently. While other young men wore long togas, Leonardo wore short, rose-colored velvet togas.

He wrote differently. Backwards. From the right side of the paper to the left. A person would have to use a mirror to read his writing.

And he wouldn't eat meat. He liked animals too much to eat anything that had once been alive. Nor could he stand the sight of caged birds. If he saw a man selling birds, he would buy them all. Then he would open the cages and watch the birds fly away. What a flurry they made! How did they do it? All his life Leonardo tried to discover their secret of flying so he could make a flying machine for himself.

For a man who liked to ask questions, Leonardo da Vinci was born at the right time—April 15, 1452. Everybody was asking questions then. The age was called the Renaissance, a time of rebirth when people who had forgotten how to be curious became curious again. They were exploring new countries, discovering, inventing, looking at old things in new ways. What was the point, Leonardo asked, in copying what had already been done? He had to bring his own experience into whatever he painted. You wouldn't catch him putting a halo around the head of a saint. How could he? He had never seen a halo.

Leonardo da Vinci turned out to be a famous artist; still, he was not just an artist. He could never be just one thing. He was an engineer, an architect, a musician, a philosopher, an astronomer. Once he fashioned a special kind of flute made of silver in the shape of a horse's head. The ruler of Florence, Lorenzo de' Medici, asked him to deliver it as a gift to the duke of Milan. This was lucky for Leonardo. He had heard that the duke of Milan wanted to honor his father with a bronze horse in front of his palace. And Leonardo wanted to be the one to make it.

Temporary bridge

Eight-gun cannon

Armored tank

This would be his mark on history. Hundreds of years later people would point to the horse. "Leonardo made that," they would say.

So he wrote to the duke, listing all the things that he could do. He could make cannons, lightweight bridges, and covered chariots that couldn't be broken or harmed. On and on he went, but he saved the most important point for the last. He could make a bronze horse. In the end, he didn't send the letter. He simply left for Milan. Never mind that he was in the midst of painting a large religious picture in Florence. Let someone else finish it. He had planned the picture and that was the important part.

War chariot

Exploding
cannonballs

Cannon

Parachute

Catapult

Leonardo was thirty years old now, handsome with curly blond hair. The duke gave him the job of working on the horse, but at the same time he was expected to take charge of entertainment in the palace. He had a beautiful singing voice, he could play musical instruments, he could juggle and ask riddles, and he was also asked to stage elaborate plays for special occasions. Whenever he had a chance, he went back to the horse.

He visited the stables, studying how a horse was put together.

He needed to understand everything about his subject. He measured and drew pictures until he knew where all the bones and muscles of a horse were. But you couldn't show all the muscles on a statue, he said, or the horse would look like a bag of turnips. You should show only those muscles the horse was using or getting ready to use.

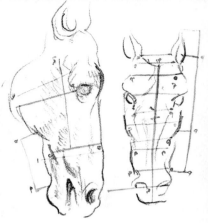

He visited statues of horses. Many were shown in an amble—left front leg moving at the same time as the left back leg. This was not easy for a horse; he had to be taught to do it. Leonardo saw one horse, however, that he described as free—left front leg and right back leg moving together, in a trot. Moreover, both ears were pointed forward. (Some horses pointed one ear back to hear the rider's orders.)

Leonardo was ready to begin.

But the duke wasn't quite ready. He wanted a much bigger horse than the one he had originally planned. One three times larger than life. Could Leonardo manage anything that large? the duke wondered. He wrote to Lorenzo, asking him to recommend someone who could do the job.

Lorenzo replied: Leonardo da Vinci was the only one.

On April 23, 1490, Leonardo wrote in his notebook: "I resumed work on the horse." The hardest part would be the casting. He collected 58,000 pounds of metal—tin and copper—which would be heated until it was fluid. This would be turned into bronze and used to cast the horse. But should he pour the bronze all at once? No one had tried a single pouring of anything this large.

In November 1493, he had completed the clay model—
twenty-four feet high. It was shown off at one of the duke's
special occasions, and it was a sensation.

But Leonardo seemed to be in no hurry to start casting. Perhaps he wasn't sure how he'd do it. Besides, he was planning a new project.

Later, in 1498, there were rumors that the French were preparing to invade Milan, and the duke wanted to be ready. And there was all the metal that Leonardo had collected. Just what the duke needed. So he sent it off to be made into cannon. Well, this is war, Leonardo reasoned. What else could they do?

When the French came in 1499, Leonardo and the duke fled. But the horse couldn't leave. There he was when the French arrived. The archers laughed. Never would they find as perfect a target, they said. Pulling back the strings on their bows, they let their arrows fly. Ping! Ping! Ping! The horse sagged. Ping!

Then it rained. And the horse became smaller and smaller.

At last it was nothing but a pile of mud stuck with arrows.

Leonardo went back to inventing and painting, but he never forgot his horse.

He still wanted to invent a flying machine. But he still couldn't do it.

His greatest disappointment, however, was his horse.

As Leonardo became older, his hair turned white and grew down to his shoulders. His beard reached to his waist.

And he became depressed. What had he achieved? he asked himself. He complained to his notebook: "Tell me," he asked, "if anything has been achieved by me. Tell me. Tell me." It was especially hard when his rival, Michelangelo, taunted him.

"You," Michelangelo said, "who made a model of a horse you could never cast in bronze and which you gave up, to your shame."

In his notebook Leonardo mourned, "I have wasted my hours."

On May 2, 1519, Leonardo da Vinci died. It was said that even on his deathbed, Leonardo wept for his horse.

In 1977 Charles Dent, an American and a big fan of Leonardo, saw a magazine article about him. When he read that Leonardo died grieving for his horse, Charles said, "Let's give Leonardo his horse."

But Charles Dent died before work was finished. Later, a sculptor from New York City, Nina Akamu, carried on with Charles's dream. Many people contributed money to help her finish. Finally, on September 10, 1999, in Milan, Italy, in front of huge crowds, the horse was unveiled.

At last Leonardo's horse was home.

Envision It! Retell

READING STREET ONLINE
STORY SORT
www.ReadingStreet.com

Think Critically

1. Imagine that you are an artist like Leonardo. How would you feel if you were unable to complete a challenging project? Why do you think you would feel this way? **Text to Self**

2. Jean Fritz's biographies put readers right there with the subject of each book. Identify examples from the selection that made you feel as if you were right beside da Vinci. **Think Like an Author**

3. What is the author's main idea in this selection? She shows how da Vinci was brilliant, but what else does she show about the kind of person he was? Look back at the text to answer the question. **Main Idea**

4. Think about what happened to the clay model of Leonardo's horse. Describe how the visual details helped you understand what happened. Look back at page 372 to help you. **Visualize**

5. **Look Back and Write** Look back at pages 376–377. Did Leonardo da Vinci's greatest dream ever come true? Provide evidence to support your answer.
   TEST PRACTICE Extended Response

Meet the Author

JEAN FRITZ

Jean Fritz writes books about history because she enjoys doing research. She says, "For every book I write, I have to read a great deal and usually travel to the place where that person lived. It's like being a detective. I want to find the truth, so I never make up anything in these books, not even conversation. If you see quotation marks, you can be sure I have a source for them."

While writing *Leonardo's Horse*, Ms. Fritz went to Italy. She was there when the twenty-four-foot bronze horse was presented as a gift from the people of the United States to the people of Italy. She says, "It was one of my most exciting adventures."

Although Ms. Fritz today lives along the Hudson River in New York, she spent her childhood in China. She heard her parents' stories about the United States and felt a need to know all she could about the United States, both past and present. Many of her biographies are about people important in U.S. history, such as George Washington, Benjamin Franklin, and Harriet Beecher Stowe.

Ms. Fritz says, "I get letters from readers sometimes who say they like the way I add 'fun' to history. I don't add anything. It's all true, because past times were just as filled with exciting events and 'fun' stories as are present times."

Here are other books by Jean Fritz.

Bully for You, Teddy Roosevelt!

Can't You Make Them Behave, King George?

Use the *Reader's and Writer's Notebook* to record your independent reading.

Objectives

- Write essays that help the reader understand key ideas and details.
- Use and understand the function of verbs (irregular verbs and active voice). • Write persuasive essays that take a position on a topic.

Let's Write It!

Key Features of a Persuasive Speech

- attempts to get support for an idea
- states the main position in the topic sentence
- uses examples and evidence to support position

READING STREET ONLINE
GRAMMAR JAMMER
www.ReadingStreet.com

Persuasive Speech

A **persuasive speech** is an attempt to get others to agree with and support your ideas. The student model on the next page is an example of a persuasive speech.

Writing Prompt Think about modern inventions. Which recent invention changed people's lives the most? Write a persuasive speech that answers this question.

Writer's Checklist

Remember, you should ...

✓ establish a position.

✓ use detailed and relevant evidence.

✓ guide and inform readers' understanding of evidence.

✓ show reasons for your argument in order of importance.

✓ use active voice to make your meaning clear to readers.

380

Computers: Modern Marvels

Computers have changed the modern world more than any other invention. Using a computer, people write reports, draw pictures, send e-mail, read the news, network, play games, create graphs, and conduct research. There is no modern invention that affects life in the same way.

Computers are so useful that they have replaced many other devices. Typewriters still can be found in museums and attics, but people rarely use them anymore, because computers are faster and easier to use. Some people even use computers to make low-cost telephone calls.

Computers also act as clocks, calendars, and file cabinets. You can find out what the weather is like all over the world at any time. You can get up-to-date baseball scores or the latest news or recent music downloads. You can even watch television programs on your computer!

In conclusion, people use computers every day to perform all sorts of tasks. They certainly have changed the way we do almost everything today.

Writing Trait
The introductory paragraph provides a clearly defined **focus** and is written with an active voice.

The **principal parts of regular verbs** are used correctly.

Genre
A **persuasive speech** uses detailed and relevant evidence to convince others of your position.

Conventions

Principal Parts of Regular Verbs

Remember Verbs have a **present** form (*I talk*), a **present participle** (*I am talking*), a **past** (*I talked*), and a **past participle** (*I have talked*). With **active voice,** the subject does the action (*Jon loves pizza*).

Objectives
● Explain how historical events or movements can affect the theme of a work of literature. ● Explain the roles and functions of characters, including their relationships and conflicts. ● Explain different forms of third-person points of view in stories.

Social Studies in Reading

Genre
Historical Fiction

● Historical fiction is a story set in a particular historical period.

● In historical fiction, the background of the story is based on fact, but the story itself is fiction.

● Historical fiction is often written with a third-person point of view. The narrator employs words such as *he, she, it,* and *they.*

● Read the story "A Job for Michelangelo." As you read, think about how the author employs elements of historical events or movements in the story.

A Job for *Michelangelo*
by Richard Foster

"Michelangelo! Michelangelo!" called Signor Buonarroti. "Where are you?"

"I'm here, Father," Michelangelo said, putting down a sculpture he was making.

His father sighed. "You are almost a grown-up. It's time to put away such foolish things. Stop dreaming of becoming an artist. That is no profession for a boy from a good family. You shall go into government, like me."

"It's just that I want to spend my life creating art," the boy replied sadly.

"Well, you can't. It's a peasant's job. Now, don't look so glum!" his father chided. "Not every boy is as lucky as you are.

382

Here we are in Florence, the city of the powerful Medici family. It is 1488. You have a wonderful future ahead of you. If you go into government, you might even get to know the Medicis!"

Later that day, Michelangelo went for a walk. He loved to study people's faces as he strolled through Florence. He stopped in the corner of a *piazza,* or neighborhood square. He took out some paper and a piece of charcoal, and began to sketch a face he had seen. He had seen the face only for a second, but he could sketch it perfectly from memory.

Suddenly he felt the presence of someone standing behind him. Michelangelo cringed. He did not want another lecture from his father.

But then he heard an unfamiliar voice. The voice said, "Not bad. Not bad at all."

Michelangelo looked up. The voice belonged to Domenico Ghirlandaio, the most famous painter in all of Florence. "How old are you, young man?"

"Thirteen," Michelangelo answered nervously.

"Thirteen, and not yet an apprentice?" Signor Ghirlandaio exclaimed. All boys in Florence were already learning a trade at this age.

"My father says I am to go into government, like him," Michelangelo explained, his voice sad and dull.

"We'll see about that," said Signor Ghirlandaio.

Let's **Think** About...

How does the historical period influence the conflict between Michelangelo and his father?
Historical Fiction

Michelangelo led Ghirlandaio to his family's home. He told a servant to ask his father to come outside.

When Michelangelo's father saw Signor Ghirlandaio, he looked surprised. After greeting the artist, he said, "It is an honor to have a visit from Florence's greatest artist. But what brings you here, good sir?"

"Your son's talent," explained Ghirlandaio. "I should like him to become my apprentice."

Signor Buonarroti was surprised. "*Your* apprentice?"

The artist nodded. "Your son has a tremendous gift. One day, he may be even a better artist than me."

"You are too kind," his father said. "But I am afraid it is quite impossible. My son will go into government or law, just as I have done. I want him to move among great men. This is a time of great wealth for Florence. I want my son to have part of that for himself."

Signor Ghirlandaio smiled at Michelangelo's father. "In times past, being an artist was the job of a peasant. That is true. But times have changed. The great Medicis are spending huge amounts of money on art. Why, I work directly with members of the Medici family. If your son works with me, so will he."

Let's **Think** About...

How is the historical movement Ghirlandaio talks about important to the story?
Historical Fiction

384

Michelangelo's father looked stunned. The Medici family was the wealthiest family in Florence. They built marvelous churches and palaces. "Did you say that my son will meet the Medici family?"

"Of course. And in time, perhaps they will sponsor him as they have sponsored me!"

"Father, please. To sculpt, to draw, to paint. It is my dream," Michelangelo pleaded.

His father took a deep breath. "Very well. You may apprentice with Signor Ghirlandaio for three years."

Things worked out very well for Michelangelo. After just one year working for Ghirlandaio, he had learned everything the master artist could teach him. After that, Lorenzo de Medici paid Michelangelo to create art. Lorenzo had a wonderful ancient art collection. Looking at ancient Roman statues gave Michelangelo many ideas. He used these ideas to create a renaissance, or a rebirth, of art.

Michelangelo became a famous and wealthy artist. More importantly, he spent his life doing what he loved: creating beautiful works of art.

Let's **Think** About...

What kind of third-person narrator is used in this story? How can you tell?
Historical Fiction

Let's **Think** About...

Reading Across Texts List some traits that made Leonardo da Vinci and Michelangelo different from other artists.

Writing Across Texts Use your list to write a paragraph that describes why da Vinci and Michelangelo were such unique artists.

385

Objectives

● Read aloud grade-level texts and understand what is read. ● Determine the meaning of English words with roots from Greek, Latin, and other languages. ● Examine the different techniques used in media. ● Listen to and interpret a speaker's messages and ask questions. ● Identify the main ideas and supporting ideas in the speaker's message. ● Use and understand the function of verbs (active voice).

Let's Learn It!

READING STREET ONLINE
ONLINE STUDENT EDITION
www.ReadingStreet.com

Vocabulary

Greek and Latin Roots

Word Structure Many English words contain roots, or word parts, from Greek, Latin, and other languages. These roots can help you figure out the meanings of words.

Practice It! The Greek root *arch* means "chief" or "first." The Latin root *capit* means "head," and the word *cocoa* comes from the Spanish word *cacao*. List words and their meanings that are formed from these roots, or roots from other languages. Then trade lists with a partner. Did you both list many of the same words?

Fluency

Rate

Partner Reading You can use different reading rates to express the mood and tone in a text. Reading more slowly adds emphasis. Reading more quickly adds energy and excitement.

Practice It! With a partner, practice reading a page from *Leonardo's Horse*. Focus on reading at an appropriate rate. Take turns reading and offering each other feedback.

Media Literacy

When you give a presentation, speak loudly and clearly.

Newscast

In a newscast, reporters tell news stories. The purpose of a newscast is to inform people about important events.

Practice It! With a group, create a newscast about Leonardo's horse. Include information about the horse that will help viewers understand its significance. Then deliver your newscast to the class, and discuss how a newscast differs from online news.

Tips

Listening . . .

- Listen to and interpret the speaker's message and gestures.

- Determine the newscast's main ideas and supporting details.

Speaking . . .

- Use and understand active voice in your newscast.

- Make eye contact with your listeners.

Teamwork . . .

- Ask for suggestions from others.

- Identify where you agree and disagree with others.

Objectives
- Listen to and interpret a speaker's messages and ask questions.
- Identify the main ideas and supporting ideas in the speaker's message.

Oral Vocabulary

Let's Talk About

Dinosaurs and Paleontology

- Share what you know about dinosaurs and paleontology.

- Listen to and interpret a classmate's knowledge of dinosaurs and paleontology.

- Determine main and supporting ideas in your classmates' messages.

READING STREET ONLINE
CONCEPT TALK VIDEO
www.ReadingStreet.com

You've learned
1 2 0
Amazing Words
so far this year!

Objectives
• Identify the facts in a text and prove that they are facts. • Set a purpose for reading a text based on what you hope to get from the text.

Envision It! Skill Strategy

Skill

Strategy

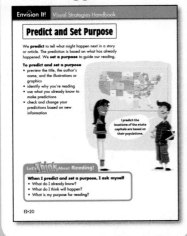

READING STREET ONLINE
ENVISION IT! ANIMATIONS
www.ReadingStreet.com

Comprehension Skill

Fact and Opinion

• You can prove statements of fact true or false by verifying them with your own knowledge, asking an expert, or checking a reference source.

• An opinion gives ideas or feelings, not facts, and cannot be proved true or false.

• A sentence may contain both a statement of fact and a statement of opinion.

• Use a graphic organizer like the one below to help you determine and verify facts in "Dinosaurs" on page 391.

> **Statement— Can it be proved true or false?**
>
> **Opinion—No** **Fact—Yes** **How to check?**

Comprehension Strategy

Predict and Set Purpose

Active readers try to predict what they will learn when they read a nonfiction article. This helps them establish a purpose for why they are reading the article. Previewing an article is a good way to predict what you will be reading and to establish your purpose for reading. Establishing a purpose for reading can help you understand a text.

DINOSAURS

By far the most fascinating creatures ever to walk the Earth were the dinosaurs. Their name comes from two Greek words that mean "terrible lizard." When you see drawings or models of certain dinosaurs, it is very easy to understand how they got their name.

Skill There are two statements of opinion in this paragraph. Identify one of them.

Types of dinosaurs Some dinosaurs were herbivores, meaning that they ate only plants. Apatosaurus and Iguanodon were herbivores. Other dinosaurs were carnivores, or meat eaters. The most feared dinosaur of all, Tyrannosaurus, was a carnivore.

Strategy Preview the title and the headings. What will this article be about? What is your purpose for reading it?

Dinosaur characteristics Dinosaurs were marked by special body features. Stegosaurus had armor it used for protection. Pterosaur had wings like a bat's. Tyrannosaurus had strong back legs but short, weak front ones.

Skill Which statements are facts in this paragraph? What could you use to check whether they are true or false?

What happened to the dinosaurs? No one knows for sure, though there are several ideas about why they disappeared. Some of these ideas are as interesting as the dinosaurs themselves.

Your Turn!

 Need a Review? See the *Envision It! Handbook* for additional help with the skill and strategy.

▶ **Ready to Try It?** Use what you learned as you read *The Dinosaurs of Waterhouse Hawkins.*

Objectives
• Determine the meanings of unfamiliar words or multiple-meaning words by using the context of the sentence.

mold

tidied

workshop

erected

foundations

occasion

proportion

READING STREET ONLINE
VOCABULARY ACTIVITIES
www.ReadingStreet.com

Vocabulary Strategy for

🎯 Homonyms

Context Clues Homonyms are words with the same spelling but different origins and meanings. You can use context to help figure out their meanings. The words and sentences around the homonym offer clues.

1. Read the words and sentences around the homonym to find clues.

2. Think about the homonym's different meanings. For example, the word *bill* can mean "a statement of money owed" or "the beak of a bird."

3. Try each meaning in the sentence and decide which meaning makes sense.

Read "The Artist of the Hour" on page 393. Use context clues to help you determine and clarify the meanings of homonyms.

Words to Write Reread "The Artist of the Hour." How would you make a model of a dinosaur? Write an explanation and the steps in your plan. Use words from the *Words to Know* list in your writing.

The Artist of the Hour

Imagine that you are an artist at work in your workshop. You have been asked to make a sculpture for the new hospital. When people look at this sculpture, they are supposed to think about freedom and hope. You have decided to make a group of birds in flight.

First, you make a clay shape of each bird. You must measure carefully to be sure the proportion of the wings to the body is just right. Then you cover the shapes with melted plastic and let it get hard. Each mold has the exact shape of the bird you made. Next, you pour cement into each mold. After it hardens, any crumbs of cement and plastic must be tidied up. Then you have a whole bird shape.

Meanwhile, you have to build foundations for the birds. These are bases made of wood or cement, with iron pipes sticking up. When they are fastened to the rods, the birds will look as though they are sailing into the sky.

You hope your work of art will be erected in the flower garden at the hospital. When it is put in place, you will be honored for your work. There will be a party to celebrate the occasion.

Your Turn!

 Need a Review? For additional help with using context clues to determine and clarify the meanings of homonyms, see *Words!*

▶ **Ready to Try It?** Read *The Dinosaurs of Waterhouse Hawkins* on pp. 394–411.

THE DINO OF WATER

By **BARBARA KERLEY**
With drawings by **BRIAN SELZNICK**

THE DINO SAURS OF WATERHOUSE HAWKINS

A **biography** is a story of a person's life written by another person. As you read about Waterhouse Hawkins, notice how the author presents major events in his life.

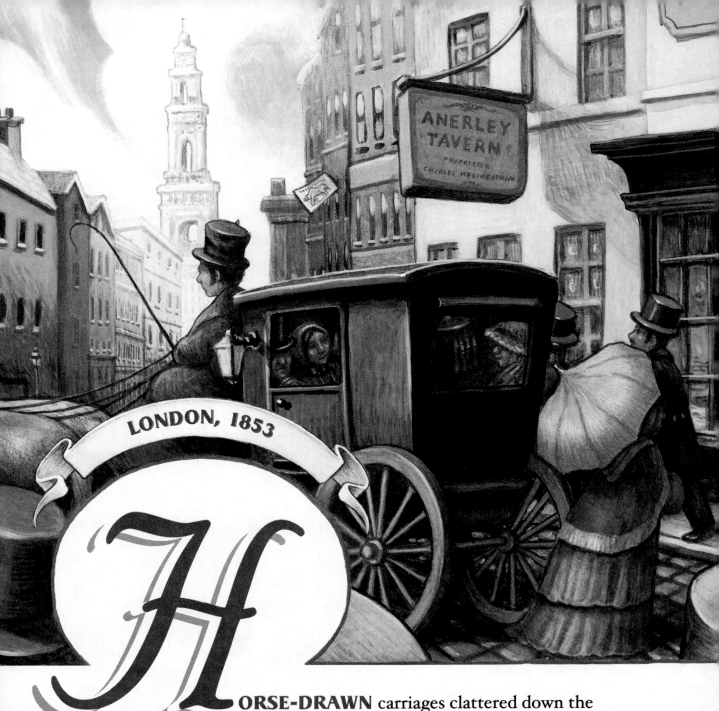

LONDON, 1853

HORSE-DRAWN carriages clattered down the streets of London in 1853. Gentlemen tipped their hats to ladies passing by. Children ducked and dodged on their way to school.

But Benjamin Waterhouse Hawkins had no time to be out and about. Waterhouse, as he liked to call himself, hurried toward his workshop in a park south of town. He was expecting some very important visitors. He didn't want to be late.

As he neared his workshop, Waterhouse thought of the hours he'd spent outside as a boy. Like many artists, he had grown up sketching the world around him. By the time he was a young man, he'd found his true passion: animals. He loved to draw and paint them. But what he really loved was sculpting models of them. Through his care and hard work, they seemed to come to life.

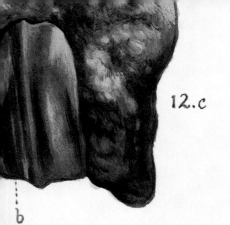

12.c

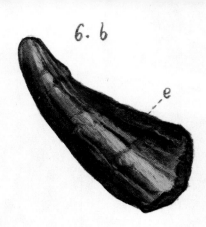

6. b

4. a

Now Waterhouse was busy with a most exciting project: He was building dinosaurs! His creations would prowl the grounds of Queen Victoria and Prince Albert's new art and science museum, the Crystal Palace.

6.c

Even though the English had found the first known dinosaur fossil many years before—and the bones of more dinosaurs had been unearthed in England since then—in *1853*, most people had no idea what a dinosaur looked like.

Scientists weren't sure either, for the only fossils were some bits and pieces—a tooth here, a bone there. But they thought that if they studied a fossil and compared it to a living animal, they could fill in the blanks.

And so, with the help of scientist Richard Owen, who checked every muscle, bone, and spike, that's exactly what Waterhouse was doing. He wanted to create such perfect models that anyone—a crowd of curious children, England's leading scientists, even the Queen herself!—could gaze at his dinosaurs and see into the past.

6 e

Waterhouse threw open the doors to his workshop. Nervously, he tidied up here and there. His assistants came, then Richard Owen.

At last, the visitors arrived: Queen Victoria and Prince Albert!

The Queen's eyes grew wide in surprise. Waterhouse's creatures were extraordinary! How on earth had he made them?

He was happy to explain: The iguanodon, for instance, had teeth that were quite similar to the teeth of an iguana. The iguanodon, then, must surely have looked like a giant iguana. Waterhouse pointed out that the few iguanodon bones helped determine the model's size and proportion. And another bone—almost a spike—most likely sat on the nose, like a rhino's horn.

Just so for the megalosaurus. Start with its jawbone. Compare it to the anatomy of a lizard. Fill in the blanks. And voilà! A dinosaur more than forty feet long.

Waterhouse was also making ancient reptiles and amphibians. While Richard Owen could imagine their shapes, it took an artist to bring the animals to life.

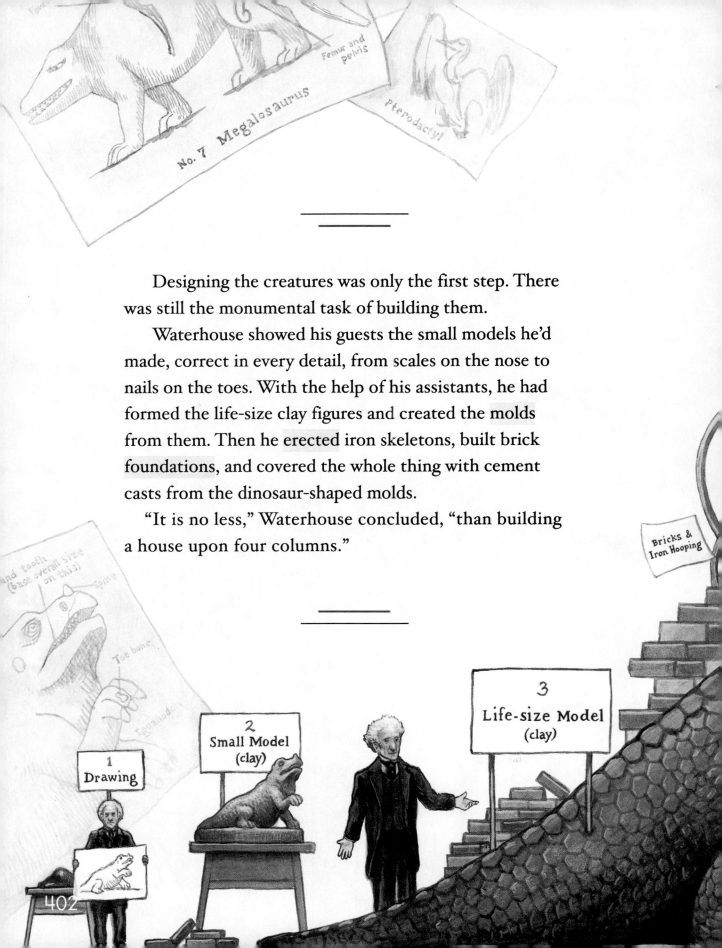

Designing the creatures was only the first step. There was still the monumental task of building them.

Waterhouse showed his guests the small models he'd made, correct in every detail, from scales on the nose to nails on the toes. With the help of his assistants, he had formed the life-size clay figures and created the molds from them. Then he erected iron skeletons, built brick foundations, and covered the whole thing with cement casts from the dinosaur-shaped molds.

"It is no less," Waterhouse concluded, "than building a house upon four columns."

No. 7 Megalosaurus

Femur and pelvis

Pterodactyl

and tooth size (base overall size on this)

Spine

Toe bone

Iguanodon

Bricks & Iron Hooping

1 Drawing

2 Small Model (clay)

3 Life-size Model (clay)

4
Mold

5
Iron Skeleton
(must support tons
of dinosaur)

6
Finished Dinosaur
(bricks, tiles and broken
stones, all held together
with cement, covered with
casts and painted)

Tiles &
Broken
Stones

403

In the weeks to follow, Waterhouse basked in the glow of the Queen's approval. But he would soon face a much tougher set of critics: England's leading scientists. Waterhouse wanted to be accepted into this circle of eminent men. What would they think of his dinosaurs?

There was only one way to find out. Waterhouse would show them. But why not do it with a little style?

A dinner party. On New Year's Eve, no less. And not just any dinner party. Waterhouse would stage an event that no one would ever forget!

He sketched twenty-one invitations to the top scientists and supporters of the day, the words inscribed on a drawing of a pterodactyl wing. He pored over menus with the caterer.

The iguanodon mold was hauled outside. A platform was built. A tent erected.

As the hour drew near, the table was elegantly set, and names of famous scientists—the fathers of paleontology—were strung above the tent walls. All was ready.

With great anticipation, Waterhouse dressed for the occasion in his finest attire. He was ready to reveal his masterpiece!

When the guests arrived, they gasped with delight!
Waterhouse smiled as he signaled for dinner to begin.
With solemn formality, the footmen served course after
course from silver platters. Up and down the steps of the
platform they carried the lavish feast: rabbit soup, fish,
ham, and even pigeon pie. For dessert, there were nuts,
pastries, pudding, and plums.

For eight hours, the men rang in the New Year. They laughed and shouted. They made speech after speech, toasting Waterhouse Hawkins. All the guests agreed: The iguanodon was a marvelous success. By midnight they were belting out a song created especially for the occasion:

THE JOLLY OLD BEAST IS NOT DECEASED
THERE'S LIFE IN HIM AGAIN!

407

The next months passed by in concrete, stone, and iron, as Waterhouse put the finishing touches on his dinosaurs. Inside the iguanodon's lower jaw he signed the work: B. HAWKINS, BUILDER, 1854. The models were now ready for the grand opening of the Crystal Palace at Sydenham Park.

Forty thousand spectators attended the regal ceremony. In the sun-filled center court, Waterhouse mingled with scientists and foreign dignitaries. At last, the Queen arrived! The crowd cheered, "Hurrah!"

Cannons boomed, music swelled, and a choir of one thousand voices sang. Waterhouse bowed before the Queen. Then she and Prince Albert invited the spectators to enjoy the amazing sights.

Waterhouse hurried to the lake and waited for the crowd to arrive.

First two, then ten, then a dozen more . . . Gasped! Shrieked! Laughed and cried: So this was a dinosaur!

AFTERWORD

In 1868, Waterhouse traveled to the United States to create the first-ever model of a complete dinosaur skeleton. The model went on display to amazed visitors of Philadelphia's Academy of Natural Sciences. Waterhouse also worked on making more dinosaur sculptures for a museum in New York City's Central Park. But before he could finish, vandals broke into his workshop, smashed the models to pieces, and buried them in the park. Today, pieces of the dinosaurs of Waterhouse Hawkins are still buried somewhere in Central Park.

Envision It! Retell

READING STREET ONLINE
STORY SORT
www.ReadingStreet.com

Think Critically

1. Waterhouse Hawkins's dinosaurs were considered a remarkable artistic and scientific achievement in the 1800s. What modern-day artistic or scientific achievement might be considered remarkable? How does it compare to Waterhouse Hawkins's dinosaurs? **Text to World**

2. This biography is about an artist and his art. It does not give personal information, such as whether Hawkins had children or liked to swim. Do you think this kind of information should be in the story or not? What do you think needs to be told in a biography?
Think Like an Author

3. Turn to pages 402 and 403. What facts did you learn about Waterhouse's method of constructing the dinosaur figure? Why do you think he expresses the opinion "It is no less than building a house upon four columns"? **Fact and Opinion**

4. Look back at page 398. What might lead readers to predict that Hawkins would one day amaze the people of Victorian England? **Predict and Set Purpose**

5. **Look Back and Write** Look back at the story. Describe the way Waterhouse Hawkins introduced the world to a new kind of creature. Provide evidence from the text to support your answer.
TEST PRACTICE Extended Response

BARBARA KERLEY and BRIAN SELZNICK

Barbara Kerley

Barbara Kerley says she got the idea for writing *The Dinosaurs of Waterhouse Hawkins* when her daughter asked how big a T. rex was. "I had no idea, so we got a book on dinosaurs from the library. In it was this incredible drawing of a dinner party, with formal waiters, candlesticks on the table, and all these elegant gentlemen stuffed into a dinosaur. I was hooked—I just had to find out the story behind that picture."

Brian Selznick

Once Ms. Kerley had written the manuscript, Brian Selznick got a call from his editor. She described *The Dinosaurs of Waterhouse Hawkins*. Mr. Selznick said the story left his head spinning, and all he could say was "I'll do it!" Mr. Selznick has also written and illustrated his own books.

Here are other books by Barbara Kerley and Brian Selznick.

A Week in the Woods by Andrew Clements, illustrated by Brian Selznick

Songs of Papa's Island by Barbara Kerley

Reading Log

Use the *Reader's and Writer's Notebook* to record your independent reading.

413

Objectives
● Write persuasive essays that take a position on a topic. ● Use and understand the function of verbs (irregular verbs and active voice).

Let's Write It!

Key Features of an Advertising Brochure

● asks readers to do something, such as buy a product or attend an event

● includes persuasive words or artwork to draw in readers

● may appeal to a specific audience

READING STREET ONLINE
GRAMMAR JAMMER
www.ReadingStreet.com

Advertising Brochure

An **advertising brochure** is a document that informs readers of an event or tries to convince them to buy a product. It is usually small in size and is often folded into parts. The student model on the next page is an example of an advertising brochure.

Writing Prompt *The Dinosaurs of Waterhouse Hawkins* tells about the introduction of dinosaur models to the world. Prepare an advertisement that entices people to come to one of the events.

Writer's Checklist

Remember, you should . . .

✓ describe the event.

✓ include details that show why the event would be important to attend.

✓ use convincing words to pull in readers.

✓ use verbs, including irregular verbs, to show a sense of action and excitement.

Step Back in Time

You have been <u>chosen</u> to attend
a New Year's Eve
dinner party like no other!

Dine on fabulous food,
meet fascinating scientists,
and best of all —
take a step back in time!

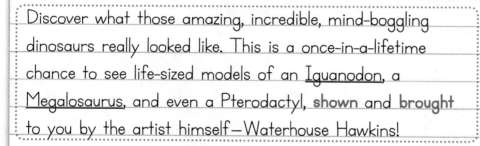

Discover what those amazing, incredible, mind-boggling
dinosaurs really looked like. This is a once-in-a-lifetime
chance to see life-sized models of an <u>Iguanodon</u>, a
<u>Megalosaurus</u>, and even a Pterodactyl, <u>shown</u> and <u>brought</u>
to you by the artist himself—Waterhouse Hawkins!

Let everyone know you're <u>going</u>! Reserve your seat today!

Genre
An **advertising brochure** tries to convince readers to attend an event or purchase a product.

Writing Trait Word Choice
Descriptive words make the event sound exciting.

Irregular verbs are used correctly.

Conventions

Principal Parts of Irregular Verbs

Remember Irregular verbs do not follow the rule of adding *-ed* to show past tense. For example, the irregular verb *write* becomes *writing* (present participle), *wrote* (past), and *written* (past participle). Use a dictionary to find irregular verb parts.

Objectives

● Identify the facts in a text and prove that they are facts. ● Use text features and graphics to gain an overview and locate information. ● Make connections between ideas within a text and across two or three texts.

Science in Reading

Genre
Expository Text

- An interview is a kind of expository text. An expository text contains facts and information about different subjects.

- In an interview, one person asks questions and the subject answers them.

- An expository text might contain graphics or illustrations that give an overview of the text's content.

- Read the interview "A Model Scientist." Look for elements that make this interview an expository text.

A Model SCIENTIST

FROM *OWL* MAGAZINE

Meet Garfield Minott. He's been making dinosaur models since he was seven years old. Back then, he made dinosaurs just for fun. Today, his passion for the prehistoric has turned into a cool and unusual dinosaur job.

Q: OWL: What exactly do you do?

A: Garfield: I'm a paleo-artist. I bring dinosaurs back to life!

Q: How do you do that?

A: I build real-life models of the dinosaurs scientists discover. My models help dinosaur scientists to gain a better understanding of these incredible creatures. I get bags of bones shipped to me from scientists, and I use these bones to plan my models. When it comes to learning about dino bones, nothing beats the real thing!

Q: What can you tell from a simple bone?

A: Lots of stuff! If you took all the muscles off of a bone, you'd be left with marks on the bone called "scarring." These marks tell me how the muscles were attached. Then, I can tell how the skin formed around the muscles. As I build up, layer after layer from the inside out, I can bring an animal back to life!

Q: How do you make your models?

A: Once I've researched in books and bones, I make a rough drawing. Then, I make a skeleton of the body out of welded steel. Next, I start layering on the muscles, which are made out of clay. When that's done, I start on the skin. If the dinosaur had scales, then I make the scales and layer them on one at a time. This could take three to five weeks. I want my dinosaur models to look as close as possible to the real thing.

Let's **Think** About...

Does the graphic of the dinosaur help you understand Garfield Minott's description about how he creates models? Why?
Expository Text

417

Let's Think About...

How is this interview organized? Why does this help you understand the interview's content?

Expository Text

Q: When did you become interested in models?

A: I've been making models ever since I was a kid growing up in Jamaica. My mom used to bake a lot and whenever she did, she would teach me how to mold things out of flour. In those days, I was crazy about lizards so that's mostly the kind of models I made.

Q: When did you get hooked on dinosaurs?

A: When I was seven years old my family moved to Canada. Because I was in a new country, I became a pretty shy kid. One day my teacher asked me what kind of animals I liked. Of course I said, "Lizards." She said, "Well, if you like lizards you must like dinosaurs." I had no idea what a dinosaur was. She took me to the library, pulled a book off the shelf, and showed me my first dinosaur. I went totally bananas!

Q: And you've been crazy about dinos ever since?

A: Yes! And I especially loved hearing all those long and crazy dinosaur names. *Tyrannosaurus rex* is my favorite. That name still makes me flip out!

Q: Did you ever imagine a career with dinosaurs?

A: When I was a kid, I had a kit that came with tiny models of dinosaurs. I used these models to play "dinosaurs" with friends. But, after a while I learned about more kinds of dinosaurs than I had in my kit—so I made the ones I didn't have out of Plasticine™. And, if my *T. rex* got hungry and ate a whole herd of models, I had to make new dinosaurs very quickly! I did this so often that I became good at building models in no time at all. That's how I became a model expert.

Let's **Think** About...

How did Garfield Minott's activities as a child lead him to become a model expert?
Expository Text

419

Q: How did model building become your job?

A: I found out about a paleo-artist who worked at the Royal Ontario Museum in Toronto. One day I went to meet him. He saw that I was interested in dinosaurs and a good model builder, so he suggested that I volunteer at the museum. I did, and I've been building models ever since.

Q: Do you wish dinosaurs still roamed Earth?

A: If they did, humans wouldn't be here. We'd be eaten! I'd like to see a live dinosaur on an island somewhere, and just observe it.

Let's Think About...

Read the last two pages and identify one dinosaur fact. How would you verify that fact?

Expository Text

420

Q: What's the coolest fact you've learned about dinosaurs?

A: Dinosaurs never stopped growing the way humans do. Some were as long as a football field! That's unbelievable. To me, dinosaurs are amazing.

Right now I'm working on a model of an Afro Titan. It's the biggest one I've ever made. I could lay down inside its head! If this dinosaur were alive, it could eat me whole in one bite.

Let's **Think** About...

Reading Across Texts Both Waterhouse and Garfield Minott enjoy what they do. Use details from each selection to show that this statement is true. Then think about how "Dinosaurs" on page 391 would help them with their art.

Writing Across Texts Present your results in three paragraphs, one for each selection.

Objectives

● Read aloud grade-level texts and understand what is read. ● Identify and explain the meaning of common idioms. ● Listen to and interpret a speaker's messages and ask questions. ● Participate in discussions by raising and considering suggestions from other group members and by identifying points of agreement and disagreement. ● Give organized presentations that communicate your ideas effectively.

Let's Learn It!

READING STREET ONLINE
ONLINE STUDENT EDITION
www.ReadingStreet.com

Vocabulary

Idioms

Context Clues An idiom is a phrase whose meaning cannot be understood from the ordinary meanings of the words that form it. For example, *at the eleventh hour* means "very late." You can use context to determine the meanings of common idioms.

Practice It! Look at the idiom "bits and pieces" on page 398 of *The Dinosaurs of Waterhouse Hawkins*. What does this idiom mean? What nearby words tell you what the idiom means? Identify and explain other common idioms in the story.

Fluency

Appropriate Phrasing

Partner Reading When you use appropriate phrasing, you group words together as you read, using punctuation as a guide.

Practice It! With your partner, practice reading a page from *Waterhouse Hawkins*. Make sure to use appropriate phrasing. Take turns reading and offering each other feedback.

Listening and Speaking

When you make a speech, use gestures to communicate your ideas.

Introduction

An introduction is an opener that announces a speaker or subject. Introductions should grab the audience's attention, and then explain what the subject is and why it is important, using details as evidence.

Practice It! Prepare a speech introducing Waterhouse's dinosaur display at the Crystal Palace. Make your introduction informative and dramatic. Use words that describe what the audience is about to see. Then present your speech to the class.

Tips

Listening . . .

- Listen to and interpret a speaker's messages and gestures.

- Ask questions to clarify a speaker's purpose.

Speaking . . .

- Speak loudly and enunciate.

- Use and understand irregular verbs.

Teamwork . . .

- Ask for and consider suggestions from other group members.

- Identify where you agree and disagree with others.

Objectives
• Listen to and interpret a speaker's messages and ask questions.
• Identify the main ideas and supporting ideas in the speaker's message.

Oral Vocabulary

Let's Talk About

Music and Musicians

- Share your opinions about music and musicians.

- Listen to and interpret a classmate's ideas about his or her favorite music.

- Determine classmates' main and supporting ideas about music.

READING STREET ONLINE
CONCEPT TALK VIDEO
www.ReadingStreet.com

You've learned
1 3 0
Amazing Words
so far this year!

Objectives

• Summarize the main ideas and supporting details in a text. • Analyze how the organization of a text affects the way ideas are related.

Envision It! | **Skill Strategy**

Skill

Strategy

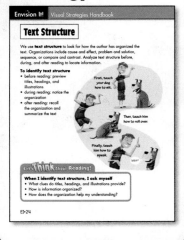

READING STREET ONLINE
ENVISION IT! ANIMATIONS
www.ReadingStreet.com

Comprehension Skill

Main Idea and Details

- The main idea is the most important idea about a topic.

- Sometimes the author tells you the main idea. Sometimes you must figure it out for yourself.

- Supporting details tell more about the main idea.

- Use a graphic organizer like the one below to help you summarize the main ideas and supporting details from "Aretha: An American Queen." Maintain the meaning of the ideas and details, and place them in logical order.

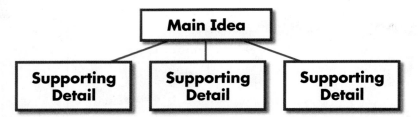

Comprehension Strategy

Text Structure

Text structure is the way a selection is organized. A selection may describe events in a sequence or in a cause-and-effect pattern. It may also use a series of main ideas and details. Active readers use text structure to help them understand what a selection is about.

Aretha
An American Queen

The United States is not ruled by a queen. There is a queen who rules in the hearts of American music lovers, though. That queen is Aretha Franklin.

Aretha Franklin was born in Memphis, Tennessee, in 1942. Both her parents were religious gospel music singers. Aretha grew up listening to gospel music. She also learned to sing it as a child.

Even when she was little, people saw that she was a talented singer. Aretha began singing on stage in her early teens. She sang with her father. Her first album, *The Gospel Sound of Aretha Franklin,* was released in 1956. She was only 14!

When Aretha turned 18, she moved to New York. Eventually, she developed her own style of singing. It came from deep inside her. It was a mixture of gospel and rhythm and blues. This music was called "soul music." Aretha sang it so well that she became known as "The Queen of Soul."

Aretha was voted into the Rock and Roll Hall of Fame in 1987. Her songs are still played on the radio today. For many people, she still rules as queen.

Skill In your own words, what is the main idea of this paragraph?

Skill What is the main idea of this paragraph? Give one detail that supports the main idea.

Strategy Explain how the sequential pattern in this text helped you understand what you read.

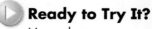
Your Turn!

⏸ **Need a Review?** See the *Envision It! Handbook* for additional help with main idea and text structure.

▶ **Ready to Try It?** Use what you learned as you read *Mahalia Jackson.*

Envision It! | Words to Know

barber

choir

teenager

appreciate
released
religious
slavery

READING STREET ONLINE
VOCABULARY ACTIVITIES
www.ReadingStreet.com

Vocabulary Strategy for

🎯 Antonyms

Context Clues Antonyms are words that have the opposite meanings of other words. For example, *fast* is an antonym for *slow*. Using context clues, or nearby words and sentences, can help you determine the meaning of an antonym.

1. Complete this analogy using one of the *Words to Know: gloomy* is to *cheerful* as *freedom* is to _____.

2. Reread the context around the word.

3. Look for an antonym that shows a contrast with the unfamiliar word.

4. Give the unfamiliar word the opposite meaning of the antonym. Does this meaning make sense in the sentence?

Read "Out of Great Pain, Great Music." Check the context of words you don't know. Look for antonyms to help you determine and clarify the meanings of unfamiliar words.

Words to Write Reread "Out of Great Pain, Great Music." Then look at the illustrations in *Mahalia Jackson.* Choose an illustration to write about. Use words from the *Words to Know* list in your writing.

Out of Great Pain, GREAT MUSIC

It is hard to understand how people in the United States ever put up with slavery, since Americans value freedom so highly. However, for some 250 years, African Americans were held as slaves. Every child of a slave, from infant to teenager, also became the owner's property. Slaves performed many jobs, from cook to field hand to barber.

Slavery caused great sorrow and pain, but it also gave rise to some of the world's most moving music. Spirituals are religious folk songs that began among slaves. They would sing these songs to help raise their spirits. Church gave them a place to express their hope for a better life to come. The choir made powerful music about that hope.

Slavery ended for African Americans some 140 years ago. But spirituals remain an important part of life for many African Americans today. People of many races and backgrounds have come to appreciate spirituals. Many people also love blues music, which also originated from the African American experience of slavery. Many African American singers have released recordings of blues music and spirituals that have sold millions of copies all around the world.

Your Turn!

❚❚ Need a Review? See *Words!* for additional support with antonyms.

▶ Ready to Try It? Read *Mahalia Jackson* on pp. 430–437.

from *The Blues Singers:*
Ten Who Rocked the World

Mahalia
JACKSON

by
Julius Lester

illustrated by
Lisa Cohen

Question of the Week
**How does an artist use
music to inspire others?**

Genre

Expository texts explain what certain things are and how they came to be. As you read, notice how the author explains a musical form known as the blues and how it came to be.

431

In this selection the author is talking to his granddaughter. He wants her to know about a kind of music that he loves, the blues.

First he explains that the blues is not just a feeling. It's a kind of music. Then he tells her about a great singer who knew all about the blues.

So what are the blues? Well, the blues are like having the flu in your feelings. But instead of your nose being stuffed up, it's your heart that feels like it needs blowing. Everybody gets the blues, even children.

But the blues is not only a feeling. It's also a kind of music that cures the blues. The words of a blues song might be sad, but the music and the beat wrap around your heart like one of your grandmother's hugs.

The roots of the blues go back to slavery. If anything would give you the blues, it was slavery. Imagine somebody owning you like I own my car. Just like I can sell my car to anybody who has the money, somebody could sell you and me the same way.

One of the ways black people fought against slavery was with the breath in their bodies. They wove hope on the air by singing songs called spirituals—songs for the spirit. Their bodies were in slavery, but it didn't mean their spirits had to be buried in sorrow as white as fog.

Slavery ended in 1865, but freedom didn't take its place. The people who had owned the slaves still owned the land. How could the slaves truly be free if they had to keep working for the same people who had owned them?

Blues music probably started something like this: Somebody was out in the field working one day. She knew she would be working from sunup to sundown on somebody's farm making fifty cents a day until the day she died. Thinking about it made her heart burn as if it had been struck by lightning. The pain was so bad she didn't know what to do, and suddenly she started singing.

> **Got a hurtin' in my heart, feels like I'm going to die,**
> **Got a hurtin' in my heart, feels like I'm going to die,**
> **I feel like a bird whose wings will never fly.**

Singing just those few words made her feel a little better, and everybody who heard her felt a little better too.

The blues IS LIFE And don't you forget it!

Aretha Franklin

Ray Charles

They took THE GOSPEL FEELING and put it into the BLUES.

Mahalia Jackson (1911–1972) was not a blues singer. She sang church songs, gospel, but she knew blues and brought the blues feeling into church music. Other people, like Ray Charles and Aretha Franklin, grew up singing gospel, too, but they took the gospel feeling and put it into the blues. The words in a gospel song and the words in the blues will be different, but both can make you start moaning like you've just bitten into the best fried chicken anybody ever made. So that's why you have to know about Mahalia Jackson. Even if she didn't sing the blues, she learned a lot from listening to blues singers, and blues singers have learned a lot from listening to her sing gospel.

Mahalia grew up in New Orleans, Louisiana, the city where jazz was born and where there is still more good music and good food per block than anyplace in the world. Her father worked on the docks during the day loading bales of cotton on boats, was a barber at night and a preacher on Sundays. When Mahalia was five years old her mother died. Her father took her to live with Mahalia Paul, an aunt who lived nearby and the woman for whom Mahalia Jackson was named. Mahalia never lived with her father again, but she saw him almost every day at his barbershop.

Mahalia grew up loving music, and the person she wanted to sing like was none other than Bessie Smith. But Mahalia's aunt was very religious, and she took Mahalia to church every day. When talking about her childhood, Mahalia said that in her church, "everybody sang and clapped and stomped their feet, sang with their whole bodies! They had the beat, a powerful beat, a rhythm we held on to from slavery days, and [the] music was so strong and expressive, it used to bring the tears to my eyes." It was in church that Mahalia first started singing.

She dropped out of school after the eighth grade and went to work doing people's laundry. Mahalia began hearing stories from relatives and friends about how good life was in Chicago, Illinois. So when she was sixteen, another aunt, Hannah, took her to Chicago to live. Once there, Mahalia joined a gospel group and a church choir while working during the day as a maid in hotels.

It was in Chicago that Mahalia got the chance to see her idol, Bessie Smith, who came to town to put on a show. Years later Mahalia remembered that Bessie "filled the whole place with her voice [and] I never went home until they put us out and closed up for the night."

Mahalia's singing brought her to the attention of Thomas A. Dorsey, who directed a number of gospel choirs in Chicago. Dorsey was the father of gospel music, but earlier in his life he had been the pianist for Ma Rainey, the blues singer Bessie Smith had traveled with. He began taking her to out-of-town churches for concerts and her reputation began to grow almost as fast as you are.

In 1946, Mahalia's first record was released. She would go on to become the most famous gospel singer in the world, and in 1976 she received (posthumously) a Grammy Lifetime

"Bessie FILLED THE WHOLE PLACE with HER VOICE [and] I never went home UNTIL they put us out and closed up for the night."

Achievement Award. Mahalia was a close friend of Martin Luther King, Jr., and at the March on Washington, he asked her to sing right before he gave his famous "I Have a Dream" speech.

Mahalia Jackson had a big voice, and she could go from a high note to a low one as easily as you put one foot in front of the other. She could hold a note until you thought she should run out of breath, and she could put together a lot of notes in a line of music that would take your breath away. And she did it as easily as a cloud floats across the sky.

When I was a teenager, I was attending a meeting in Chicago with my church youth group. Mahalia came to our meeting and sang a few songs. I knew who she was, and I'm sorry now that I didn't have sense enough to appreciate listening to one of the greatest singers of the twentieth century. I hope you won't make the same mistake if you get a chance to hear some of the great singers of today.

Envision It! | Retell

READING STREET ONLINE
STORY SORT
www.ReadingStreet.com

Think Critically

1. The slaves who began singing the blues and spirituals hundreds of years ago had good reasons for singing the blues. List some of their reasons. Why do you think people sing blues music today? Are their reasons similar to those of the slaves? Explain. **Text to World**

2. Think about how you would describe your favorite singer's voice to a friend. Now read the paragraph on page 437 about Mahalia Jackson's voice. How well does the author describe it? **Think Like an Author**

3. This selection is about blues music and how it relates to slavery and people's feelings. Look back at pages 432–433 and explain the main idea. **Main Idea**

4. The selection tells about two different kinds of music and a powerful singer. List the order in which the topics are described. Then discuss how the topics are related to each other. **Text Structure**

5. **Look Back and Write** Look back at the text. How did Mahalia Jackson use the blues in a new and different way? Provide evidence from the text to support your answer.

TEST PRACTICE Extended Response

438

Julius Lester

Julius Lester says, "I write because the lives of all of us are stories. If enough of those stories are told, then perhaps we will begin to see that our lives are the same story. The differences are merely in the details."

Mr. Lester has published more than thirty books and won many honors for his children's books, including the Newbery Honor Medal. When he was growing up in the 1940s and 1950s, he never dreamed he would one day become a writer. He wanted to be a musician. After recording two albums and hosting radio and television shows, he turned to writing. In addition to his work as a writer, he teaches at the University of Massachusetts. His photographs of the Civil Rights movement were part of an exhibition at the Smithsonian Institution.

It is important to Mr. Lester to help African American children become aware of their heritage. In his books for young people, he doesn't focus on the history of wars and politics, but rather on the lives and experiences of ordinary people.

More books by Julius Lester:

Black Cowboy, Wild Horses

The Knee-High Man and Other Tales

Reading Log

Use the *Reader's and Writer's Notebook* to record your independent reading.

Objectives
● Write a personal narrative that conveys your thoughts and feelings about an experience. ● Use and understand the function of verbs (irregular verbs and active voice).

Let's  Write It!

Key Features of a Description

● creates a vivid mental picture

● may appeal to the five senses through imagery

● uses precise words and vivid adjectives

**READING STREET ONLINE
GRAMMAR JAMMER**
www.ReadingStreet.com

Description

A **description** is a vivid account or explanation of something. The student model on the next page is an example of a description.

Writing Prompt *Mahalia Jackson* describes the voice of a talented singer. Think about music or another unique sound. Now write a description of that sound, using vivid sensory words.

Writer's Checklist

Remember, you should . . .

✓ include specific details.

✓ organize your writing in a way that makes sense.

✓ use powerful adjectives and precise words to create vivid images.

✓ use troublesome verbs correctly.

440

Playing with Heart

I took piano lessons last fall. Although I was a beginner, I loved the way the music sounded. The first song I learned to play was "Twinkle, Twinkle Little Star." When I practiced, I **set** the sheet music on the stand and began to play. The song wasn't too hard, even for a beginner. I taught myself to play the song using a steady rhythm and lively style.

Then I thought I wanted to experiment with the song a little, so I varied the rhythm. I **let** my fingers lead the way. Sometimes the song felt soothing and pleasant. At other times the sound became intense and edgy.

Finally, I tried varying the loudness. When I **laid** my fingers quietly on the keys, I almost couldn't hear the song. It sounded faint, delicate, and fragile. Then, as I played a little louder, the song grew bold and thunderous.

"What's going on in there?" Mom yelled.

"I'm practicing the piano!" I yelled back.

"Do you have to play that raucously?" Mom asked.

"No," I replied, and went back to playing quietly.

Genre
A **description** creates a vivid picture of an event.

Writing Trait Word Choice
The writer uses precise words and vivid adjectives.

Troublesome Verbs are used correctly.

Conventions

Troublesome Verbs

Remember Some pairs of verbs are confusing because they have similar meanings or look alike. For example, *lay* means *put* or *place*, while *lie* means *rest* or *recline*. Other **troublesome verbs** are *sit/set* and *let/leave*.

441

Objectives

• Examine how poets use sound effects to reinforce meaning in poems. • Make connections between and among texts.

Social Studies in Reading

Genre
Poetry

- Poets may use sound effects to reinforce meaning in a poem and to appeal to our senses. Alliteration is two or more words with the same beginning sound repeated.

- Another effect is called onomatopoeia. Onomatopoeia is a word that imitates the sound it represents.

- Some poems have rhyme, while others do not. For poems that rhyme, the rhyming pattern a poem follows is called rhyme scheme.

- Read the poems in "Perfect Harmony." Look for sound effects in each of the poems.

Perfect Harmony
by Charles R. Smith, Jr.

The author's poems are inspired by his work with The Boy's Choir of Harlem, in New York City. This choir of young African American men performs for audiences around the world.

442

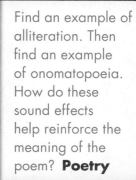

Let's **Think** About...

Find an example of alliteration. Then find an example of onomatopoeia. How do these sound effects help reinforce the meaning of the poem? **Poetry**

FOcus

Feet apart
arms at sides
chest puffed out
head held high

w a i t i n g

to release butterflies
inside.

Eyes focus
like
the calm
before the storm
ready to erupt
before I perform
toes tingle
feet quake
muscles twitch

hands shake
while
throat hums
hummmmmmms
hummmmmmmmmmmmms
so that
my voice may
awake.

Focus
I must
focus
to channel my
electricity
and relax

r e l a x
r e l a x

before I set
the butterflies
free.

Deep Breaths

Let's **Think** About...

Does this poem have a rhyme scheme? Do you think rhyme would add to the poem's meaning? **Poetry**

Ex-
hale
s l o w.
In-
hale
d e e p.
Thoughts focus.
Ready.
Release.

Breath
breathes life
into words
on a page
gives them
a stage
to showcase
sound
and express
rage
drown sorrows
and engage
ears
with musical
notes
that jump
leap

and
shout
from throats
voicing words
floating
on air
built up
in lungs
singing
singing
a song
that began
with a breath
transformed
from air
to notes
to words
in voice
waiting
to be
sung.

Energy spent.
Ex-
hale
and
done.

Let's **Think** About...

Reading Across Texts Think about the ways Mahalia and the poems' narrator use their bodies when they sing.

Writing Across Texts Make a list of tips that Mahalia Jackson and the poets might give to people who want to sing with great energy and power.

Objectives

● Read aloud grade-level texts and understand what is read. ● Listen to and interpret a speaker's messages and ask questions. ● Give organized presentations that communicate your ideas effectively. ● Participate in discussions by raising and considering suggestions from other group members and by identifying points of agreement and disagreement. ● Write analogies with antonyms and synonyms you know. ● Follow, restate, and give oral instructions.

Let's **Learn** It!

READING STREET ONLINE
ONLINE STUDENT EDITION
www.ReadingStreet.com

Vocabulary

Antonyms

Context Clues Context clues can help you figure out the meanings of words. Antonyms, or words that are opposite in meaning, are one kind of context clue. You can use antonyms and analogies to determine the meanings of unfamiliar words.

Practice It! In one of this week's readings, find an unfamiliar word that has an antonym as a context clue. Write an analogy using the unfamiliar word and the antonym. Then say what you think the unfamiliar word means.

Fluency

Rate

Partner Reading You can use different rates to call attention to the rhythm of a text. Slow down for emphasis, and speed up to express energy. Use line breaks to create rhythm.

Practice It! With a partner, practice reading a page from *Mahalia Jackson*. Focus on bringing out the rhythm in the text. Take turns reading and offering each other feedback.

446

Listening and Speaking

When you give directions, use gestures to communicate.

Give Directions

When you give directions, you describe how to do an activity. The purpose of directions is to teach others how to make an item or do an activity.

Practice It! In a group, create step-by-step directions on organizing a concert. Do your own research or reread *Mahalia* to find details on the organizational sequence of a concert. Present the directions to the class, repeating each step when necessary.

Tips

Listening . . .

- Listen to the speaker's messages and pay attention to gestures.

- Ask questions when you follow each step.

Speaking . . .

- Speak at a natural rate and enunciate as you speak.

Teamwork . . .

- Consider others' suggestions.

- Find areas of agreement, and compromise when you disagree.

Objectives
• Listen to and interpret a speaker's messages and ask questions.
• Identify the main ideas and supporting ideas in the speaker's message.

Oral Vocabulary

Let's Talk About

Special Effects

- Share what you know about special effects.

- Listen to and interpret a classmate's ideas about special effects.

- Determine classmates' main and supporting ideas about effects.

READING STREET ONLINE
CONCEPT TALK VIDEO
www.ReadingStreet.com

You've learned

1 4 0

Amazing Words

so far this year!

449

Objectives
- Use text features and graphics to gain an overview and locate information. • Interpret information in maps, charts, illustrations, graphs, timelines, tables, and diagrams.

Envision It! | Skill Strategy

Skill

Strategy

READING STREET ONLINE
ENVISION IT! ANIMATIONS
www.ReadingStreet.com

Comprehension Skill

🎯 Graphic Sources

- A graphic source, such as a picture, diagram, or chart, organizes information and helps you understand what you read.

- Before reading, preview the graphic sources in a selection to help you gain an overview of the text's contents.

- As you read, compare the information in the text with the graphic source.

- Use an organizer like the one below as you read "Computer Art and What It Takes" on page 451. As you read, use the graphics to locate and interpret information.

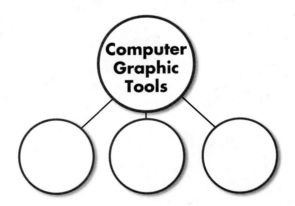

Comprehension Strategy

🎯 Important Ideas

When you read, try to identify the important ideas of a selection. The important ideas are the essential information, facts, and details that help you understand what an author is writing about.

Computer Art
AND WHAT IT TAKES

These days, computers can create art that you find in video games or on TV. This type of art is called computer graphics.

It does not take much to create a computer graphics system. Graphics software allows you to create the pictures. A computer hard drive stores the graphics, or pictures, and lets you work with them. A monitor shows you the pictures.

You also need a mouse and a keyboard to input commands. Equipment, such as a digital pad, a camera, a scanner, or a light pen, may be needed to input pictures. If you want to make a copy of the pictures on paper, you will need a printer too.

Skill Preview the picture below. What does it tell you about the article's contents?

Skill Which items mentioned in the text are shown in the picture below?

Strategy What is the most important idea of this paragraph?

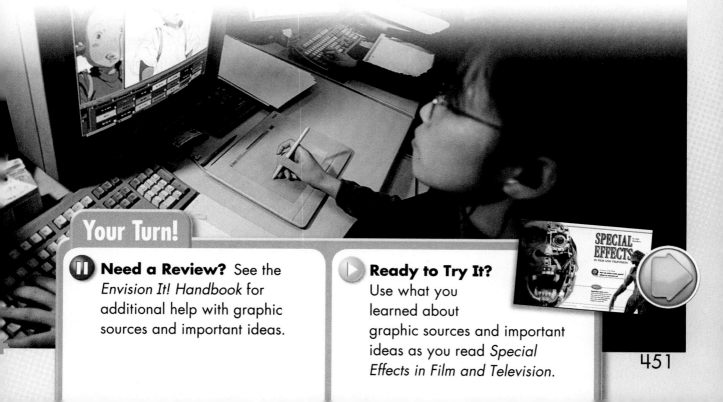

Your Turn!

⏸ **Need a Review?** See the *Envision It! Handbook* for additional help with graphic sources and important ideas.

▶ **Ready to Try It?** Use what you learned about graphic sources and important ideas as you read *Special Effects in Film and Television*.

SPECIAL EFFECTS
IN FILM AND TELEVISION

Objectives
• Determine the meaning of English words with roots from Greek, Latin, and other languages.

Envision It! | Words to Know

landscape

miniature

prehistoric

background
reassembled

READING STREET ONLINE
VOCABULARY ACTIVITIES
www.ReadingStreet.com

Vocabulary Strategy for

Affixes: Prefixes pre-, re-

Word Structure A prefix is a word part that is added to the beginning of a base word. For example, *pre-* means "before." If you *prearrange* something, you arrange it before it happens. The prefix *re-* means "again." If you *reheat* soup, you warm it up again. Both *pre-* and *re-* are from Latin.

1. Look at a word to see if it has a base word you know.

2. Check to see if a prefix has been added to the base word.

3. Ask yourself how the prefix changes the meaning of the base word.

4. Try the meaning in the sentence. Does it make sense?

Read "Visiting the Past" on page 453. Use your knowledge of prefixes to help you determine the meanings of *prehistoric, reassembled, reproduce,* and other unfamiliar words.

Words to Write Reread "Visiting the Past." What place have you visited that uses special effects? Write a paragraph about it using the *Words to Know.*

VISITING THE PAST

While we were on vacation, our family visited an incredible theme park. My parents had preplanned our trip to this exciting park. It had models that reproduce scenes from the past. Once we entered the park, we split up and went our own ways.

I went straight to the exhibit of prehistoric times. Paintings of huge, strange plants recreated the feeling of an ancient landscape. The model dinosaurs were life-sized, looked real, and even moved! A tape of background noises, such as animal cries and splashes, added to the realism. In one large room, artists had shaped a past world in miniature.

When we reassembled as a family for lunch, my brother described the Old West community he had visited. It had a whole street from a mining town—complete with general store, hotel, and jail. He rode a cart into a deep tunnel. Down there, the exhibit showed how miners worked. Occasionally, he said, you felt a tremor and heard a boom. Somehow they reproduced the explosions when ore was blasted from a mountain! We agreed that this was the best theme park we have ever visited.

Your Turn!

⏸ **Need a Review?** See *Words!* for additional support with prefixes.

▷ **Ready to Try It?** Read *Special Effects in Film and Television* on pp. 454–463.

SPECIAL EFFECTS IN FILM AND TELEVISION

454

SPECIAL EFFECTS

by Jake Hamilton

IN FILM AND TELEVISION

Question of the Week

How do artists create special effects to entertain us?

Genre

Expository texts explain what certain things are and how they came to be. As you read, notice how the author explains how artists make miniature models for movie sets.

IN MINIATURE

Special effects (SFX) is the art of making the impossible into a fantastic reality. Special effects has always pushed the boundaries of human imagination. It keeps today's movie and television audiences glued to their seats in starry-eyed wonder.

The art of miniature model-making has always been an important part of special effects in movies. Some movie stories have big, spectacular, action-filled scenes. They may call for fights between dinosaurs, explosions on the Golden Gate Bridge, or an armed force charging through the desert. Movie-makers can save time and money by making models for these scenes. This article tells the story of the building of a miniature landscape for a television show.

400-foot (120 m) film magazine with running time of $4\frac{1}{4}$ minutes at normal speed

Prime lens interchangeable with the zoom lens

Matte box reduces lens flares.

Concept model is 1 ft × 1 ft (0.3 m × 0.3 m)

1 A General Idea

A special effects team must build a prehistoric world in a workshop. The team's first step is to make a "concept" model of this mini-world. The model will give a general view of what the finished product will look like. This model shows that the landscape will include a fallen tree and a circular lake.

2 Getting Larger

The movie-makers study this concept model to decide on the size and shape of the finished product. Then they make a larger and more detailed "prototype" model. This gives them a clearer picture of how the finished product will look. The prototype comes in sections that are fitted together like puzzle pieces. This 2 ft × 2 ft (0.6 m × 0.6 m) prototype is fully painted and fitted with bushes and trees. Now the team can work on the final product.

Cameraman's eyepiece

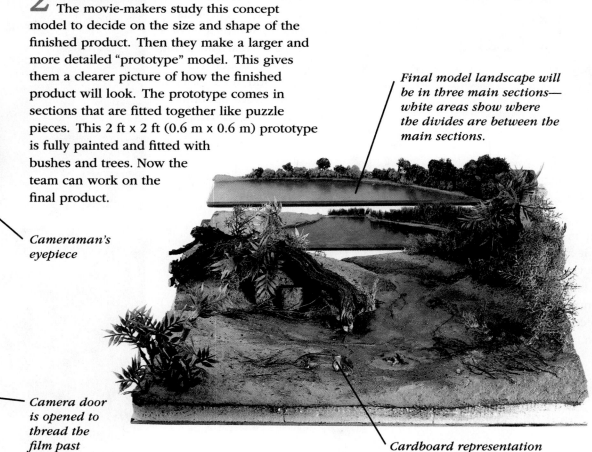

Final model landscape will be in three main sections— white areas show where the divides are between the main sections.

Camera door is opened to thread the film past the gate.

Cardboard representation of early reptile

Getting Started

The full-size miniature model will be
24 ft x 24 ft (7.2 m x 7.2 m). Building it will **3**
take real cooperation among all the SFX team
members. The model's base is made of the kind
of plastic used in fast food cups and boxes.
Model-makers carve the plastic surface to make
hills and valleys and rivers and lakes. They use
references such as pictures of trees and rocks
to guide them. These model-makers are using
photographs of a dry riverbed as a guide.

*Model-makers carve details in
ground of model's front section.*

*Miniature trees and bushes are
modeled with plastic and paint,
as well as real pieces of greenery.*

4 Carving It Out

Here, the model-makers
are cutting out the area of
the huge circular lake at the
heart of the model. They
will then add more surface
detail and mark out other
features in the landscape.

Rebuilding **5**

The model is cut into sections
so it can be taken on trucks to the
television studio. Since the model is
so large and detailed, each section
is numbered. That way, when the
pieces reach the studio they
can be reassembled easily.

*Rebuilding the landscape
is just like putting a huge
jigsaw puzzle together.*

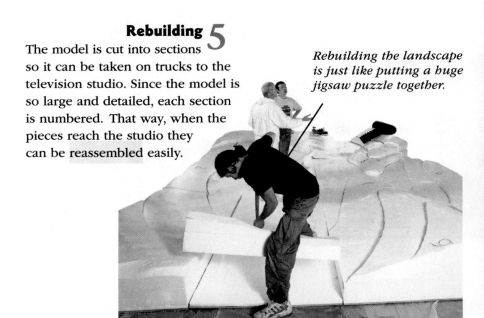

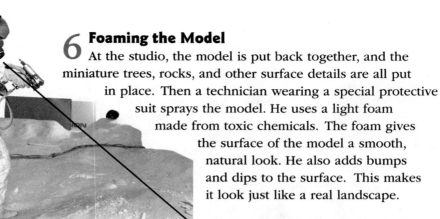

6 Foaming the Model

At the studio, the model is put back together, and the miniature trees, rocks, and other surface details are all put in place. Then a technician wearing a special protective suit sprays the model. He uses a light foam made from toxic chemicals. The foam gives the surface of the model a smooth, natural look. He also adds bumps and dips to the surface. This makes it look just like a real landscape.

To protect against toxic fumes, the technician wears a respirator.

7 In the Studio

Putting the miniature landscape back together takes a great deal of attention to detail. Every last tree, bush, and rock must be exactly in place. A huge painted backdrop of blue sky streaked with clouds has been placed on the far wall. Lights positioned overhead will give the landscape more texture and shadow.

Technician's head pops up between two of the main landscape sections.

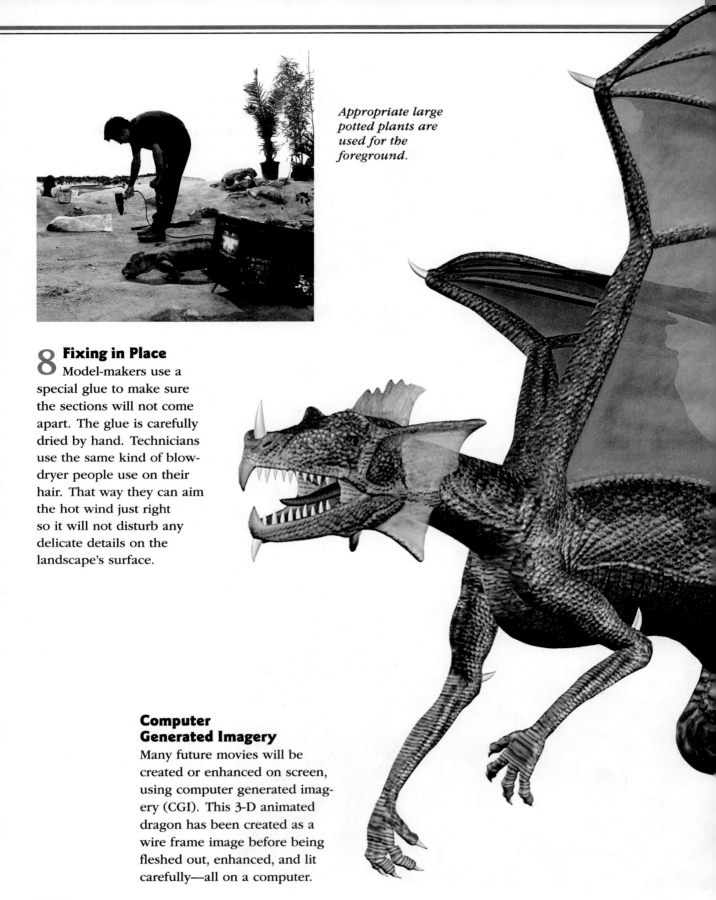

Appropriate large potted plants are used for the foreground.

8 Fixing in Place

Model-makers use a special glue to make sure the sections will not come apart. The glue is carefully dried by hand. Technicians use the same kind of blow-dryer people use on their hair. That way they can aim the hot wind just right so it will not disturb any delicate details on the landscape's surface.

Computer Generated Imagery

Many future movies will be created or enhanced on screen, using computer generated imagery (CGI). This 3-D animated dragon has been created as a wire frame image before being fleshed out, enhanced, and lit carefully—all on a computer.

REPTILE MODELING

Early reptiles were needed to inhabit the prehistoric scene, so miniature models were prepared. After it was agreed which reptiles to model, including Moschops (left), each one was sculpted carefully in nondrying clay, which is easy to shape. The model is attached to metal leg stands, and the smallest details are added at this stage, including horned backbones, razor-sharp claws, and scaled reptile skin.

The model-maker sprays the model with plastic sealer to make it possible to release the fiberglass of the mold from the clay later on. A dividing wall of clay is then placed around the model (right) so that when the mold is made it can be split into two halves.

The mold is filled with foam latex and the result is this white-faced reptile. The model-makers can now paint its skin with different textures of green and yellow. The creature is hollow in the middle so that SFX technicians can get their arms up and inside to operate it without the viewer seeing.

Foam latex model of a Lystrosaur

Water makes Lystrosaur glisten on film.

The final image of one reptile perched on a fallen log in the miniature landscape looks incredibly realistic. The creature has also been given small eyes, pointed claws, and fanged teeth.

461

Tricks of the Trade

The model-makers go to great lengths to make a miniature look as realistic as possible. Here, they are working on a slight depression in the surface that was carved out for a lake. It is filled with water to a depth of just 1.5 in. (4 cm). The model-makers are layering the shallow water with fabric to make it look more like a deep lake.

Model-makers refer to television monitor for camera's eye view.

Large, potted trees are used for foreground section.

Real log is used in foreground of landscape.

Toy Soldiers

Director Steven Spielberg used a miniature model to plan shots for the film *Raiders of the Lost Ark*. Directors often use miniature models to plan the way a scene should look, including actors' movements, the scenery, and any special lighting or camera angles.

Spielberg decides where to position the camera for the desert shot.

Sand dunes are constructed from polystyrene and beach sand.

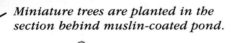

Miniature models of tents, tanks and other vehicles are used.

Miniature trees are planted in the section behind muslin-coated pond.

Landscape is supported on timber platform.

Sand used on ground of miniature and to cover cracks in model surface.

Finally Ready

It has taken most of the day to reassemble the entire miniature landscape. Now the scene is ready for filming. During filming, SFX team members beneath the platform can reach up and move the reptile models around from below. Notice how the trees in the background section of the landscape are much smaller than the trees in the foreground section. This makes the scene seem to roll back away rapidly into the distance. The large painted backdrop and studio lighting add to the effect of a vast prehistoric landscape roamed by early reptiles.

Objectives
● Provide evidence from text to support understanding. ● Read independently for a sustained period of time and paraphrase the reading, including the order in which events occur.

Envision It! Retell

Think Critically

1. Think of special effects you have seen in movies or on television. How does reading the explanations and looking at the visual images in *Special Effects in Film and Television* help you understand how artists create special effects? Give an example of a special effect you have seen and describe how artists may have created it. **Text to World**

2. The selection includes photographs to help readers visualize the process that the author describes. What are some steps and tools that are not shown? Do you think showing them would make the selection better? Explain. **Think Like an Author**

3. Think of a few additional captions for the photographs in the selection.
   Graphic Sources

4. Think about the title of this selection. Then skim through the selection and list several important ideas about special effects that the author provides to readers.
   Important Ideas

5. **Look Back and Write** Look back at pages 457–463. The selection shows how artists use special effects to re-create dinosaurs and landscapes. Write a summary of how special-effects artists make movies look so realistic. Provide evidence from the text to support your answer.

   TEST PRACTICE Extended Response

Jake Hamilton

Jake Hamilton has always loved movies. As a boy, he saw every film he could and spent hours in movie theaters. Today, as a successful journalist, Mr. Hamilton gets to watch movies as part of his job. He is a film critic for newspapers and magazines. He also reviews movies for the BBC World Service. This is his first book for young people.

Many people working in the film industry helped Mr. Hamilton in the making of the book *Special Effects in Film and Television*. The special effects departments of major film studios allowed him behind the scenes to see how they work. They showed him how special effects are staged. He was able to photograph the equipment used to create those awesome effects.

Here are other books about special effects.

***Computer Animation From Start to Finish* by Samuel G. Woods**

***Virtual Reality* by Holly Cefrey**

Use the *Reader's and Writer's Notebook* to record your independent reading.

Reading Log

Objectives

● Use and understand the function of prepositions and prepositional phrases. ● Write essays with strong introductions and conclusions. ● Write essays with specific facts, details, and examples in an organized way.

Let's Write It!

Key Features of an Expository Text

● has a clear introduction

● supports main idea or topic sentences with details

● sums up the main points with a conclusion

READING STREET ONLINE
GRAMMAR JAMMER
www.ReadingStreet.com

Expository Text

Expository text gives information about a topic. The student model on the next page is an example of expository text that compares and contrasts two things.

Writing Prompt Think about which form of entertainment you prefer: watching a movie or watching a television program. Compare and contrast the two, using specific details to make your point.

Writer's Checklist

Remember, you should . . .

☑ clearly state your position.

☑ provide strong details and examples to show why your choice is best.

☑ write with an appropriate compare-and-contrast structure.

☑ use effective transitions and a varied sentence structure.

☑ use prepositions correctly.

466

Movies: The Best Form of Entertainment

Movies are better than television programs. Movies have fewer interruptions or distractions, better sound and visual images, and are simply more enjoyable overall.

First, if you go into a movie theater, movies are shown on a big screen. Your attention is focused on the screen. On TV, images are smaller, and there are more distractions—especially during weeknights at home, when busy family members talk or walk in front of the screen. Commercials also constantly interrupt television shows. This makes it hard to focus on the story. Movies might have previews before the film starts, but the movie itself is uninterrupted.

Also, because movies seem to have bigger budgets, they usually have better sound quality and special effects.

Finally, I simply feel more cozy watching a dramatic movie at night with friends—movies are longer than television shows, so you know you have more time to relax!

Therefore, it is easy to see why I prefer movies. They have fewer interruptions, better features, and are longer!

Writing Trait Organization
Paragraphs are linked by transitions, and there is a clear introduction and conclusion.

Genre
This **expository text** compares and contrasts two things.

Prepositions and **prepositional phrases** are used correctly.

Conventions

Prepositions and Prepositional Phrases

Remember A **preposition** shows the relationship between a noun or a pronoun and another word in the sentence. (The book is *on* the table.) Prepositions or **prepositional phrases** convey location, direction, time, or provide details.

Objectives
● Analyze whether Web sites and other digital media are formal or informal.

21st Century Skills
INTERNET GUY

Use quotes in a **search engine.** "Capital of Texas" only finds pages with all the words together. *Capital of Texas* finds every page with at least one word. Which is best?

● Search engines are tools that help Internet users find Web sites.

● Each search engine has a small window in which you can type keywords. Keywords are words you type in to pinpoint what you are looking for.

● The sites you find in your search may use formal or informal language. Formal language is businesslike, while informal language is friendly.

● Read "Searching for Animation." Think about the kind of language used on each site. Is it formal or informal?

Searching for Animation

Matt does an Internet search to find out more about animation. He starts by typing the keyword "animation" into a search engine and then clicking on the SEARCH button.

Matt gets a long list of Web sites. He uses his mouse and the scroll bar to scroll through the results until he gets to the 27th item on the list.

File   Edit

      www.url.here

Search   "animation"   GO!

> Search Results: "animation"

25. <u>Animation World</u> - Site provides a look at the latest happenings in the world of animation.

26. <u>Animation Express</u> - We have dozens of Web-based animation shorts, updated twice-weekly.

27. <u>Drawn to be Wild</u> - Check out this information about animation and find out about its history, meet some famous animators, and learn the tricks of the trade.

Matt would like to learn tricks of the animation trade. So he clicks on the link <u>Drawn to be Wild</u>.

Is the language in this list formal or informal? Do you think the sites contain informal language? Why or why not?

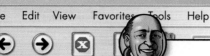

The next thing he sees on his computer screen is this:

THE UK'S ANIMATION CELEBRATION

Welcome to Drawn to be Wild. Here you can find
a wealth of information about films and animators.

Learn to Be Wild

Facts, figures and history about the world of animation

Ask Brian

Many children had questions for our Drawn to be Wild
expert Brian Sibley. Read a selection of them here.

Other Web Sites

Kids' sites on the Web that we think you'll like

Matt clicks on <u>Learn to Be Wild</u>, and up pops an article
about how animation tricks the eye. Read from the article
that Matt found by searching the Internet.

A Trick of the Eye

by Brian Sibley

No matter how they are made, all animated films
work because of an optical illusion called "persistence of
vision." The simplest example of this visual trick is the old-
fashioned "flip-book." These books present a sequence of
line illustrations, one after the other. Each one is slightly
different, so that when the book is "flipped," the pictures

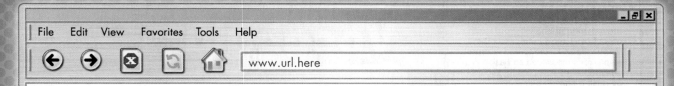

appear to move. What really happens is that the eye holds onto an image for a fraction of a second after seeing it. Then, when that image is replaced with another — and then another and another — the eye tells the brain that those drawings are moving.

Every movie ever made, whether animated or live-action, works in just this way. Film is really just a long strip of pictures, called frames. Like the drawings in a flip-book, each frame is slightly different from the one before and after. A motion picture camera is designed to photograph 24 still frames every second. Then, when developed and edited, that film is passed through a projector at the same speed. That way, what we see (or think we see) are moving pictures.

The difference with an animated film is that the camera works on a "stop-frame" system. It takes single static pictures. The animator has to provide the illusion of movement by drawing 24 separate pictures (or, in the case of model animation, by moving each puppet 24 times) for every single second of film.

for more practice

Get Online!
www.ReadingStreet.com
Use a search engine to find out about digital cinema.

21st Century Skills Online Activity
Log on and follow the directions for using search engines to find out more about digital cinema.

471

Objectives

● Read aloud grade-level texts and understand what is read. ● Determine the meaning of English words with roots from Greek, Latin, and other languages. ● Listen to and interpret a speaker's messages and ask questions. ● Participate in discussions by raising and considering suggestions from other group members and by identifying points of agreement and disagreement. ● Use and understand the function of prepositions and prepositional phrases.

READING STREET ONLINE
ONLINE STUDENT EDITION
www.ReadingStreet.com

Vocabulary

Prefixes *pre-*, *re-*

Word Structure A prefix is a word part added to the beginning of a word to change its meaning. You can use prefixes to determine the meanings of words. The prefix *pre-* means "before." The prefix *re-* means "again."

Practice It! Work with a partner to create and define a list of words that begin with the Latin prefixes *pre-* or *re-* from stories you've read this year. You can use a dictionary or glossary to find more words and to check their meanings. Now look at the parts of speech each prefix is added to. What patterns do you see?

Fluency

Accuracy

Partner Reading Accuracy is being able to read without stopping at difficult words. You can increase your reading accuracy by previewing and identifying unfamiliar words before reading.

Practice It! With your partner, practice reading a section from *Special Effects*. Practice pronouncing any difficult words first. Then read the paragraphs aloud three times. Take turns reading aloud and giving feedback.

472

Listening and Speaking

When you take part in discussions, identify points of agreement.

Advertisement

An advertisement is an announcement that promotes a product, service, or event in order to sell it to people. Advertisers persuade customers to buy the product or go to the event.

Practice It! With a partner, create an advertisement for the movie described in *Special Effects*. Give the movie a title and choose a cast. Then create an ad to persuade people to go to the movie. Present your ad to the class.

Tips

Listening . . .

- Interpret the ad's message.
- Ask questions to clarify the ad's purpose.

Speaking . . .

- Make eye contact with your audience to communicate your ideas.
- When you speak, use natural gestures.
- Use and understand the function of prepositions.

Teamwork . . .

- Ask for and consider suggestions from others.

473

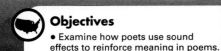

Objectives

● Examine how poets use sound effects to reinforce meaning in poems.

Poetry

- Rhyme scheme is the pattern of words that sound alike in a poem. Rhyme scheme can draw a reader's attention to important words or lines.

- Alliteration is the repetition of consonant sounds at the beginning of words. Poets use alliteration to call attention to important words or ideas.

- Alliteration also adds a musical quality to a poem that makes it fun to read.

- As you read, listen for the rhyme scheme and for examples of alliteration. How do these reinforce each poem's meaning?

George Washington Carver
Inventor, Scientist, Teacher
1864?–1943

Chemistry 101

by Marilyn Nelson

A canvas apron over his street clothes,
Carver leads his chemistry class into
the college dump. The students follow, a claque
of ducklings hatched by hens. Where he
sees a retort, a Bunsen burner,
a mortar, zinc sulfate, they see
a broken bowl, a broken lantern,
a rusty old flatiron, a fruit jar top.
Their tangle of twine, his lace.
He turns, a six-inch length of copper tubing
in one hand. "Now, what can we do with this?"
Two by two, little lights go on.
One by hesitant one, dark hands are raised.
The waters of imagining, their element.

The Bronze Horse

by Beverly McLoughland

The museum guard is fast asleep
Chin on his chest in his fold-up chair,
The bronze horse paws at the marble floor
His muscles quiver, his nostrils flare

His bronze mane flows as though a breeze
Has blown through the door, while the breath of sun
In the empty room holds summer fields
Of tender green, where the horses run.

And feeling his bronze soul come to life,
He lifts one foot from the marble floor,
Nuzzles the silence which stirs to hear
Hoofbeats echo through the open door.

Let's Think About...

In "Chemistry 101," the poet uses alliteration throughout the poem. Do you think this adds meaning or makes the poem fun to read?

Let's Think About...

Which lines rhyme in each stanza of "The Bronze Horse"? Why do you think the poet uses this rhyme scheme?

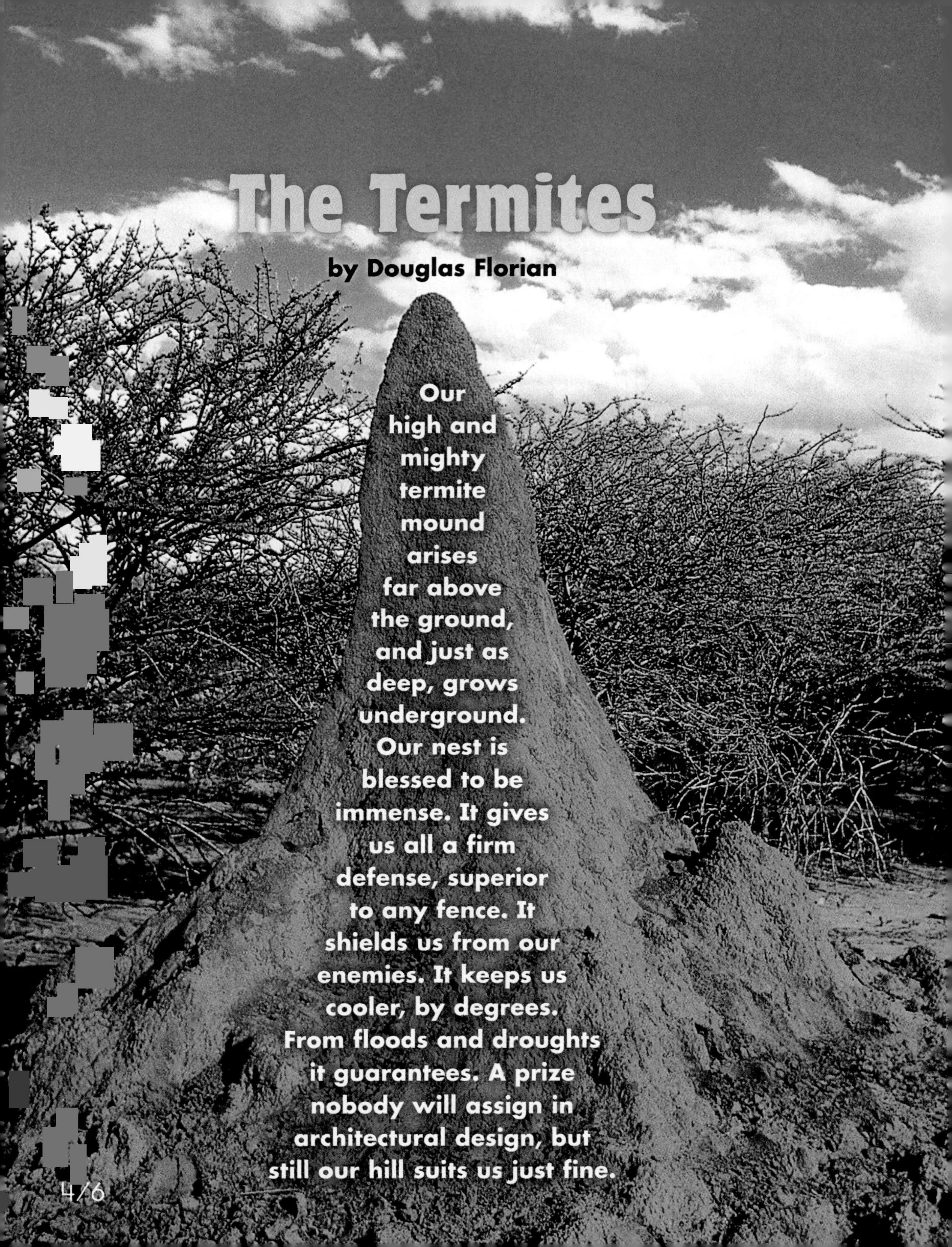

The Termites

by Douglas Florian

Our
high and
mighty
termite
mound
arises
far above
the ground,
and just as
deep, grows
underground.
Our nest is
blessed to be
immense. It gives
us all a firm
defense, superior
to any fence. It
shields us from our
enemies. It keeps us
cooler, by degrees.
From floods and droughts
it guarantees. A prize
nobody will assign in
architectural design, but
still our hill suits us just fine.

Stairs

by Oliver Herford

Here's to the man who invented stairs
And taught our feet to soar!
He was the first who ever burst
Into a second floor.

The world would be downstairs today
Had he not found the key;
So let his name go down to fame,
Whatever it may be.

How to Use This Glossary

This glossary can help you understand and pronounce some of the words in this book. The entries in this glossary are in alphabetical order. There are guide words at the top of each page to show you the first and last words on the page. A pronunciation key is at the bottom of page 479. Remember, if you can't find the word you are looking for, ask for help or check a dictionary.

The entry word is in dark type. It shows how the word is spelled and how the word is divided into syllables.

The pronunciation is in parentheses. It also shows which syllables are stressed.

Part-of-speech labels show the function or functions of an entry word and any listed form of that word.

an·ces·tor (an′ses′tər), NOUN. person from whom you are descended, such as your great-grandparents: *Their ancestors had come to the United States in 1812.* ❑ PLURAL **an·ces·tors.**

Sometimes, irregular and other special forms will be shown to help you use the word correctly.

The definition and example sentence show you what the word means and how it is used.

Aa

a·chieve (ə chēv′), v. to carry out to a successful end; accomplish; do: *Have you achieved your purpose?* ❑ v. **a·chieved, a·chiev·ing.**

al·gae (al′jē), N. PL. group of related living plants and monerans found mostly in water, which can be as small as scum on rocks or as large as seaweeds.

algae

ap·plaud (ə plȯd′), **1.** v. to show approval by clapping hands, shouting, etc.: *The audience applauded with great enthusiasm at the end of the play.* **2.** v. to be pleased with; approve of: *My parents applauded my decision to stay in school.* ❑ v. **ap·plauds.**

ap·pre·ci·ate (ə prē′shē āt), v. to think highly of; recognize the worth or quality of; value; enjoy: *Almost everybody appreciates good food.* ❑ v. **ap·pre·ci·ated, ap·pre·ci·at·ing.**

ar·chi·tect (är′kə tekt), N. person who designs and makes plans for buildings. (*Architect* comes from two Greek words, *archi* meaning "chief" and *tekton* meaning "builder.")

as·ton·ish (ə ston′ish), *v.* to surprise greatly; amaze: *We were astonished by the child's remarkable memory.* ❑ *v.* **as·ton·ished, as·ton·ish·ing.**

Bb

back·ground (bak′ ground), *N.* the part of a picture or scene toward the back: *The cottage stands in the foreground with the mountains in the background.*

ban·dan·na or **ban·dan·a** (ban dan′ə), *N.* a large, colorful handkerchief, often worn on the head or around the neck: *She wore a red bandanna while she worked in the hot sun.*

bar·ber (bär′bər), *N.* person whose business is cutting hair and shaving or trimming beards.

bar·ren (bar′ən), **1.** *ADJ.* not able to produce offspring: *a barren fruit tree; a barren animal.* **2.** *ADJ.* not able to produce much: *a barren desert.*

be·hav·ior (bi hā′vyər), *N.* manner of behaving; way of acting: *Her sullen behavior showed that she was angry.*

ben·e·fac·tor (ben′ə fak′tər), *N.* person who has given money or kindly help. (*Benefactor* comes from two Latin words, *bene* meaning "well" or "good" and *facere* meaning "do.")

brace·let (brās′lit), *N.* band or chain worn around the wrist or arm for ornamentation or identification.

brand (brand), **1.** *N.* a certain kind, grade, or make: *Do you like this brand of flour?* **2.** *v.* to mark by burning the skin with a hot iron: *The cowboys branded the cows.* ❑ *v.* **brand·ed, brand·ing.**

bronze (bronz), *N.* a dark yellow-brown alloy of copper and tin often used for sculptures and for medals: *A bronze went to the swimmer who came in third.*

browse (brouz), **1.** *v.* to read here and there in a book, library, etc. **2.** *v.* to look for information on the Internet. **3.** *v.* to feed on leaves and other vegetation; graze ❑ *v.* **brows·ing.**

Cc

can·non (kan′ən), *N.* a big gun, especially one that is mounted on a base or wheels.

cannon

a	in hat	ėr	in term	ô	in order	ch	in child	ə	= a in about
ā	in age	i	in it	oi	in oil	ng	in long	ə	= e in taken
â	in care	ī	in ice	ou	in out	sh	in she	ə	= i in pencil
ä	in far	o	in hot	u	in cup	th	in thin	ə	= o in lemon
e	in let	ō	in open	u̇	in put	ᴛʜ	in then	ə	= u in circus
ē	in equal	ȯ	in all	ü	in rule	zh	in measure		

can·teen (kan tēn′), *N.* a small container for carrying water or other drinks.

choir (kwīr), *N.* group of singers who sing together, often in a church service.

com·pres·sion (kəm presh′ən), *N.* act or process of compressing. ❑ *N. PL.* **com·pres·sions.**

con·ceal (kən sēl′), *v.* to put out of sight; hide: *The murky water concealed the crabs.* ❑ *v.* **con·cealed, con·ceal·ing.**

con·fed·er·a·cy (kən fed′ər ə sē), **1.** *N.* **the Confederacy,** the group of eleven Southern states that seceded from the United States in 1860 and 1861. **2.** *N.* union of states or countries or a group of people joined together for a special purpose; league. ❑ *N. PL.* **con·fed·er·a·cies.**

con·fi·dence (kon′fə dəns), *N.* firm belief in yourself; self-confidence: *Years of experience at her work have given her great confidence.*

con·struct (kən strukt′), *v.* to put together; fit together; build: *construct a bridge.* ❑ *v.* **con·struct·ed, con·struct·ing.**

Dd

dain·ti·ly (dān′ti lē), *ADV.* with delicate beauty; freshly and prettily: *She daintily wiped her mouth with her napkin.*

deaf·en (def′ən), **1.** *v.* to make deaf: *A hard blow on the ear can deafen someone for life.* **2.** *v.* to stun with noise: *A sudden explosion deafened us for a moment.* ❑ *ADJ.* **deaf·en·ing.**

de·pressed (di prest′), *ADJ.* gloomy; low-spirited; sad. (*Depressed* comes from the Latin word *depressum,* meaning "pressed down.")

de·vas·ta·tion (dev′ə stā′shən), *N.* the act of laying waste; destroying.

dis·tri·bu·tion (dis′trə byü′shən), *N.* the act of giving some to each, of dividing and giving out in shares.

drift·wood (drift′wùd′), *N.* wood carried along by water or washed ashore from the water.

driftwood

Ee

e·rect (i rekt′), *v.* to put up; build: *That house was erected forty years ago.* ❑ *v.* **e·rec·ted, e·rec·ting.**

Ff

fab·u·lous (fab′yə ləs), **1.** *ADJ.* wonderful; exciting. **2.** *ADJ.* not believable; amazing: *The painting was sold at a fabulous price.*

fash·ion (fash′ən), *v.* to make, shape, or form: *He fashioned a whistle out of wood.* ❑ *v.* **fash·ioned, fash·ion·ing.**

fast·ball (fast′bȯl′), *N.* a pitch thrown at high speed with very little curve.

fate (fāt), *N.* what becomes of someone or something: *The Revolutionary War decided the fate of the United States.*

fear·less (fir′lis), *ADJ.* without fear; afraid of nothing; brave; daring.

foun·da·tion (foun dā′shən), **1.** *N.* part on which the other parts rest for support; base: *the foundation of a house.* **2.** *N.* basis: *This report has no foundation in fact.* **3.** *N.* a founding or establishing: *The foundation of the United States began in 1776.* ❑ *N. PL.* **foundations.**

Gg

glim·mer (glim′ər), **1.** *N.* a faint, unsteady light: *The candle glimmered and went out.* **2.** *N.* a faint idea or feeling: *a glimmer of hope.*

glo·ry (glôr′ē), *N.* great praise and honor given by others to someone or something; fame: *Their heroic acts won them glory.*

gnaw (nȯ), *v.* to bite at and wear away: *A mouse has gnawed the cover of this box.* ❑ *v.* **gnawed, gnaw·ing.**

gnaw

grat·i·tude (grat′ə tüd), *N.* kindly feeling because of a favor received; desire to do a favor in return; thankfulness. (*Gratitude* comes from the Latin word *gratia*, meaning "favor.")

grum·ble (grum′bəl), *v.* to mutter in discontent; complain in a bad-tempered way; find fault: *He grumbled about the rainy weather.* ❑ *v.* **grum·bled.**

Hh

ham·mock (ham′ək), *N.* a hanging bed or couch made of canvas, cord, etc. It has cords or ropes at each end for hanging it between two trees or posts. ❑ *N. PL.* **ham·mocks.**

head·land (hed′lənd), *N.* narrow ridge of high land jutting out into water; promontory.

ho·gan (hō′gän′), *N.* dwelling built with logs and covered with earth, used by the Navajo.

insistent • lurch

Ii

in·sist·ent (in sis′tənt), **1.** *ADJ.* continuing to make a strong, firm demand or statement; insisting: *In spite of the rain, she was insistent on going out.* **2.** *ADJ.* impossible to overlook or disregard; compelling attention or notice; pressing; urgent: *Her insistent knocking on the door woke us.* **3.** *ADJ.* persistent; repeated; steady: *The insistent drip has worn a hollow in the stone.* ❏ *ADV.* **in·sist·ent·ly.**

in·spect (in spekt′), **1.** *v.* to look over carefully; examine: *The engineers inspected the new road.* **2.** *v.* to look over officially; examine formally: *Government officials inspect factories and mines to make sure that they are safe for workers.* ❏ *v.* **in·spect·ing.**

in·ten·tion·al (in ten′shə nəl), *ADJ.* done on purpose; meant; planned; intended: *His being late was intentional.* ❏ *ADV.* **in·tent·ion·al·ly.**

Jj

jos·tle (jos′əl), **1.** *v.* to shove, push, or crowd against; elbow roughly: *We were jostled by the crowd at the entrance to the circus.* ❏ *v.* **jos·tled, jos·tling.**

Kk

kelp (kelp), *N.* any of various large, tough, brown seaweeds.

Ll

lair (lâr), *N.* den or resting place of a wild animal.

lair

la·ment (lə ment′), **1.** *v.* to feel or show grief for; mourn aloud for: *We lament the dead.* **2.** *v.* feel sorry about; regret: *She lamented his absence.* ❏ *v.* **la·ment·ed, la·ment·ing.**

land·scape (land′ skāp), **1.** *N.* view of scenery on land. **2.** *N.* picture showing a land scene.

lin·ger (ling′gər), *v.* to stay on; go slowly, as if unwilling to leave: *He lingers after the others leave.* ❏ *v.* **ling·ered, ling·er·ing, ling·ers.**

lul·la·by (lul′ə bī), *N.* soft song to lull a baby or young child in a cradle to sleep.

lurch (lėrch), *v.* lean or roll suddenly; stagger: *The injured animal lurched forward.* ❏ *v.* **lurched.**

Mm

mag·ni·fy (mag′nə fī), *v.* to cause something to look larger than it actually is; increase the apparent size of an object: *A microscope magnifies bacteria so that they can be seen and studied.* ❑ *v.* **mag·ni·fied, mag·ni·fy·ing.**

magnify

me·sa (mā′sə), *n.* a small, high plateau with a flat top and steep sides, common in dry regions of the western and southwestern United States.*(Mesa comes from a Latin word meaning "table": The flat top of a mesa looks like a table.)* ❑ *N. PL.* **me·sas.**

midst (midst), *n.* in the middle of.

min·i·a·ture (min′ē ə chúr *or* min′ə chər), *ADJ.* a reduced image or likeness: *miniature furniture for a dollhouse.*

min·ute¹ (min′nit), **1.** *N.* a short time; instant: *I'll be there in a minute.* **2.** *N.* an exact point in time: *The minute you see her coming, please tell me.*

mi·nute² (mī nüt′), **1.** *ADJ.* very small; tiny: *Even a minute speck of dust makes him cough.* **2.** *ADJ.* going into or concerned with small details: *minute instructions.*

mock (mok), *v.* to laugh at; make fun of: *The student was punished for mocking the kindergartner.* ❑ *v.* **mocked, mock·ing.**

mold¹ (mōld), *n.* a hollow shape in which anything is formed, cast, or solidified, such as the mold into which melted metal is poured to harden into shape, or the mold in which gelatin is left to stiffen.

mold² (mōld), *n.* a fuzzy growth, often greenish in color, that appears on food and other things when they are left too long in a warm, moist place.

Nn

Nav·a·jo (nav′ə hō), *n.* an individual or group of Native American people living primarily in New Mexico, Arizona, and Utah. ❑ *N.PL.* **Nav·a·jo** or **Nav·a·jos.**

neu·tral (nü′trəl), *n.* position of gears when they do not transmit motion from the engine to the wheels or other working parts.

nor·mal·ly (nôr′mə lē), **1.** *ADV.* in a normal way: *to act normally.* **2.** *ADV.* if things are normal: *Children normally begin to lose their baby teeth when they are six years old.*

occasion • proportion

Oo

oc·ca·sion (ə kā′zhən), **1.** *N.* a particular time: *We have met them on several occasions.* **2.** *N.* a special event: *The jewels were worn only on great occasions.*

out·field (out′fēld′), **1.** *N.* the part of a baseball field beyond the diamond or infield. **2.** *N.* the three players in the outfield.

outfield

Pp

phi·los·o·pher (fə los′ə fər), *N.* a person who attempts to discover and understand the basic nature of knowledge and reality. (*Philosopher* comes from the Greek word *philosophia*, meaning "love of wisdom.")

pitch (pich), **1.** *v.* to throw or fling; hurl; toss: *They were pitching horseshoes.* ❑ *v.* **pitched, pitch·ing. 2.** *N.* thick, black, sticky substance made from tar or turpentine, used to fill the seams of wooden ships, to cover roofs, to make pavements, etc.

pre·his·tor·ic (prē′hi stôr′ ik), *ADJ.* Of or belonging to periods before recorded history: *Some prehistoric people lived in caves.*

prehistoric

pre·vi·ous (prē′vē əs), *ADJ.* coming or being before; earlier: *She did better in the previous lesson.*

pro·ces·sion (prə sesh′ən), *N.* something that moves forward; persons marching or riding: *The opening procession started at noon.*

proj·ect (proj′ekt), **1.** *N.* a plan; scheme; effort; undertaking: *a project for better sewage disposal.* **2.** *N.* a special assignment planned and carried out by a student, a group of students, or an entire class.

pro·por·tion (prə pôr′shən), **1.** *N.* a proper relation among parts: *The dog's short legs were not in proportion to its long body.* **2.** *N.* relation of two things in magnitude, size, number, amount, or degree compared to another: *Each girl's pay will be in proportion to the other's.*

pry·ing[1] (prī′ing), *ADJ.* looking or searching too curiously; unpleasantly inquisitive.

pry·ing[2] (prī′ing), *v.* moving or forcing open with a lever: *He was prying into my business.*

Qq

quar·rel (kwôr′əl), **1.** *N.* an angry dispute; a fight with words: *The children had a quarrel over the candy.* **2.** *v.* to fight with words; dispute or disagree angrily: *The two friends quarreled, and now they don't speak to each other.* 3. *v.* to disagree: *Most people did not quarrel with the jury's decision.* ❑ *v.* **quar·reled, quar·rel·ing.**

Rr

ra·vine (rə vēn′), *N.* a long, deep, narrow valley eroded by running water.

re·as·sem·ble (rē′ə sem′ bəl), *v.* come or bring together again. ❑ *v.* **re·as·sem·bled, re·as·sem·bling.**

re·bel·lion (ri bəl′yən), **1.** *N.* armed resistance or fight against your government; revolt. **2.** *N.* resistance or fight against any power or restriction.

rec·om·mend (rek′ə mend′), *v.* to speak in favor of; suggest favorably: *The teacher recommended him for the job.* ❑ *v.* **rec·om·men·ded, rec·om·men·ding.**

re·lease (ri lēs′), *v.* to permit to be published, shown, sold, etc. ❑ *v.* **re·leased, re·leas·ing.**

re·li·gious (ri lij′əs), *ADJ.* much interested in the belief, study, and worship of God or gods; devoted to religion: *He is very religious and prays often.*

re·source·ful (ri sôrs′fəl), *ADJ.* good at thinking of ways to do things; quick-witted: *The resourceful children mowed lawns to earn enough money to buy new bicycles.*

ri·val (rī′vəl), *N.* person who wants and tries to get the same thing as another or who tries to equal or do better than another; competitor: *The two girls were rivals for the same class office.*

Ss

sa·cred (sā′krid), **1.** *ADJ.* worthy of reverence: *the sacred memory of a dead hero.* **2.** *ADJ.* not to be violated or disregarded: *a sacred promise.* (*Sacred* comes from a Latin word *sacrare,* meaning "holy.")

sea ur·chin (sē′ ėr′chən), *N.* any of numerous small, round sea animals with spiny shells. ❑ *N. PL.* **sea ur·chins.**

sea urchin

485

shell·fish (shel′fish′), *N.* a water animal with a shell. *Oysters, clams, crabs, and lobsters are shellfish.*

sin·ew (sin′yü), *N.* tendon.

slav·er·y (slā′vər ē), *N.* the condition of being owned by another person and being made to work without wages.

som·ber (som′bər), **1.** *ADJ.* having deep shadows; dark; gloomy: *A cloudy winter day is somber.* **2.** *ADJ.* sad; gloomy; dismal: *His losses made him somber.*

stal·lion (stal′yən), *N.* male horse.

steed (stēd), **1.** *N.* horse, especially a riding horse. **2.** *N.* a high-spirited horse.

steed

stern·ly (stèrn′ lē), *ADV.* strictly; firmly: *The teacher frowned sternly.*

sur·vey (sər vā′ *for* VERB; sèr′vā *for* NOUN), **1.** *v.* to look over; view; examine: *The foreman surveyed the work when it was done.* **2.** *N.* a general look; view; examination; inspection: *We were pleased with our first survey of the house.* **3.** *N.* a formal or official inspection, study, poll, etc.: *The institute conducted a survey of public opinion.* **4.** *N.* a careful measurement: *His survey showed that the northern boundary was not correct.* ❑ *v.* **sur·veyed, sur·vey·ing.**

Tt

teen·ag·er (tēn′ā′jər), *N.* person in his or her teens, ages 13 through 19.

thieve (thēv), *v.* to steal. ❑ *v.* **thieved, thiev·ing.**

ti·dy (tī′dē), *v.* to put in order; make neat: *I tidied the room.* ❑ *v.* **ti·died, ti·dy·ing.**

tidy

tra·di·tion (trə dish′ən), N. custom or belief handed down from generation to generation: *According to tradition, Betsy Ross made the first American flag.* ❑ N. PL. **tra·di·tions.**

tur·quoise (tėr′koiz *or* tėr′kwoiz), **1.** N. sky-blue or greenish-blue mineral often used as a gem: *Native Americans are known for their artistry with turquoise.* **2.** ADJ. sky blue or greenish-blue: *Her favorite colors are turquoise and red.*

tweez·ers (twē′zərz), N. small pincers for pulling out splinters or hairs, picking up small objects, etc.

Uu

un·ion (yü′nyən), **1.** N. act of uniting or condition of being united: *The United States was formed by the union of thirteen former British colonies.* **2.** N. **the Union, a** the United States of America, **b** those states that supported the federal government of the United States during the Civil War. **3.** any of many groups of workers joined to protect and promote their common good; labor union or trade union.

u·nique (yü nēk′), **1.** ADJ. having no like or equal; being the only one of its kind: *a unique specimen of rock, a unique experience.* **2.** ADJ. INFORMAL very uncommon or unusual; rare; remarkable. ❑ ADV. **u·nique·ly,** N. **u·nique·ness.**

Vv

vein (vān), **1.** N. membranous tubes forming part of the system of vessels that carry blood to the heart. **2.** N. a small, natural channel within the Earth through which water trickles or flows. ❑ N. PL. **veins.**

Ww

weak·ness (wēk′nis), N. a weak point; slight fault: *Putting things off is her weakness.*

wind·up (wīnd′up′), N. (in baseball) a swinging movement of the arms while twisting the body just before pitching the ball.

work·shop (wėrk′shop′), **1.** N. space or building where work is done. **2.** N. group of people working on or studying a special project.

Unit 1

Red Kayak

compressions / compresiones*
grumbled / refunfuñó
insistently / insistentemente*
intentionally / intencionalmente
minute / minuto*
neutral / neutro*
normally / normalmente

Thunder Rose

branded / marcados
constructed / construyó
daintily / con elegancia
devastation / devastación*
lullaby / nana
pitch / brea
resourceful / ingeniosa
thieving / (hábitos de) robar
veins / venas*

Island of the Blue Dolphins

gnawed / royeron
headland / promontorio
kelp / algas
lair / guarida
ravine / barranco
shellfish / mariscos
sinew / tendón

* English/Spanish Cognate: A **cognate** is a
  word that is similar in two languages and
  has the same meaning in both languages.

Satchel Paige

confidence / confianza
fastball / bola rápida
mocking / burlón
outfield / jardín
unique / único
weakness / debilidad
windup / windup (movimiento para lanzar)

Ten Mile Day

barren / estéril
deafening / ensordecedor
lurched / tambaleó
previous / anterior
prying / apalancando
surveying / inspeccionando

Unit 2

At the Beach

algae / algas*
concealed / ocultado
driftwood / madera flotante
hammocks / hamacas*
lamented / lamentó *
sea urchins / erizos de mar
sternly / severamente
tweezers / pinzas

Hold the Flag High

canteen / cantimplora
Confederacy / Confederación*
glory / gloria*
quarrel / pelea
rebellion / rebelión*
stallion / semental
union / Unión*

The Ch'i-lin Purse
astonished / asombrada
behavior / comportamiento
benefactor / benefactora*
distribution / distribución*
gratitude / gratitud*
procession / procesión*
recommend / recomendar *
sacred / sagrado
traditions / tradiciónes*

A Summer's Trade
bandana / pañuelo
bracelet / brazalete*
hogan / hogan (choza)*
jostled / empujó
mesa / meseta*
Navajo / Navajo*
turquoise / turquesa*

The Midnight Ride of Paul Revere
fate / destino
fearless / intrépido
glimmer / destello
lingers / se entretiene
magnified / ampliado
somber / sombrías
steed / corcel

Unit 3

The Fabulous Perpetual Motion Machine
applauds / aplaude*
browsing / hojeando
fabulous / fabuloso*
inspecting / inspeccionando
project / proyecto*

Leonardo's Horse
achieved / logrado
architect / arquitecto*
bronze / bronce*
cannon / cañón*
depressed / deprimido
fashioned / elaboró
midst / (en) medio (de)
philosopher / filósofo*
rival / rival*

The Dinosaurs of Waterhouse Hawkins
erected / erigió
foundations / cimientos
mold / molde*
occasion / ocasión*
proportion / proporción*
tidied / ordenó
workshop / taller

Mahalia Jackson
appreciate / apreciar
barber / barbero*
choir / coro
released / se publicó
religious / religiosa*
slavery / esclavitud
teenager / adolescente

Special Effects in Film and Television
background / fondo
landscape / paisaje
miniature / miniatura*
prehistoric / prehistórico*
reassembled / reensamblados*

Acknowledgments

Text

Grateful acknowledgment is made to the following for copyrighted material:

Anderson Literary Agency

"The Microscope" by Maxine W. Kumin first published in *The Atlantic Monthly, 1963*. Copyright © 1968 by Maxine W. Kumin. Used by permission.

Bayard Presse Canada, Inc a div of Owl Kid Books

"A Model Scientist" adapted from *Owl Magazine, May 1996 Owl*. Used by permission of Bayard Presse Canada, Inc.

Beverly McLoughland

"The Bronze Horse" from *Cricket Magazine* by Beverly McLoughland, Cricket, Nov. 1990. Used by permission of the author.

Buck Tilton

"7 Survival Questions" by Buck Tilton from *Boys' Life, p. 16, April 2001*. Used by permission of Buck Tilton.

Cedric McClester

"For Peace Sake" by Cedric McClester, 1990. For more poems by Cedric McClester go to Poetry.com. Used by permission of the author.

Dorling Kindersley

From **Special Effects in Film and Television** by Jake Hamilton. © 1998 Dorling Kindersly.

Dutton Children's Books a div of Penguin Group (USA)

From *Red Kayak* by Priscilla Cummings, copyright © 2004 by Priscilla Cummings Frece. Used by permission of Dutton Children's Books, A Division of Penguin Young Readers Group, A member of Penguin Group (USA) Inc., 345 Hudson Street, New York, NY 10014. All rights reserved.

Farrar, Straus & Giroux & Linda Fang

"The Ch'i-lin Purse" from *The Ch'i-lin Purse* by Linda Fang. Copyright © 1963 by Linda Fang. Used by permission.

Franklin Watts a div of Scholastic, Inc

"Measuring Tornados" (originally titled "Storm Chasers") by Trudi Strain Trueit. Copyright © 2002 Franklin Watts, a Division of Scholastic, Inc. All rights reserved. Used by permission of Franklin Watts, an imprint of Scholastic Library Publishing, Inc.

Front Street & Wordsong an imprint of Boyds Mills Press

"Chemistry 101" from *Carver: A Life In Poems* by Marilyn Nelson. Copyright © 2001 by Marilyn Nelson. Published by Wordsong, an imprint of Boyds Mills Press. Reprinted by permission.

Gina MacCoby Literary Agency & G.P. Putnam's Sons a div of Penguin Group (USA)

"Leonardo's Horse" by Jean Fritz, and illustrated by Hudson Talbott. Text copyright © 2001 by Jean Fritz. Illustrations Copyright © 2001 by Hudson Talbott. Used by permission.

Handprint Books, Inc & Chronicle Books

Illustrations from *The Midnight Ride of Paul Revere* by Henry Wadsworth Longfellow, graved and painted by Christopher Bing, © 2001 Christopher Bing. Used by permission.

HarperCollins Publishers

"Full Day" from *Come With Me: Poems For A Journey* by Naomi Shihab Nye. Text copyright © 2000 by Naomi Shihab Nye. Greenwillow Books. "Hold the Flag High" by Catherine Clinton. Text copyright © 2005 by Catherine Clinton. Illustrated by Shane W. Evans. Illustrations copyright © 2005 by Shane W. Evans. Used by permission of HarperCollins Publishers.

Henry Holt & Company, LLC

Text and illustrations from *Ten Mile Day and the Building of the Transcontinental Railroad* written and illustrated by Mary Ann Fraser. Copyright © 1993 by Mary Ann Fraser. Reprinted by arrangement with Henry Holt and Company, LLC.

Houghton Mifflin Harcourt Publishing Company

"The Termites" from *Insectlopedia* by Douglas Florian. Copyright © 1998 by Douglas Florian. From *Thunder Rose* by Jerdine Nolen, illustrated by Kadir Nelson. Text copyright © 2003 by Jerdine Nolen, Illustrations copyright © 2003 by Kadir Nelson. Reproduced by permission of Houghton Mifflin Harcourt Publishing Company. All rights reserved.

Houghton Mifflin Harcourt Company & McIntosh and Otis, Inc

From *Island Of The Blue Dolphins* by Scott O'Dell. Copyright © 1960, renewed 1988 by Scott O'Dell. Reprinted by permission.

Hyperion Books

From *Perfect Harmony: A Musical Journey With The Boys Choir Of Harlem* by Charles Smith Jr. Copyright (c) 2002 by Charles Smith Jr. Reprinted by permission of Hyperion Books for Children. All rights reserved.

Hyperion Books & Julius Lester

"Mahalia Jackson" from *The Blues Singers: Ten Who Rocked The World* by Julius Lester. Copyright © 2001 Julius Lester. Illustrated by Lisa Cohen. Reprinted by permission.

Marian Reiner Literary Agent

"Two People I Want to Be Like" from *If Only I*

Could Tell You by Eve Merriam. Copyright © 1983 by Eve Merriam.

Margaret K. McElderry books an imprint of Simon & Schuster Children's Publishing Division & Janet Wong

Reprinted with the permission of Janet S. Wong from *Good Luck Gold and Other Poems* by Janet S. Wong. Copyright © 1994 Janet S. Wong. Used by permission.

Random House Children's Books a div of Random House, Inc

"The Eagle and the Bat" by Lame Deer from *The Sound of Flutes and Other Indian Legends* by Richard Erdoes and illustrated by Paul Goble. Copyright © 1976 by Richard Erdoes. Illustrations copyright © 1976 by Paul Goble. Used by permission of Random House Children's Books, a division of Random House, Inc.

Salina Bookshelf

"A Summer's Trade" by Deborah W. Trotter. Copyright © 2007 by Deborah W. Trotter. Illustrations copyright © 2007 by Irving Toddy. Used by permission of Salina Bookshelf, Inc.

Scholastic, Inc

"At the Beach" from *Salsa Stories* by Lulu Delacre. Copyright © 2000 by Lulu Delacre.

"Dinosaurs of Waterhouse Hawkins" from *The Dinosaurs of Waterhouse Hawkins* by Barbara Kerley Kelly, illustrated by Brian Selznick. Text copyright © 2001 by Barbara Kerley Kelly, illustrations copyright © 2001 Brian Selznick. Scholastic Inc./Scholastic Press. Reprinted by permission.

Sheil Land Associates

Extract from *A Trick Of The Eye* by Brian Sibley © Brian Sibley, 2000. Reproduced by permission of Sheil Land Associates Ltd.

Simon & Schuster Books for Young Readers an imprint of Simon & Schuster Children's Publishing Division

Reprinted with the permission of Simon & Schuster Books for Young Readers, an imprint of Simon & Schuster Children's Publishing Division, from *Satchel Paige* by Lesa Cline-Ransome. Text copyright © 2000 Lesa Cline-Ransome.

Note: Every effort has been made to locate the copyright owner of material reproduced on this component. Omissions brought to our attention will be corrected in subsequent editions.

Acknowledgments

Illustrations

Cover: Greg Newbold, **EI2–EI25** Dan Santat; **26–39** Ron Mazellan; **56–58** Darryl Ligasan; **88–100** E.B. Lewis; **104–106** Maryjo Koch; **170–172** Greg Newbold; **182–194** Michael Steirnagle; **198** Amanda Hall; **236–249** Ed Young; **254** Chi Chung; **330–343** Gerardo Suzan; **416–420** Phil Wilson; **W2–W15** Dean MacAdam.

Photographs

Every effort has been made to secure permission and provide appropriate credit for photographic material. The publisher deeply regrets any omission and pledges to correct errors called to its attention in subsequent editions.

Unless otherwise acknowledged, all photographs are the property of Pearson Education, Inc.

Photo locators denoted as follows: Top (T), Center (C), Bottom (B), Left (L), Right (R), Background (Bkgd)

18 (C) ©Charles Marion Russell/Getty Images, ©Rob Howard/Corbis; **20** (BL) ©Bob Daemmrich/PhotoEdit, (B) ©Robert W. Ginn/PhotoEdit, (BC) ©i2i Images /Jupiter Images; **24** (T) ©Ian Edelstein/Alamy Images, (C) ©izmostock/Alamy Images, (C) ©Matthias Kulka/zefa/Corbis; **46** (B) Getty Images; **50** (B) ©Eric Nguyen/Corbis, (BL) ©Galen Rowell/Corbis, (BC) Jupiter Images; **54** (T) ©Dennis Kirkland/Jaynes Gallery/Alamy Images, (C) ©Mark & Audrey Gibson/PhotoLibrary Group, Ltd., (B) ©Tomas Van Houtryve/Corbis; **78** (Bkgd) ©International Stock Photography/Taxi/Getty Images; **79** (TL, CL) ©Jim Reed/Corbis;

82 (B) ©Ron Sanford/Corbis; **83** (CC) ©Brian Finke/Getty Images, (BR) ©Mischa Photo Ltd/Getty Images; **86** (B) ©Heather Angel/Natural Visions/Alamy Images, (C) ©Radius Images/Jupiter Images, (T) ©W. Perry Conway/Corbis; **110** (BL) ©Stefan Zaklin/epa/Corbis, (B) ©Dimitri Lundt/Corbis; **111** (BR) ©AP Photo; **114** (T) ©Bananastock /Jupiter Images, (B) ©Cut and Deal Ltd/Alamy, (C) ©Kim Karpeles/Alamy Images; **117** (TC) Legends Archive; **134** (TL) ©Focus On Sport/Getty Images, (T) ©Stockbyte; **135** (B) ©DK Images; **136** (TL) ©Bettmann/Corbis; **137** (BC) ©Focus On Sport/Getty Images; **140** (BC) ©AbleStock/Index Open, (B) Corbis; **141** (BR) ©AP Photo; **144** (C) ©allOver photography/Alamy Images, (B) ©Mike Goldwater/Alamy Images, (T) ©TMI/Alamy Images; **162** (BR) ©Carl & Ann Purcell/Corbis; **163** (TC) ©Scott T. Smith/Corbis; **164** (CR) ©Topham/The Image Works, Inc., (B) Corbis; **165** (CR) ©Huntington Library/SuperStock; **176** (B) ©David Young-Wolff/PhotoEdit, (BC) ©John Neubauer/PhotoEdit; **177** (BR) Tom Carter/PhotoEdit; **180** (C) ©ImageState/Alamy Images, (T) ©Michael Gilday/Alamy Images, (B) Jupiter Images; **181** ©Roland Seitre/Peter Arnold, Inc.; **202** (B) ©Duomo/Corbis, (BC) ©Joe Rosenthal/Corbis; **203** (BC) ©Transtock/Corbis; **206** (C) ©image100/Corbis, (T) ©Joan Comalat/PhotoLibrary Group, Ltd., (B) PhotoLibrary; **224** ©Walter B. McKenzie/Getty Images; **225** ©Corbis; **230** (B) ©Jim Cummins/Corbis, (BL) ©Louise Gubb/Corbis; **231** (TR) ©Dennis Hallinan/Jupiter Images; **234** (C) ©Jose Luis Pelaez Inc./Jupiter Images, (B) ©Mark & Audrey Gibson/PhotoLibrary Group, Ltd., (T) ©Misty Bedwell/Design Pics/Corbis; **258** (BL) ©SW Productions/Brand X/Corbis;

259 (BR) ©Moodboard Micro/Corbis; 262 (B) ©Christoph von Haussen/PhotoLibrary Group, Ltd., (T) ©Jean J. Trome Talbot/PhotoLibrary, (C) PhotoLibrary; 280 (BL) ©Mark Wilson/ Pool/epa/Corbis, (B) ©Michael Newman/ PhotoEdit; 281 (BR) ©Kevin Lamarque/Corbis; 290 (BR) ©Hans Neleman/Getty Images; 291 (TR, BR, BL) ©Hans Neleman/Getty Images; 292 (B) ©Jon Feingersh/Blend Images/Getty Images, (C) ©Jorgen Larsson/Nordic Photos/ Getty Images, (T) ©Randy Faris /Jupiter Images; 318 (C) ©Images/Corbis; 320 (C) ©Images/ Corbis; 322 (B) ©Brownie Harris/Corbis, (C) ©Richard Cummins/Corbis, ©The Gallery Collection/Corbis; 324 (BL) ©Rick Friedman/ Corbis, (B) JLP/Jose Luis Pelaez/Corbis; 325 (BR) ©Bettmann/Corbis; 328 (T) ©David P. Hall/Corbis, (C) ©Randy Faris/Corbis, (B) Getty Images; 349 (B) ©Neil Guegan/Getty Images; 350 (B) Jupiter Images; 354 (B) ©Jeff Greenberg/ PhotoEdit; 355 (TR) ©Bill Bachmann/Alamy Images, (CR) Mark Wilson/Getty Images; 358 (B) ©Gary Cralle/Getty Images, (C) ©ian nolan/ Alamy Images, (T) ©Steve Chenn/Corbis; 360 (Bkgd) ©Randall Fung/Corbis; 388 (B) ©IIHS/ AP Images; 389 (TR) ©Layne Kennedy/Corbis, (CR) De Agostini Picture Library/Getty Images; 392 (T) ©Joel Sartore/National Geographic/ Getty Images, (C) ©Martin Poole/Getty Images, (B) ©Neil Beckerman/Getty Images; 417 (BR) ©Kevin Kelly; 424 (B) ©Chad Ehlers/Stock Connection/Jupiter Images, (BL) Tim Pannell/ Corbis; 425 (BR) Catherine Karnow/Corbis; 428 (C) ©Alex Segre/Alamy Images, (B) ©Ian Shaw/ Alamy Images, (T) Getty Images;

443 (TR) The Boys Choir of Harlem, Inc.; 448 (CL) ©Buddy Mays/Corbis, (BC) ©Image Source Limited, (B) ©Jeff Greenberg/Alamy Images; 452 (B) ©Kevin O'Hara/PhotoLibrary Group, Ltd., (C) ©Margaret O'Grady/PhotoLibrary Group, Ltd., (T) ©Martin Sundberg/Photolibrary; 454 (C) ©Jim Henson's Creature Shop/DK Images; 455 (R) ©Millennium FX Ltd/DK Images; 456 (B) ©Mike Valentine (BSC)/DK Images; 457 (TL, BR) ©Millennium FX Ltd/DK Images; 458 (TR, R, CL, BC) ©Millennium FX Ltd/DK Images; 459 (TL) ©Millennium FX Ltd/DK Images; 460 (TL) ©Millennium FX Ltd/DK Images, (R) ©Turbo Squid, Inc.; 461 (TC, CR, CC, BR) ©Millennium FX Ltd/DK Images; 462 (TC, B) ©Millennium FX Ltd/DK Images; 463 (TR) ©Paramount/Everett Collection, Inc.; 468 (C) ©American Artist; 469 (CR) Getty Images; 470 (TR, CL) ©American Artist, (BL) ©Matthias Kulka/Corbis; 474 (Bkgd) ©Steve Drake/Solus Photography/Veer, Inc., (TR) Getty Images; 475 (Bkgd) ©Stuart McClymont/Getty Images; 476 (Bkgd) ©Walter Bibikow/Index Stock Imagery; 477 (Bkgd) ©Pete Turner/Getty Images; 478 ©Peter Steiner/ Alamy; 479 Getty Images; 480 (BL) ©FogStock/ Index Open, (TR) Getty Images; 481 ©Everett Johnson/Index Open; 482 Digital Vision; 483 (T) ©Elmer Frederick Fischer/Corbis, (BR) Tracy Morgan/©DK Images; 485 (L) Getty Images, (R) Image Source/Getty Images; 486 ©Patrik Giardino/Corbis; 487 Getty Images; 488 (R) ©PhotoLibrary/Index Open, (L) ©Tetra Images/ Alamy; 489 (R) ©Blend Images/Alamy, (L) Paul Springett/©DK Images; 490 (L) ©Image Source, (R) Susanna Price/©DK Images; 491 Getty Images.

WORDS! | Vocabulary Handbook

Antonyms

Synonyms

Base Words/Root Words

Prefixes

Suffixes

Context Clues

Related Words

Word Origins: Roots

Multiple-Meaning Words

Dictionary

Thesaurus

Antonyms

An antonym is a word that has the opposite meaning of another word. *Day* is an antonym for *night*.

Smooth   **Bumpy**

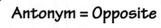

Antonym = Opposite

Strategy for Antonyms

1. Identify the word for which you want to find an antonym.
2. Think of other words or phrases that have the opposite meaning.
3. Use a thesaurus to help you find antonyms.
4. Use a dictionary to check antonyms' meanings so that you use the word that best communicates your ideas.

Synonyms

Synonyms are two or more words that have the same meaning or nearly the same meaning.

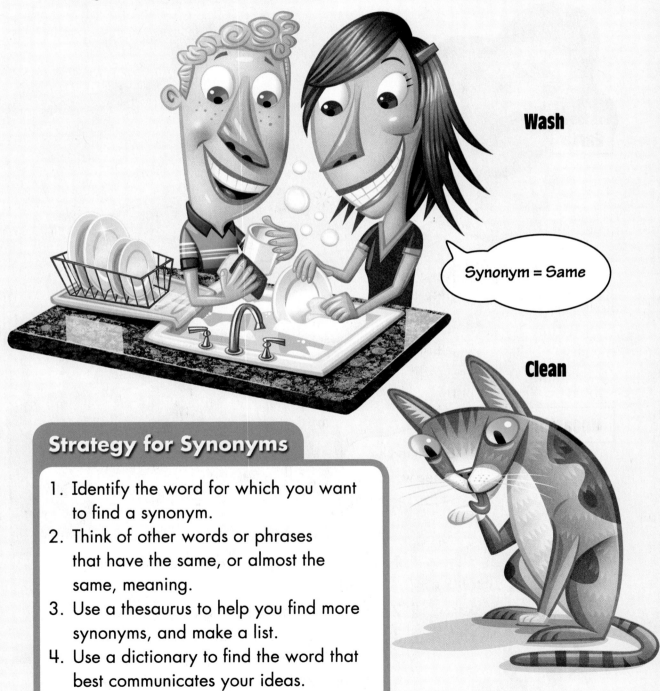

Wash

Synonym = Same

Clean

Strategy for Synonyms

1. Identify the word for which you want to find a synonym.
2. Think of other words or phrases that have the same, or almost the same, meaning.
3. Use a thesaurus to help you find more synonyms, and make a list.
4. Use a dictionary to find the word that best communicates your ideas.

W•3

Base Words/Root Words

A base word, also called a root word, is a word that can't be broken into smaller words.

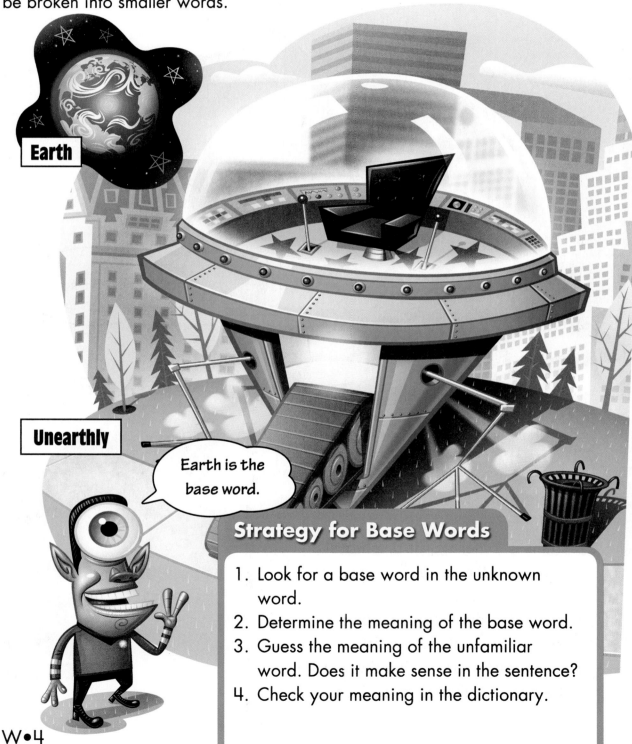

Earth

Unearthly

Earth is the base word.

Strategy for Base Words

1. Look for a base word in the unknown word.
2. Determine the meaning of the base word.
3. Guess the meaning of the unfamiliar word. Does it make sense in the sentence?
4. Check your meaning in the dictionary.

Prefixes

A prefix is a word part added onto the front of a base word to form a new word.

Formal

Informal

Strategy for Prefixes

1. Look at the unknown word and identify the prefix.
2. What does the base word mean? If you're not sure, check the dictionary.
3. Use what you know about the base word and the prefix to figure out the meaning of the unknown word.
4. Use the dictionary to check your guess.

Common Prefixes and Their Meanings

un–	not
re–	again, back
in–	not
dis–	not, opposite of
pre–	before

Suffixes

A suffix is a word part added to the end of a base word to form a new word.

Sleeve

Sleeveless

Common Suffixes and Their Meanings

Suffix	Meaning
-ly	characteristic of
-tion	act, process
-able	can be done
-ment	action or process
-less	without

Strategy for Suffixes

1. Look at the unknown word and identify the suffix.
2. What does the base word mean? If you're not sure, check a dictionary.
3. Use what you know about the base word and the suffix to figure out the meaning of the unknown word.
4. Use a dictionary to check your guess.

Context Clues

Context clues are the words and sentences found around an unknown word that may help you figure out a word's meaning.

I saw many animals at the zoo! I saw an elephant, a lion, capybaras, and a monkey.

Strategy for Context Clues

1. Look for clues in the words and phrases around the unknown word.
2. Take a guess at the word's meaning. Does it make sense in the sentence?
3. Use a dictionary to check your guess.

Related Words

Related words are words that all have the same base word.

Illustrate

Reillustrate

Illustrator

Strategy for Related Words

1. Find the base word in your unknown word.
2. Identify the meaning of the base word.
3. Guess the meaning of the unfamiliar word. Does it make sense in the sentence?
4. Use a dictionary to check your guess.

W•8

Word Origins: Roots

Many English words contain Greek and Latin roots.

Telescope

Automobile

Television

Latin Roots

dent	tooth
dict	to say; to speak
scrib	to write
sub	under; below
tract	to pull
vis	to see

Greek Roots

auto	self
bio	life
micro	very small
ology	the study of
phon	sound; voice
scope	see
tele	far

Strategy for Roots

1. Using what you know about roots, guess the meaning of the unknown word.
2. Does your guess make sense in the sentence?
3. Use a dictionary to check your guess.

W•9

Multiple-Meaning Words

Multiple-meaning words are words that have different meanings depending on how they are used. Homonyms, homographs, and homophones are all multiple-meaning words.

Homographs

Homographs are words that are spelled the same but have different meanings and are sometimes pronounced differently.

Wind

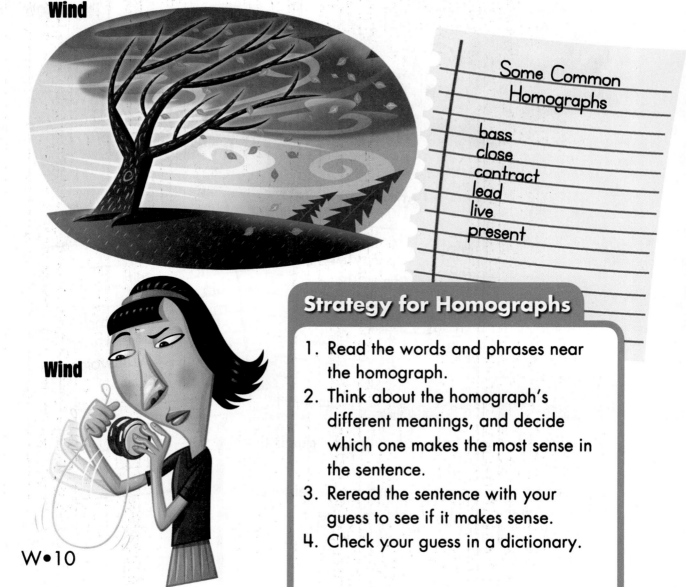

Some Common Homographs

bass
close
contract
lead
live
present

Wind

Strategy for Homographs

1. Read the words and phrases near the homograph.
2. Think about the homograph's different meanings, and decide which one makes the most sense in the sentence.
3. Reread the sentence with your guess to see if it makes sense.
4. Check your guess in a dictionary.

Homonyms

Homonyms are words that are pronounced the same and have the same spelling, but their meanings are different.

Pitcher

Pitcher

Strategy for Homonyms

1. Read the words and phrases near the homonym.
2. Think about the homonym's different meanings, and decide which one makes the most sense.
3. Reread the sentence with your guess to see if it makes sense.
4. Use a dictionary to check your guess.

Some Common Homonyms

pen
duck
mail
ear
bank
bark

Homophones

Homophones are words that are pronounced the same way but have different spellings and meanings.

Eight

Ate

Some Common Homophones

ate	eight
bored	board
brake	break
knight	night
weight	wait

Strategy for Homophones

1. Think about the different spellings and meanings of the homophone.
2. Check a dictionary for the definitions of the words.
3. Use the word that best fits your writing.

This chart can help you remember the differences between homographs, homonyms, and homophones.

Understanding Homographs, Homonyms, and Homophones

	Pronunciation	Spelling	Meaning
Homographs	may be the same or different	same	different
Homonyms	same	same	different
Homophones	same	different	different

address

Homograph

address

duck

Homonym

duck

Homophone bear

bare

Dictionary

A dictionary is a reference book that lists words alphabetically. It can be used to look up definitions, parts of speech, spelling, and other forms of words.

punc•tu•al ❶ (pungk′ chü əl), ❷ *ADJECTIVE.* ❸ prompt; exactly on time: ❹ *He is always punctual.* ❺ ✱ *ADVERB* **punc′tu•al•ly.**

❶ Pronunciation

❷ Part of speech

❸ Definitions

❹ Example sentence

❺ Other form of the word and its part of speech

Strategy for Dictionary

1. Identify the unknown word.
2. Look up the word in a dictionary. Entries are listed alphabetically.
3. Find the part of the entry that has the information you are looking for.
4. Use the diagram above as a guide to help you locate the information you want.

Thesaurus

A thesaurus is a book of synonyms. A thesaurus will also list antonyms for many words.

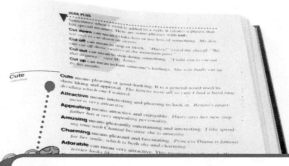

cute
adjective
attractive, appealing, amusing, charming, adorable, enchanting.
ANTONYMS: plain, ugly

Strategy for Thesaurus

1. Look up the word in a thesaurus. Entries are listed alphabetically.
2. Locate the synonyms and any antonyms for your word.
3. Find the word with the exact meaning you want.